In this book, David Novak conducts a historical, philosophical, and theological reflection on the central Jewish doctrine of Israel's election by God, also known as the idea of the chosen people. Historically, he analyzes the great change in modern Jewish thought brought about by Spinoza's inversion of the doctrine: that it was not God who elected Israel, but Israel who elected God. The development of that inversion is illustrated by the thought of the German philosopher-theologian Hermann Cohen. Philosophically, Novak explores the ontological implications of the two differing theologies of election. Theologically, he argues for the correlation of election and revelation, and maintains that a theology of election is required in order to deal with two central questions, namely: Who are the Jews, and how are Jews to be related to the world? The constructive picture which results leads to a new understanding of Jewish modernity.

THE ELECTION OF ISRAEL

THE
ELECTION OF ISRAEL

The idea of the chosen people

DAVID NOVAK

*Edgar M. Bronfman Professor of Modern Judaic Studies,
University of Virginia*

CAMBRIDGE
UNIVERSITY PRESS

Published by the Press Syndicate of the University of Cambridge
The Pitt Building, Trumpington Street, Cambridge CB2 1RP
40 West 20th Street, New York, NY 10011–4211, USA
10 Stamford Road, Oakleigh, Melbourne 3166, Australia

First published 1995

Printed in Great Britain at the University Press, Cambridge

A catalogue record for this book is available from the British Library

Library of Congress cataloguing in publication data
Novak, David, 1941–
The election of Israel: the idea of the chosen people / David Novak.
p.   cm.
Includes bibliographical references and index.
ISBN 0 521 41690 6
1. Jews – election, doctrine of – history of doctrines.
2. Jews – identity.   I. Title.
BM613.N68   1995
296.3′11–dc20   94–31954   CIP

ISBN 0 521 41690 6 hardback

To the memory of
George and Clara Eller Krulewitch
"Your children are like olive plants round about your table."
Psalms 128:3

Contents

Preface

I have learned over the years that theological reflection oscillates between personal isolation and communal participation. A theologian has to live an isolated life for much of the time because he or she is attempting to formulate a vision not yet seen by others of what lies beneath the surface of his or her tradition. But a theologian must also be a participant in a community or communities of discourse, being present in the attempt to answer some of the questions that have been raised by colleagues there. It is often impossible to identify the source of one's questions accurately, either inside or outside of oneself. Indeed, it seems better not to try to make any such identification. For too much identification with one's solitary vision might confuse theology with prophecy, and too much identification with one's communal response might confuse theology with ideology.

This book deals with a question that has concerned me for much of my life: What does it mean to be a Jew in the world, to be chosen by God, and is that true? And this book is equally about that same question as it concerns serious Jews – and non-Jews who have come in contact with Jews or Judaism or both. This question, whether mine or that of others, has obscure beginnings. I have been thinking about it since whenever I learned that my being a Jew means to be something distinct. The Jews – and many non-Jews – have been thinking about it since whenever the Jews became distinctly recognizable.

Nevertheless, the raising of this question that had led to the writing of this book does have some identifiable beginnings.

Personally, it seemed to be required by the trajectory of my own theological project, especially after I dealt with the question of what makes the emergence of Judaism possible in my books *The Image of the Non-Jew in Judaism* and *Jewish–Christian Dialogue*. In these books, I argued that the preconditions in the world that make this emergence possible do not explain its reality. So, without getting on to that most central issue, my claims about preconditions would become unfulfilled promises if I did not soon deal with *the* Jewish reality: God's election of Israel.

In the case of the communities of discourse to which I belong, my discussion in this book has a history. The Academy for Jewish Philosophy, of which I am a proud and active member, designated the question of election as the topic of its 1990 annual meeting to be held at Temple University in Philadelphia. This indicated to me renewed interest by a group of Jewish intellectuals in an issue that has always concerned me. So, in response to the call for papers, I delivered a paper in June of that year entitled "The Election of Israel: Outline of a Philosophical Analysis." That paper has been subsequently published in a collection of papers given at that annual meeting (and that of 1991), *A People Apart: Chosenness and Ritual in Jewish Philosophical Thought*, ed. Daniel H. Frank (Albany, N.Y., 1993). I am most grateful to my colleagues in the Academy for Jewish Philosophy who reacted to my paper with their suggestions and criticisms. The names of Elliot Dorff, Daniel Frank, Martin Golding, Steven Katz, Peter Ochs, Norbert Samuelson, Joseph Cohen, and Kenneth Seeskin come readily to mind. Also, at the annual meeting of the Academy in June 1993 at Northwestern University in Evanston, I delivered an earlier version of the chapter on Spinoza. In addition to some of the names just mentioned, I recall with gratitude the comments of David Shatz, Robert Gibbs, and Martin Yaffe.

In December of 1991, the section on Constructive Jewish Theology of the Association for Jewish Studies allowed me to present another version of the original paper on election (that has now been transformed into the introduction and conclusion of this book) at the annual meeting in Boston. I am grateful to David Blumenthal, who organized this session, and to Arthur Green and Michael Wyschogrod, who critically reacted to the paper. In the case of Michael Wyschogrod, our many conversations on this topic, which go back to our days together in the philosophy department of Baruch College of the City University of New York, have found explicit expression in the beginning of the conclusion.

At the time of writing this newer version of the original paper, Raphael Jospe was kind enough to share with me his as yet unpublished paper on the doctrine of election, which was most helpful to me. Also, when I was working on the section on Judah Halevi, Barry Kogan was most generous in sharing with me parts of his forthcoming translation of *Kuzari* and to comment on some of the points I make there. I learned much from his sound scholarship and gentle criticism.

The Dulles Colloquium on theology of the Institute on Religion and Public Life in New York brings together an extraordinary group of Christian and Jewish theologians for intense discussions several times each year. In 1991 and again late in 1993, I was able to present various sections of drafts of this book. These sessions have shown me more than any other experiences of mine in interfaith dialogue that Jews and Christians can engage in rewarding discourse about questions of faith, and that such discourse moves far beyond suspicion, condescension, patronizing, or minimization of *the* difference between our respective communities. I thank all of the members of the Colloquium, and especially Richard John Neuhaus (the president of the Institute and leader of the Colloquium), George Weigel, Fritz Rothschild, Robert Jenson, Russell Hittinger, Thomas Oden, Avery Dulles (in whose honor the Colloquium is convened), Edward Oakes, James Nuechterlein, and George Lindbeck.

Since 1989 I have been fortunate to learn and teach in an exceptional academic setting in the Department of Religious Studies of the University of Virginia. Conversations with colleagues, particularly with Robert Wilken, Nathan Scott, Gary Anderson, Daniel Westberg, and Eugene Rogers, have been resonating in my mind throughout the two years that I have spent in actually writing this book. In addition, I note with pride what I have learned from discussions with my students, especially two of my present doctoral students, Robert Tuttle and James Danielson.

Because of the specifically theological thrust of this book, I was surprised (pleasantly, to be sure) when the Woodrow Wilson International Center for Scholars in Washington, D.C., an agency of the United States Government, accepted my proposal of this topic and awarded me a fellowship for the academic year 1992/3. About one-half of the book was researched and written while I was in residence at the Center. For a remarkably supportive and stimulating environment, I thank the Center and its staff. I most fondly remember my many and helpful lunchtime discussions with Michael Lacey of the Center's staff, and some of the other fellows, especially Joseph Hamburger.

Since settling in Richmond, Virginia some five years ago, I have had the great privilege and pleasure to lead a Bible-study group that meets every Sunday morning in different homes. Many of the thoughts presented here have been tested and refined with the members of this group, especially the "regulars," Martin Graham, Leatrice and Bernard Kaplan, Brian Milner, Stephen Meyers, Charles Krumbein, Anita and Robert Schneider, Shelia and Marvin Weger, Morris Yarowsky, Robin Zeiger, and Jacob Joffe.

In addition to all the names mentioned above, I want to thank David Weiss Halivni, Lenn Goodman, Eugene Borowitz, Warren Poland, and Lewis Ford for all that I have learned from our many conversations over the years. I also want to thank my editor at Cambridge University Press, Alex Wright, for his cooperation in the writing and production of this book, and Pauline Marsh for her superb copy-editing of the typescript. As for my immediate family: Melva, Marianne, Jacob, and Noam, I hope they know by now what treasures they have given to me, which include what they have contributed to my work and my ability to do it.

Finally, the dedication. I do not remember just when the question of the election of Israel first presented itself to me. But

I do remember who first taught me to appreciate election itself, the privilege of being one of the chosen people. This book, therefore, is dedicated to the memory of George and Clara Eller Krulewitch – Uncle George and Aunt Clara – who loved being Jews and at whose Seder table I received my first and best lessons in how to celebrate what God does for and with his people.

Charlottesville, Virginia

Abbreviations

B. = Talmud Bavli (Babylonian Talmud)
M. = Mishnah
R. = Rabbi
T. = Tosefta
Tos. = Tosafot
Y. = Talmud Yerushalmi (Palestinian Talmud)

General note

All translations, unless otherwise noted, are by the author.

Two philosophically formulated terms appear regularly throughout this book and call for an explanation *ab initio*.

1. *Constitution*: "I use it in the fundamental sense that Husserl did – a reconstruction of a datum within consciousness, as opposed to representation in the empirical sense in which a datum is posited as being viewed as it immediately appears. See Husserl, *Ideas*, sec. 86 . . . I differ from Husserl in that the basis of this constitution is not the ego qua cogito, but a standpoint within Judaism as a living tradition to which I am primarily bound" (D. Novak, *Jewish–Christian Dialogue: A Jewish Justification* [New York, 1989], 159, n. 24. See also D. Novak, *Jewish Social Ethics* [New York, 1992], 3–5).

2. *Relation*: By this term I mean "relation" in the sense of the German *Verhältnis*, namely, the connection of constituted essences as parts of a larger whole. Hence essences or ideas are "related"; and if the relation is symmetrical, they are "correlated." I contrast this with the term "relationship," which is used in the sense of the German *Beziehung*, namely, the interaction *between* persons. The structure of this interaction flows *from what is between* the persons and does not function as a prior enclosing totality of any kind. See D. Novak, "Buber's Critique of Heidegger," *Modern Judaism* (1985), 5:131–132.

Introduction

THE FUNDAMENTAL QUESTION OF JEWISH IDENTITY

From the very beginnings of our history until the present time, we Jews have been involved in a continuing process of self-definition. We have never stopped asking ourselves the most fundamental question of our identity: Who is a Jew? Others too have asked us the same question from time to time, but before they can be given an answer, we always need to answer our own question to ourselves first.[1] The question to ourselves is more urgent inasmuch as others can usually live coherently without definitions about who are those who are other than themselves. But we cannot live coherently as insiders without such a definition. It is *the* question of our own identity.

In our own day, the question "Who is a Jew?" is being asked again with special urgency. In the Diaspora, the question is asked every time a Jew deliberates over the ready modern option of remaining part of the Jewish people or separating from it, and every time a non-Jew deliberates whether to seek admission to the Jewish people or not. In the State of Israel, the question "Who is a Jew?" has been a major political issue, since the "Law of Return" (*hoq ha-shevut*) that guarantees admission and citizenship to any Jew is vaguely formulated. On a number of occasions, the question has been the subject of landmark decisions of the Israeli Supreme Court.[2] Surely, the answer to

---

[1] See, e.g., B. Sanhedrin 18a re Zeph. 2:1; *Bemidbar Rabbah* 19.4 re Num. 19:1ff.
[2] See pp. 197–199 below.

I

this question will largely determine how we understand both what separates us from the rest of the world and what connects us to it.

Even though we have always been both separated from and connected to the rest of the world, new contexts of these relations call for renewed answers to the fundamental question of identity. Obviously, much has changed in both our situation and that of the world itself since the time when the questions of our separation from the world and our connection to it could usually be answered by pointing – both literally and figuratively – to the walls and gates of the Ghetto. For this reason, the answer to the fundamental identity question must be reformulated anew, even though it must also be ultimately the same as the fundamental answer that has always been given from Jewish tradition. For without that historical continuity, any answer to the identity question can only be invented rather than discovered. But since we Jews surely have a history, invention of our identity would hardly strike us – or anyone who knows anything about us – as authentic. So at this point in our history, how do we interpret to ourselves and then to the world the two most dominant facts of modern Jewish existence: the political emancipation of the Jews in the Western democracies, and the establishment of a Jewish state in the land of Israel? How we interpret these facts largely depends on how we answer anew to and for ourselves the perennial question: Who is a Jew?

Now there are three levels on which one can attempt to answer this most basic question of Jewish identity. At the first level, a legal answer can be offered. For almost two thousand years at least, one could correctly say that a Jew is someone who either (1) is born of a Jewish mother, or (2) has been properly converted to Judaism.[3] On legal grounds, the former case is rather easy to ascertain, except in rare instances of doubtful parentage.[4] The latter case is often more difficult to ascertain because the issues of the validity of conversion pro-

---

[3] See B. Yevamot 47b; B. Kiddushin 68b re Deut. 7:4.
[4] See, e.g., B. Pesahim 3b and Tos., s.v. "v'ana."

cedures and the validity of those conducting them can be the subject of dispute more readily.[5] Nevertheless, in both cases, Jewish law still has the resources for supplying a cogent answer to the "Who is a Jew?" question, that is, when it is asked as a matter of specific practice. Such a question might be: May I as a Jew marry this person or not? Or it might be: May this person be counted as a member of our Jewish congregation or not?

The legal answer to the "Who is a Jew?" question, although necessary, is still not fully sufficient, however. For the question "Who is a Jew?" is more deeply asked on what might be seen as the second level: the essential level. That is, the deeper question is not "Who is *this* person before me now: a Jew or not?" The deeper question is: *Who are the Jews? What* is it that makes them what they are and what they are to be? The category itself must be defined before we can be sure just who is a member of it and why. Without an answer to this most basic question, the insufficiency of the legal answer mentioned above soon becomes evident. Thus if one says: Jewish law has determined that one either born of a Jewish mother or properly converted to Judaism is a Jew, one can still ask two questions: (1) What is it about the Jewish mother that enables her to confer this Jewish identity on her child? (2) And what is it about a Jewish tribunal that enables it to confer Jewish identity on someone who heretofore has not been considered to be a Jew? In both cases, whether of birth or of conversion, one can further ask: Does the law itself simply create this identity by fiat, or does the law recognize and structure a reality that is prior to its own workings?

The latter question is what I would call the essential one. It is deeper and thus more important than the merely legal question. As such, it must be stated in such a way that we can derive a deeper answer than the one that simply posits legal fiat as final. For it would seem that the question of Jewish identity is not simply one that can be attributed to the workings of the law but, rather, one which the law itself recognizes as prior. It is certainly more foundational than any ordinary question of

[5] See Maimonides, *Mishneh Torah*: Isurei Bi'ah, 13.14ff.

law. It does not seem to be a merely legal creation. It seems that in this area, the law recognizes a reality that must be constituted in a prelegal mode before the law itself can deal with it cogently.

Taking this prelegal, essential, question with utmost seriousness, we could say that the Jews comprise a unique community in the world, a fact that is then recognized and structured by our law. However, is that community simply a natural fact or simply a historical fact? Is it to be approached biologically or culturally? Many in the modern world, both inside and outside the Jewish people, have attempted to answer the fundamental question of Jewish identity along these essentialist lines.

The historical approach to this essential question is usually preferred to the biological approach because the latter seems to lead straight into the pseudo-biology that justifies modern racism. Since Jews have been the world's greatest victims of this type of racism, it stands to reason why most of us, and most of the world who are morally sensitive, want to avoid the biological approach to the essential question of Jewish identity. But if our preference is for the historical approach, we must then take into consideration the phenomena of conscious human experience and free human action. That is because history is the temporal realm in which they occur.[6] Both of these phenomena are essentially social; both involve interpersonal relationships. Here we come to the third and deepest level of the fundamental identity question: the existential level. It cannot be answered by pointing to anything but personal phenomena. But *with whom* does this historical relationship occur? Certainly, it is one with ourselves inasmuch as we are a people. But if it is only an interhuman relationship, then what gives it the total existential claim that serious Jews sense it makes on every Jew? Could any human or group of humans make such a total claim?[7]

At this point, as I shall be contending throughout this book, the most adequate answer is the theological one. It is the only

---

[6] See pp. 23–26; 200–207 below.

[7] Thus it does not explain the requirement of martyrdom if one is given the choice of remaining a Jew or entering any other religious tradition. See p. 195 below.

complete answer to the existential question: *With whom* do the Jews live their life in the world, and *how* does this coexistence make them *what* they are and are to be? It answers that God elects Israel, that God chooses the Jewish people for a continuing covenantal relationship with himself for which he gave them the Torah. Therefore, the answer to the legal question *Who is a Jew?* depends on the answer to the deeper essential question of *What is a Jew?*, which in turn depends on the ultimate existential question of *With whom are the Jews what they are?*.[8] So the ultimate answer to any question of Jewish identity is theological, the one that points to the factors of election and covenant, the one that points to God's relationship with his people.[9] More specific answers, legal or otherwise, will have to be consistent with this ultimate answer in order to be truly cogent.

Of course, there are other answers that Jews and non-Jews, especially in modern times, have given to the fundamental question of Jewish identity. During the course of this book, I shall examine a number of them, those offered by some important modern Jewish thinkers. However, I shall simultaneously argue that they are not as adequate to the reality of Jewish life or as coherent for the requirements of Jewish action as is the classical biblical–rabbinic doctrine of the election of Israel: the idea of the chosen people.

THE PHILOSOPHICAL RETRIEVAL OF THE CLASSICAL DOCTRINE

The question now before us is whether the classical doctrine of the election of Israel is readily at hand, or whether it requires a method of retrieval.[10] Those who see it as being readily at hand

---

[8] See pp. 128–136 below.

[9] "It is impossible to discuss chosenness adequately without first explaining what the Jewish people has been placed on this earth to do. And that task would entail the presentation of coherent conceptions of God, revelation, covenant, etc. What is needed, in other words, is not history or sociology, but theology" (Arnold M. Eisen, *The Chosen People in America* [Bloomington, Ind. and London, 1983], 179).

[10] For the issue of philosophical retrieval, see Paul Ricoeur, *The Symbolism of Evil*, trans. E. Buchanan (New York and Evanston, 1967), 351ff.

are most often those who think that the legal answer to the "Who is a Jew?" question is sufficient and final. However, as we just saw, the legal answer itself leads directly into theological discussion of "What are the Jews?" It is not too hard to show the necessity of theological clarification for the operation of the Halakhah itself, especially on this essential point.[11] So, if one accepts the necessity of theology to explicate the workings of normative Jewish practice more fully, then one cannot say that the classical doctrine of the election of Israel is readily at hand. It requires theological reflection. Nevertheless, is the reflection of theology all that is needed?

A major assumption of this book is that the retrieval of the classical theological doctrine of the election of Israel requires philosophy, that is, the most cogent retrieval of it must be done philosophically. But what is meant here by "philosophy," and why is it needed for the retrieval of the classical doctrine?

What is meant here by "philosophy" is the systematic search for the deepest truth the world has to offer. It is the attempt to discover what is most fundamental in the realms of theory and practice, of science and politics, which are the realms in which intelligent people operate in the world in which they find themselves. It is the search for the most fundamental structures available to human reason.

Philosophy must be a religious concern for anyone who accepts the teaching that the same God who gave Israel the Torah created the world, and that creation and revelation are not totally disparate.[12] This is especially evident in classical treatments of the election of Israel. For here it is taught that the creator of the world chooses the Jewish people for a unique relationship. However, no matter how special that relationship is, it is still one that occurs *in the world*, a world which God still governs and for which God still cares.[13] Philosophy, then, both in its scientific concerns and its political concerns, is also the concern of the theologian. Philosophy becomes his or her

---

[11] See D. Novak, *Law and Theology in Judaism* (2 vols., New York, 1974, 1976), 1:1ff., 2:xiiiff.

[12] See Maimonides, *Guide of the Perplexed*, 1.65.

[13] See R. Bahya ibn Pakudah, *Hovot Ha-Levavot*: sha'ar ha-behinah.

concern precisely at the point when the question of the congruity of revelation and creation – Torah and the world – arises. Thus to deny the legitimacy of philosophy, let alone its requirement, is to ignore one of the ways (albeit not the primary way) in which we humans are related to God. Nevertheless, the theologian must understand both the range of philosophy for him or her as well as its limits. This will depend on whether or not the congruity of the Torah and the world is truly a situation where two separate phenomena are congruous *with* each other and not a reduction where one is taken as a subset *of* the other.

When the world is reduced to the level of the Torah alone, there is no room for philosophy at all. All wisdom comes from specific revelation, and philosophy is considered to be an intrusion from a realm that is ultimately an illusion. This elimination of room for philosophy has been most consistently advocated by the kabbalists. Modern research about their origins has shown that they were, to a certain extent, reacting against what they considered to be the worldly excesses of the rationalist theologians of the Middle Ages, those who were influenced by the Greek philosophers and their Arab followers.[14] Their desire for the most complete isolation of the Jewish people from the world has been paralleled by an intellectual effort to remove the worldliness of the world from Jewish religious consideration.

The fact that the Jews have been thrown into the modern world so categorically has made the theology of the kabbalists seem irretrievably fantastic. Despite great scholarly efforts in our own time to prevent their writings and doctrines from suffering total neglect by modern, worldly Jews, what has been retrieved is a cultural legacy, not a normative teaching. That is largely because of the worldliness of the modern Jews, even of those who are still pious and learned. Our problem today is certainly not that the world has been reduced to the Torah, that creation has been reduced to revelation. Our problem is the exact reverse.

[14] See Gershom Scholem, *Major Trends in Jewish Mysticism*, 3rd rev. ed. (New York, 1961), 22ff.

The retrieval of the classical doctrine of election (and its correlate, the doctrine of revelation) must be philosophical because its most powerful modern denial has been conducted philosophically. Beginning with the archetypal modern philosopher Baruch Spinoza, the denial of the plausibility – let alone the truth – of the classical Jewish doctrine of the election of Israel has appeared far more evident to intelligent people in the world than the doctrine itself, one to which they see only unworldly traditionalists adhering.[15] Therefore, if traditionalists want to counter external charges of myopia, and the internal charge that we are ignoring the relationship we have with God as the creator of the world, then we must expose the roots of the modern denial of the election of Israel. This must be done for the sake of cogently retrieving the classical doctrine in all its power and richness. That exposure, to be adequate – let alone convincing – must be philosophical. One must know what and how to answer its deniers, and that can only be done in the world with the deepest wisdom the world itself has to offer.[16] For its deniers have influenced the way we think in more ways than we are often aware of.

However, despite the large role theology must grant to philosophy and its methods, it must not give philosophy a foundational role. Such a concession would, in effect, be an attempt to reduce the Torah to the world. In one way or another, it would be apologetics. Too much of modern Jewish thought has done just that. And, as we shall see in the first three chapters of the book, this ultimately led these modern Jewish thinkers to pay far more homage to the legacy of Spinoza – the great denier of Judaism and the Jewish people – than they ever wanted to do. In this book, greatly helped by both the theories and example of Franz Rosenzweig, I shall attempt to make use of philosophy and its insights and methods as *ancilla theologiae* –

---

[15] The most persistent and influential advocate of this position was Mordecai M. Kaplan (d. 1983) throughout his long and active career. See, e.g., *Judaism as a Civilization* (New York, 1934), 257; *The Religion of Ethical Nationhood* (New York, 1970), 154.

[16] See M. Avot 2.14 and R. Israel Lipschütz, *Tiferet Yisra'el* thereon, n. 130.

the "handmaiden of theology."[17] For my main purpose here is
to clear the ground so that the classical sources, the Bible and
the rabbinic writings, may once again speak with their full
power and richness to the Jewish people in the world, and even
to the world itself. But we must be outspoken in insisting that
the Torah can never and, therefore, must never be justified by
the world or anything in it. The Torah comes from God, and it
is for God's sake that it is given to us. The world is made by
God, and God has given his Torah in the world, but the Torah
always teaches us more than the world does.[18]

So far, I have indicated the role that philosophy is to play *for*
theology; however, it also plays a role *in* theology. Here I see
philosophy functioning in theology as phenomenology.

If philosophical analysis is concerned with the explication of
the essences of phenomena, namely, that without which the
phenomenon could not appear as it does, then philosophical
analysis of the doctrine of the election of Israel is certainly
appropriate.[19] This doctrine is ubiquitous in traditional Jewish
expression, especially in the liturgy, which is that form of
Jewish expression Jews are mandated by Halakhah to recite
regularly and thereby affirm regularly. Since the phenomenon
at hand is verbal (being theo*logical* expression), its philosophical analysis is, specifically, the employment of metatheological
statements that "unpack" as it were the more cryptic theological statements themselves. This is done in order to (1)
expose the basic logical relations they contain and which give
them their essential structure; (2) draw out the ontological
implications that seem to be at work around these statements
themselves; (3) develop the wider suggestions these propositions have for the intellectual and political situation of those
now reciting them and affirming their truth.

---

[17] For the origin of this term and concept, see H. A. Wolfson, *Philo* (Cambridge, Mass.,
1947), 1:145ff.
[18] See M. Avot 3.7 and comments of R. Obadiah Bertinoro and R. Yom Tov
Lippmann Heller, *Tosfot Yom Tov* thereon.
[19] See Edmund Husserl, *Ideas*, secs. 78–79, trans. W. R. B. Gibson (New York, 1962),
200ff.

BASIC PROPOSITIONS

Before beginning the daily study of the Torah, and before one is called to the public reading of the Torah in the synagogue service, Halakhah mandates the recitation of a specific blessing (*berakhah*). Like all blessings, it is both a direct second-person statement to God and an indirect third-person statement for whomever happens to hear it. The blessing states: "Blessed are You Lord our God, king of the world, who has chosen us from among all peoples (*asher bahar banu mi-kol ha'amim*) and who has given us his Torah (*ve-natan lanu et torato*)." This statement is an elementary Jewish proposition in the legal sense inasmuch as its recitation has never been disputed in the history of the Halakhah.[20] Its recitation has liturgical permanence. Theologically, it is an elementary proposition because, as I shall argue later, it is irreducible to any other theological proposition. Such an elementary proposition, especially in the theological sense, calls for philosophical analysis.[21]

The basic logical relations exposed by philosophical analysis in this theological proposition are as follows: (1) Israel is related to God because of God's election of her; (2) Israel is related to God because of God's revelation of the Torah to her; (3) Israel is disjunct from the nations of the world because of God's election of her.

From this logical breakdown (the original meaning of "analysis"), two key questions emerge: (1) What is the relation of the election of Israel to the giving of the Torah? (2) Is Israel's disjunction from the nations of the world determined by her election alone, or by her election *and* her being given the Torah? Later on, I shall try to show how these two questions themselves are correlated and that the answer to one necessarily entails the

---

[20] See B. Berakhot 11b and Rashi, s.v. "ve-hi me'ulah"; *ibid.*, 21a re Deut. 32:3; Y. Berakhot 7.1/11a; Nahmanides, *Addenda to Maimonides' Sefer Ha-Mitsvot*, pos. no. 15. It seems that originally there were separate blessings for the election of Israel and the giving of the Torah. See T. Kippurim 3.18 and my late revered teacher Saul Lieberman, *Tosefta Kifshuta*: Mo'ed (New York, 1962), 80–801.

[21] Re elementary propositions, see Ludwig Wittgenstein, *Tractatus Logico-Philosophicus* (London, 1961), 4.2–4.23.

answer to the other. Before that can be done, however, a number of ontological implications must be seen.

At the outset, we should be aware that the doctrine of the election of Israel implies that the relationship between God and Israel is essentially historical. It is a continuing temporal process initiated by a free act of the creator God. The alternatives to this uniquely elective relationship are threefold.

First, God is not related to Israel because of natural necessity in the way that children are related to their biological parents because of natural necessity. For although this type of relationship begins at a point in time and is, therefore, temporal, that does not imply that it is the result of a particular choice. Only the latter can be properly termed *historical*; hence everything historical is temporal, but not everything temporal is historical.[22] Furthermore, even if the relationship is chosen by the parents (who either "wanted" the child by virtue of their own autonomy, or who chose to observe the Scriptural commandment, "Be fruitful and multiply"[23]), although not of course by the children, it does not imply that the choosing members of this relationship also have a prior and continuing relationship with a larger number of possible objects of choice. By contrast, God chooses Israel, but God is and remains the creator and the sustainer of the nations of the world, indeed of the entire universe. God could have chosen some other people, or no people at all.

Second, God's election of Israel is not the same as the modern institution of child adoption. For, although the relationship between these persons cannot be considered one of natural necessity (as is often the case between biological parents and their offspring), nevertheless, even if the adopting parents do have the choice of *which* child they want, they are not choosing from among their own creation.

---

[22] For the difference between historical time (*rega/sha'ah*) and physical time (*zeman*), see R. Judah Loewe (Maharal), *Gevurot Ha-Shem* (Cracow, 1582), intro., 2 and chap. 41; also, *Netsah Yisra'el* (Prague, 1599), chaps. 27–28; p. 25, n. 6 below.

[23] Note that the commandment to procreate (Gen. 9:1; see M. Yevamot 6.6; B. Yevamot 65b and Tos., s.v. "ve-lo"; Rabbenu Nissim [Ran] on *Alfasi*: Kiddushin, chap. 2, beg.) is spoken *to* the first human pair (*lahem*) as opposed to the creation of

Third, unlike either biological or adoptive parenting, the election of Israel involves not only the free act of God but also the free act of Israel. The fact of election designated by the word "covenant" (*berit*) is not a bilateral pact jointly initiated by both God and Israel together.[24] It is, rather, a historical reality created by God to be accepted by Israel. Nevertheless, this historical reality would have no human meaning without Israel's subsequent free acceptance of it and participation in it. For this reason, then, the fact of covenantal election is more often compared to a marriage than it is to parenting. God is more often seen to be like Israel's lover than her parent, more like her husband than her father. Yet even here there is an important difference. Marriage is both initiated and sustained by the natural necessity of eros in both partners. In the covenant, conversely, there is more freedom inasmuch as the divine partner is not bound by any necessity at all, which is a point emphasized by the doctrine of *creatio ex nihilo*.[25] The relationship between God and Israel is often more political than familial. That is why, it seems to me, the model of God as king is more often used in rabbinic teaching, much more often than the model of God as either parent or spouse. But even here, God does not become king because of the acceptance of his kingship by his subjects, as is the case with ordinary kingship as a form of finite human authority. Hence, to refer to God as "father," "lover," or even "king" is essentially metaphorical.

It would seem that a philosophically constituted theory of the doctrine of the election of Israel must be one where history

---

the animal instinct to procreate, which is only spoken *about* them (see Nahmanides, *Commentary on the Torah*: Gen. 1:22).

24 See Novak, *Jewish Social Ethics* (New York, 1992), 33ff.

25 See Yehezkel Kaufmann, *The Religion of Israel*, trans. M. Greenberg (Chicago, 1960), 127–128, 298–301. Of course, one can easily show that the strict doctrine of *creatio ex nihilo* might well not be literally biblical. Along these lines, see Jon D. Levenson, *Creation and the Persistence of Evil* (San Francisco, 1988), 3ff. Nevertheless, it is an understandable development from these biblical texts that emphasize the transcendence of God. See Maimonides, *Mishneh Torah*: Yesodei Ha-Torah, 1.7–9; *Guide of the Perplexed*, 2.13; also, R. Isaac Abrabanel, *Rosh Amanah*, chap. 16, ed. Kellner, 112–113. If God is not the free creator of *everything*, then something else is coeval with God. See J. O. Haberman, *Philosopher of Revelation: The Life and Thought of S. L. Steinheim* (Philadelphia, 1990), 301. Cf. Gersonides, *Milhamot Ha-Shem*, 4.2.1.

can be taken as a realm separate from nature, although not unrelated to it. It is the realm where a relationship with God, conscious and free, is possible. In the case of the election of Israel, it might be helpful to see the scheme of such relationships as being that of the interaction between one singularity and another singularity, and the interaction between a singularity and a more general horizon. This can be illustrated by looking at the following text from the Talmud:

Rav Nahman bar Isaac said to Rav Hiyya bar Avin: These *tefillin* of the Master-of-the-world, what are written inside of them? He said to him: "Who is like your people Israel, a singular (*goy ehad*) on earth!" (II Samuel 7:23/I Chronicles 17:21) ... God said to Israel: You have made me uniquely beloved in the world (*hativah ahat ba'olam*) and I have made you uniquely beloved in the world. You have made me uniquely beloved in the world as Scripture states, "Hear O' Israel: the Lord is our God, the Lord alone (*ehad*)" (Deuteronomy 6:4).[26]

The three components of this text are God, Israel, and the world. If I may continue this theological reflection in a more philosophical way, let me say that God has singled out Israel over and above the greater generality of the world. The world itself cannot recognize this singling out for what it truly is. The world can only recognize Israel's relationship with her "god" as being peculiar, but having no relevance for the world. All that it can recognize is difference. Hence Balaam states about Israel that she is "a people who dwells alone (*levadad*) and is not considered important (*yit'hashav*) by the nations" (Numbers 23:9). Hence Haman states to the contemporary ruler of most of the world about the Jews in his realm that they are "a singular people (*am ehad*) dispersed and separated among all the peoples in all the provinces of your kingdom, and their norms are different from those of every other people" (Esther 3:5). Hence Pharaoh states that Israel's "god" can make no valid claims on him: "Who is the Lord (YHWH) that I should listen to his voice to release Israel; I do not recognize (*lo yad'ati*) the Lord" (Exodus 5:2).

---

[26] B. Berakhot 6a. See A. Kohut, *Aruch Completum* (9 vols., New York, n.d.), 3:372, s.v. "hatav"; also, B. Hagigah 3a, Rashi, s.v. "hativah ahat."

From this we see that Israel's general relationship with the world is distinct from her singular relationship with God, and that God's general relationship with the world is distinct from his singular relationship with Israel. Nevertheless, one's view of both of these relationships is ultimately connected. That is, how one views God's singular relationship with Israel is going to determine how one views God's general relationship with the world – and vice versa.[27]

The connection of the singular relationship between God and Israel and the general relationship between God and the world is indicated by the presence of the Torah in all of them. Although God has chosen Israel and not the world for this singular relationship and Israel has responded accordingly, God has not deprived the world of Torah. In Scripture and rabbinic tradition, God gave the complete Torah to Israel and a partial Torah to the world.[28] Furthermore, everything in this partial Torah is included in the complete Torah, even though there is much more in the complete Torah than in the partial one.[29] And, although Israel's singular relationship with God is different from her general relationship with the world, both relationships are governed by the same divine law: the former one by the Torah's more specific precepts, the latter by its more general precepts. Employing some of the methods of phenomenological philosophy will best enable us to constitute cogently these separate yet connected relationships for Jewish theology.

ESSENTIAL PRECLUSIONS OF THE CLASSICAL DOCTRINE

The essentially free historical character of the covenantal relationship between God and Israel is basically precluded by two very different views of Judaism. What both of these views do have in common, in spite of their vast differences otherwise, is their essentially ahistorical view of the relationship between God and man and/or God and Israel. As we shall presently see,

[27] See D. Novak, *Jewish–Christian Dialogue* (New York, 1989), 115ff.
[28] For the extensive treatment of this whole topic, see D. Novak, *The Image of the Non-Jew in Judaism* (New York and Toronto, 1983).
[29] See Maimonides, *Mishneh Torah*: Melakhim, 9.1.

these ahistorical views essentially preclude a constitution of the classical biblical–rabbinic doctrine of the election of Israel.

The most radical preclusion of election comes from the philosophy of the archetypal modern Jewish renegade, Baruch Spinoza. He began the process of disconnecting philosophy from historical revelation. For Spinoza (as we shall see in greater detail in the next chapter), truth is that which is necessary and universal. It is not something revealed by a free act from above at a certain time. Instead, it is eternal and discoverable at any time, that is, of course, by anyone intelligent and desirous enough to discover it. Eternity and history are mutually exclusive ideas. But if this were all that Spinoza asserted, he could still be seen as continuing the tradition of the rationalist theology of the Middle Ages. Thus Maimonides, to cite a major example, takes revelation to be the highest level of intellection of eternal truth that is possible for finite intelligence. For him and the others in this theological tradition, the Jewish vision of the eternal truth about God still holds a privileged historical position, however.[30] The Torah contains within itself the eternal truth in esoteric form (*sitrei torah*).[31] This truth can be decoded, at least by those properly prepared to do so with a philosophically grounded hermeneutic. Although this type of rationalist theology does not in fact constitute the event of revelation apart from the event of the human discovery of eternal truth, it continues to allot a privileged epistemological (if not ontological) position to both the people of Israel and the Torah of Israel in the universal apprehension of that truth.[32] And, as we shall see in the second chapter, two centuries after Spinoza, Hermann Cohen attempted much the same thing, although operating from a quite different philosophical base.

Spinoza's radical project cleared the way for Jewish secularism and the atheism it fundamentally assumes. For Spinoza, a relationship with an intelligible and scientifically legitimate

---

[30] See Maimonides, *Commentary on the Mishnah*: Shemonah Peraqim, intro.; *Mishneh Torah*: Avodah Zarah, 11.16 and *Qiddush Ha-Hodesh*, 17.24.

[31] See Maimonides, *Guide of the Perplexed*, 3, intro. re B. Pesahim 119a.

[32] See pp. 228–230 below.

God and a relationship with the Jewish people as traditionally constituted were mutually exclusive. He opted, then, for God over Israel. In that sense, he was anything but the atheist later generations thought him to be. Jewish secularism, on the other hand, by opting for the Jewish people, while at the same time assuming that if there is a God it can only be like the God of Spinoza, thereby opted for the Jewish people over God. And more radical than either Spinoza or the Jewish secularists are those Jews who have consistently embraced Marxism. For Marxist premises leave no room for either God or Israel.[33]

The point in common between Spinoza, who willingly left the Jewish people, and the secularists, who remained with her, is that the transcendent God of the Bible, the Rabbis, the rationalist theologians, and the kabbalists is consistently denied. Accordingly, the election of Israel is necessarily denied as well. Only the transcendent God could possibly have chosen her. Spinoza, and those who are his heirs if not his actual disciples, already precluded the existence of this God from their worldview.

For Spinoza and the Jewish secularists, the doctrine of the election of Israel affirmed too much and, therefore, had to be dropped. On the other hand, it did not affirm enough for that view of Judaism which became the predominant Jewish theology for at least five centuries: Kabbalah. Although the researches of the late Gershom Scholem and his disciples and successors have shown how Kabbalah is, to a certain extent, conditioned by history, taken on its own terms, Kabbalah itself is radically ahistorical – indeed, acosmic. Whereas for Spinoza *deus sive natura* means that God is wholly immanent within nature and nature wholly immanent within God, for Kabbalah, conversely, the essential connection of God, Torah, and Israel means that nature qua cosmic order is wholly immanent *within* God, who both includes it and also transcends it. Hence it is a type of panentheism.[34]

In Kabbalah, there are no external relationships between

---

[33] Thus in his early essay *On the Jewish Question*, Marx's atheism and anti-Semitism are presented in tandem. See *Zur Judenfrage* (Berlin, 1919).

[34] See, esp., *Zohar*: Aharei-Mot, 3:73a.

God and his separate creation; all external relationships are in truth internal relations within the Godhead itself. Anything outside the Godhead can only be considered demonic (*sitra ahra*).[35] Everything real is in truth a manifestation of the Godhead. In fact, Israel is the only human manifestation of the Godhead; she is the microcosm, and the full ten *sefirot* are the macrocosm of panentheistic being.[36] Accordingly, Israel and humanity are in essence synonymous. There is no humanity outside Israel. In this divine scheme, the nations of the world have no human reality for all intents and purposes.[37]

In this ontological scheme, it is clear why the doctrine of the election of Israel cannot be constituted. Election implies that God chose Israel from among all the nations that he created, and that God did so as a transitive act in history. However, if all relations are in truth internal relations of emanation (*atsilut*) within the Godhead itself, it seems that there can be neither *creatio ex nihilo* nor history.[38] And without *creatio ex nihilo* and without history, Israel's relationship with God could not be the result of an act of free choice any more than one could choose the bodily parts to which he or she is necessarily connected. Israel is the Godhead in miniature. She is actually more than human because, in essence, she has always been part of God.

This does not mean, however, that one can exclude Kabbalah from a philosophical constitution of Jewish theology as one can exclude the thought of Spinoza. Spinoza himself not only left Judaism (which makes a severe problem for any appropriation of his thought for Jewish theology), but also left the Jewish people (which poses just as severe a problem for those Jewish secularists for whom he became a cultural hero). Kabbalah and the kabbalists, conversely, have played just too important a role in the history of Judaism and the Jewish people for that kind of exclusion. Indeed, I would say that any

---

[35] See Gershom Scholem, *Pirqei-Yesod Be-Havanat Ha-Kabbalah Ve-Simleiha*, trans. Y. Ben-Shlomoh (Jerusalem, 1980), 187ff.

[36] See *Zohar*: Ber'esheet, 1:20b; also, I. Tishby, *Mishnat Ha-Zohar* (2 vols., Jerusalem, 1961), 2:3ff.

[37] See pp. 216–218 below.

[38] See Gershom Scholem, "Schöpfung aus Nichts und Selbstverschränkung Gottes," *Eranos Jahrbuch* (1956), 25:108ff.

theological reflection (philosophical or not) on Judaism that does not incorporate at least some kabbalistic elements is deficient.[39] Nevertheless, I do not believe that Kabbalah need be taken as presenting to us elementary theological propositions. Kabbalah, like medieval rationalist theology, is itself a second-order constitution of elementary theological propositions from Scripture and the works of the Rabbis. But unlike Scripture and the works of the Rabbis, one can be more selective in using kabbalistic concepts, as is also the case when using the concepts of medieval rationalist theology. One ought not eliminate either discipline *ab initio*, however.[40] Thus even though I cannot incorporate Kabbalah at this point in my theological reflection on the election of Israel, I shall incorporate another aspect of Kabbalah at a later point in this book.[41] I cannot incorporate Kabbalah at this point in my reflection because in our time, with the ubiquitous presence of historical thinking, it seems to me that the doctrine of the election of Israel must be constituted primarily upon those classical sources where history is taken to be real. Today's Jews are just too worldly for Kabbalah to become the locus of our theology.

PARTICULARISM AND ELECTION

Jewish secularism, in its modern emergence as a unique phenomenon, has amply shown that one can maintain Jewish particularism – at least in theory – without basing it on the theological doctrine of the election of Israel by God.

In its more benign manifestations, which usually emphasize Jewish "peoplehood," this secularism has simply assumed that national distinctions are part of the "natural" order of things, which is itself a category confusion between the determination

---

[39] See Aimé Pallière, *The Unknown Sanctuary*, trans. L. W. Wise (New York, 1985), 169–170, where Pallière reports the critique of the theology of R. Samuel David Luzzatto (d. 1865) made by Pallière's teacher and Luzzatto's younger Italian colleague, R. Elijah Benamozegh (d. 1900), for its neglect of Kabbalah. See also the new introduction to this translation of Pallière's work by D. Novak, x–xiv.

[40] Cf. note of R. Abraham ben David of Posquieres (Rabad) on Maimonides, *Mishneh Torah*: Teshuvah, 3.7.

[41] See below, pp. 120, n. 34; 251–252.

of biology and the freedom of history. Thus, on this belief, the Jews are distinct from other peoples just like the Chinese or the French or the Zulus are distinct, that is, by "cultural" criteria such as language, customs, etc. Nevertheless, the utter naïveté of this confusion of biology and history should be quickly apparent. For even Jewish secularism seems to be committed to the survival of the Jewish people. But Jewish survival could necessarily be maintained by means of this model only if one were operating on the premises of an Aristotelian-type biology, which posits the permanence of species. Since Darwin, though, no reputable biologist has held this view. Species wax and wane in response to the process of natural selection. Hence to assume that the Jews are like a natural species presents no grounds for assuming Jewish survival, or even arguing against assimilation, when either individual or collective survival seems to warrant it. At this time, the inability of secular Zionism to answer the question why Jews should emigrate to or even remain in the State of Israel, when they can probably survive just as well elsewhere, aptly demonstrates the practical significance of this point.

In its more virulent manifestations, especially those overtly nationalistic, Jewish secularism has affirmed the distinctiveness of the Jewish people to be the result of election in history. But in this view of Jewish distinctiveness, that election is not an act of God. Instead, it is the act of the enemies of the Jewish people, those who throughout our history have wanted to murder us all. In the most recent version of this view, Hitler, not the Lord, becomes the final arbiter of who is a Jew and why Jews cannot lose their distinctive identity even if they want to. This is inevitably what comes out from those current views of Jewish history that make the Holocaust the central orienting event for Jews.[42] But the irony of this view, whether secularist Jewish nationalists acknowledge it or not, is that its most original enunciation did not come from a Jew at all, but from

---

[42] This emerges even in the works of Jewish theologians who make the Holocaust the linchpin of their theology. See Emil L. Fackenheim, *God's Presence in History* (New York, 1970), 81; *To Mend the World* (New York, 1982), 201ff.; Arthur A. Cohen, *The Tremendum* (New York, 1981), 10–11.

the atheistic French philosopher Jean-Paul Sartre in his
seminal book *Anti-Semite and Jew.*[43]

I mention all this because a philosophical constitution of the
theological doctrine of the election of Israel has competitors.
One cannot assume that the assumption of Jewish particularity
necessarily leads one into the realm of theology. Such a theological approach as the one advocated here must, therefore, be
ever cognizant of the claims of both benign and virulent Jewish
secularism and nationalism. It must, therefore, show how the
election of Israel by God radically differs from the anemic
survivalism of those who think cultural survival is a natural
necessity, and from the more full-blooded survivalism of those
who think the selection of the Jews by Hitler or anyone like him
gives us the identity we need.

Neither of these types of secularist survivalism provides
much of a philosophical challenge to the traditional doctrine of
election. That is why I have not devoted a separate chapter to
them. Hence the argument of this book will begin with Spinoza
and from him move on to Cohen. The transitional figure will
be Franz Rosenzweig, who revived concern with election and
revelation themselves and who had every bit as much philosophical ability as Spinoza and Cohen. Taking full advantage
of the philosophical opening provided by Rosenzweig (yet
differing from him on some subsequent points in his constitution of the doctrine), I shall come to the heart of this book:
the chapter on the retrieval of the biblical sources of the
doctrine. There I shall attempt to show how the Bible can be
read philosophically without, however, seeing it as a philosophical book. The next chapter will then attempt to show how
the Rabbis, both in their aggadic imagination and halakhic
legislation, enhanced the election of Israel and gave the Jewish
people a truly active role in the covenant with God. The last
chapter per se will deal with two medieval views of election,

---

[43] Originally published as *Réflexions sur la question juive* (Paris, 1946). However, the
English translator, George J. Becker (New York, 1965), has captured Sartre's
argument quite well in the very syntax of the English title he chose, *Anti-Semite – and
Jew.* Hence Sartre speaks of "the authentic Jew who thinks of himself as a Jew
because the Anti-Semite has put him in the situation of a Jew" (p. 150).

those of Judah Halevi and Moses Maimonides. In this chapter I shall attempt to show why their views of election cannot be retrieved for a truly normative role in contemporary Jewish theology. Finally, in the conclusion, I shall attempt to put forth my own theological view of election, building on the research and critical analysis of the preceeding chapters. Unfortunately, there is no room here for me to discuss the application of my theory to some of the grave moral and political issues facing the Jewish people and its identity after the Holocaust and the reestablishment of Jewish national sovereignty in the land and State of Israel. Perhaps such discussion will come in a future book.

CHAPTER I

Spinoza and his challenge

SPINOZA'S INVERSION OF THE DOCTRINE

No authentically philosophical attempt to recover the doctrine of the election of Israel and thereby explicate its truth for our time can hope to begin rigorously without first confronting Spinoza and then overcoming him. For it was Spinoza who presented what is still the most profound rejection of the traditional meaning of this doctrine. His rejection was one that greatly influenced almost every subsequent modern thinker who dealt with it. This was even the case with those Jewish thinkers who chose to remain part of the Jewish people, even as Spinoza had chosen to leave the Jewish people. It was even the case with those thinkers who were very much opposed to just about everything else in Spinoza's philosophy. It was even the case with those thinkers who probably never even read Spinoza carefully or even read him at all. The power of this rejection is that it was not a simple dismissal of the doctrine. Instead, it was a radical inversion of its traditionally accepted meaning, a deconstruction of it, if you will. In the traditional version of the doctrine, it is God who elects Israel and institutes the covenantal relationship with her. Spinoza, conversely, inverts this relationship and asserts that in truth it was Israel who elected God and instituted the covenantal relationship with him.

This inversion of meaning was accomplished by an explicit reading of the doctrine's biblical sources, a reading he thought far more convincing than that of the Jewish tradition theretofore. However, the real power of the inversion is that it is based on the very foundation of Spinoza's whole philosophy, his intellectual vision of God. Any philosophical attempt to recover the doctrine for our time cannot be truly cogent if it does not confront and overcome Spinoza's inversion of its meaning at its very roots and then proceed from them along Spinoza's own trajectory. Too many Jewish thinkers, who opposed Spinoza's rejection of Judaism and defection from the Jewish people, still did not go far enough in their confrontation with the philosophical foundation of all this. Accordingly, because they did not fully confront him, in the end they were not really able to overcome his rejection of what lies at the very core of Judaism.

THE GOD OF SPINOZA AND HIS RELATIONS

It is clear why the God of Spinoza cannot be attributed with the capacity for election in general and the actual election of Israel in particular. Election is the choice by one person of another person out of a range of possible candidates. This choice then establishes a mutual relationship between the elector and the elected, in biblical terms a "covenant" (*berit*). Election also promises its ultimate purpose will be fulfilled, which is to bring the whole world finally into the covenant, that is, "redemption" (*ge'ulah*). Election is much more fundamental than just freedom of choice in the ordinary sense, where a free person chooses to do one act from a range of possible acts. Instead, the elector chooses another person *with whom* he or she will both act and elicit responses, and then establishes the community *in which* these acts are to be done, and then promises that *for which* the election has occurred. The content of these practical choices is governed by law (*Torah*), but there could be no such coherent standards of action without the prior context of election, the establishment of covenantal community, and the promise of ultimate purpose.[1] Covenantal elec-

---

[1] For the inclusion of the meaning of *Torah* within that of *berit*, see Abraham Joshua Heschel, *The Prophets* (Philadelphia, 1962), 230.

tion, therefore, requires an ontology that can constitute possibility, mutual relationship, and purpose. All three of these modes, however, are precluded from the ontology of Spinoza. All of them as external relations intend transcendence, something that Spinoza's immanence of internal relations cannot bear.

For Spinoza, God is the foundation of a system of complete necessity. On the purely ontological level, there is no possibility at all. Everything is exactly as it should be. Accordingly, God is *causa immanens*, which is to be understood as a cause totally correlated with all its effects necessarily.[2] The effects inhere within the cause as much as the cause inheres within the effects. Neither of them has any reality apart from this nexus. Since there is no gap at all between them, there is no possibility. Without possibility, it is meaningless to talk about election.[3] Even when Spinoza uses the term "choice," which we shall see is in fact a metaphor, he does not mean that God had any other option. God himself is only free *from* any outside influences because in truth there are none. But God is not free *for* anything other than ultimately immutable eternity.[4]

It is even more meaningless to talk about mutual relationship emerging from election on the ontological level. For mutuality presupposes not only that the elector is free to elect anyone, but also that the elected have the capacity to respond to their being elected, that they have the power to contribute to the continuing relationship themselves. But for Spinoza, if the cause is bound by necessity, *a fortiori* so is the effect.[5] Here

---

[2] "Except for God, there neither is, nor can be conceived, any substance . . . modes can neither be nor conceived without substance . . . except for substances and modes there is nothing." *Ethics*, I, prop. 15, in *The Collected Works of Spinoza*, trans E. Curley (2 vols., Princeton, 1985), 1:420. And: "outside God there can be no substance, i.e., a thing which is in itself outside God . . . God, therefore, is the immanent, not the transitive cause of all things, q.e.d." *Ibid.*, I, prop. 18/1:428. And: "God was not before his decrees and cannot be without them." *Ibid.*, I, prop. 33, schol. 2/1:437. See *The Correspondence of Spinoza*, ed. and trans. A. Wolf (London, 1928), 343.

[3] See S. Zac, *Philosophie, théologie, politique dans l'œuvre de Spinoza* (Paris, 1979), 179; "Spinoza et l'état hébreux," in *Speculum Spinozanum: 167–1977*, ed. S. Hessing (London, 1978), 553.

[4] See *Ethics*, I, def. 7 and prop. 32.

[5] See H. A. Wolfson, *The Philosophy of Spinoza* (2 vols., Cambridge, Mass., 1934), 1:319–322, 422.

there is no mutuality, only subordination. Neither causes nor effects in any way chose their status. All ontological relations are those of cause and effect.

Finally, Spinoza cannot admit any purpose on the ontological level inasmuch as purpose presupposes a radical gap between the past, the present, and the future. What is yet to come is not simply the inevitable outcome of what has already come to be. Instead, it lies beyond what has ever been as its hidden horizon. In the biblical sense, it can only be promised by God and hoped for by humans. As for the past, because it does not inevitably and unilaterally lead into the future, those in the present cannot look to it as an unambiguous prediction of what is yet-to-come. Only part of the past can ever be recovered, namely, that part which is revealed to those in the present as precedent for what is to be experienced and done here and now, and which is to lead the elect somehow or other into the promised future.

Purpose involves an essential temporality which Spinoza cannot admit. As it was for the medieval Aristotelians, so it was for Spinoza: time is a form of change, and what is eternal cannot by definition change.[6] To do so would fatally compromise God's total perfection. Even causality, which as Kant later showed presupposes the irreducibility of time (a *then* b, the "then" signifying the temporal gap between cause and effect), is for Spinoza to be understood *more geometrico*, namely, as the atemporal relation between lines and figures in geometry, or the equally atemporal relation of ground and

---

[6] "By eternity I understand existence itself ... Exp.: For such existence, like the essence of a thing, is conceived as an eternal truth, and on that account cannot be explained by duration or time, even if duration is conceived to be without beginning or end" (*Ethics*, I, def. 8/1:409.) For a critique of Spinoza's denigration of time, written by a thinker influenced by Einstein's revolution in physics, see Samuel Alexander, *Spinoza and Time* (London, 1921), 21ff. Yet it should be noted that Einstein himself considered himself a Spinozist. As he stated in response to a query from a prominent New York Rabbi in 1929, "I believe in Spinoza's God who reveals himself in the orderly harmony of what exists, not in a God who concerns himself with the fate and actions of men" (quoted in R. W. Clark, *Einstein: The Life and Times* [New York, 1971], 413–414). Thus, although an affirmation of historical reality presupposes an affirmation of the reality of time, the latter does not necessarily entail the former. See pp. 200–207; 262–263 below; p. 11, n. 22 above.

consequent in formal logic.[7] To use Kantian terms, the relation is analytic, not synthetic.

Election itself presupposes not just possibility, which can be mathematically conceived, but *historical* possibility, namely, it takes place within distinct temporal events. In a system of thought where what is real can only be seen *sub specie aeternitatis*, the essential temporality presupposed by covenantal election, revelation, and redemption is necessarily precluded. They can only be seen *sub specie durationis*.[8] Thus in his discussion of election, Spinoza wants to separate the eternal "word" of God – a word not uttered in literal words – totally from anything pertaining to history, which is the only realm after all where eventful words can be uttered.[9] Being unable to provide us with immutable definitions, history cannot be known by deductive means, that is, *more geometrico*.[10] Hence it is not a science, but only a form of practical surmisal, something useful (as opposed to veridical) in the active pursuit of political ends rather than in the knowledge of natural causes. It deals with plausible meaning, not clear and distinct truth.[11]

THE POLITICAL ESSENCE OF ELECTION

If one remained at the level of Spinoza's ontology alone, it would be impossible even to think about the biblical doctrines of election, covenant, and redemption. Yet Spinoza has a good

---

[7] See *Ethics*, III, pref.; also, Stuart Hampshire, *Spinoza*, rev. ed. (Middlesex, 1987), 39ff.; H. E. Allison, *Benedict de Spinoza* (Boston, 1975), 69ff. Cf. Kant, *Critique of Pure Reason*, trans. N. Kemp Smith (New York 1929) B248ff.; Hermann Cohen, *Das Prinzip der Infinitesimal-Methode und seine Geschichte* (Frankfurt-on-Main, 1968), 70.

[8] See *Ethics*, V, prop. 23.

[9] "The common people, prone to superstition and prizing the legacy of time (*quod temporis*) above eternity itself, worship the books of Scripture rather than the Word of God." *Tractatus Theologico-Politicus* (hereafter *TT-P*), pref., trans. S. Shirley (Leiden and New York, 1989), 54–55; Latin text, *Opera*, ed. J. van Vloten and J. P. N. Land (4 vols., The Hague, 1914), 2:90. See also chap. 1/p. 60; chap. 15/p. 230.

[10] See *Ethics*, I, App./p. 441; II, prop. 47; III, pref. Cf. *TT-P*, chap. 7/p. 141: "Scripture frequently treats of matters that cannot be deduced from principles known by natural light; for it is chiefly made up of historical narratives and revelation."

[11] "For the point at issue is merely the meaning of texts (*sensu orationum*), not their truth ... All these details ... should be available from an historical study of Scripture." *TT-P*, chap. 7/p. 144. See also chap. 15/p. 232. For the distinction between the *vero ratio* of philosophy and the *sensus* of theology, see chap. 15/p. 228;

deal to say about them when he is not discussing ontology. How, then, does he make this considerable transition? How are ontology and history related?

In his *Tractatus Theologico-Politicus* Spinoza deals with these doctrines and carefully shows how his interest in them is not divorced from his ontological concerns. For even though reality conceived *sub specie aeternitatis* is wholly determined by prior causes, with no room at all for temporality and its possibilities, most of human reality cannot be so conceived. This is due to human ignorance. As long as humans are ignorant of the true sequence from cause to effect in their own lives, living in noetic gaps, as it were, they will have to invert the ontological order when ordering their own lives. That is, they will have to look upon the anticipated results of their actions as the determining teleological principle of them rather than looking upon their actions as part of a causal chain from which the results are subordinate effects inevitably. In other words, considerations of *for which* take practical precedence over considerations of *from which*.[12] In the realm of human action, consideration of final causes is simply unavoidable.

This is especially the case in the political realm. When it comes to the fulfillment of human political needs, humans must have purposes in mind if they are to accomplish anything in concert. This is because Spinoza believes that human societies, unlike individual human bodies and individual human minds, are not natural entities.[13] Instead, they are human inventions; they are essentially artificial constructs created by human imagination for certain previously conceived purposes. That is why they cannot be conceived in the perspective of strict causality (*causa sui*), namely, *sub specie aeternitatis*. Therefore,

and Leo Strauss, "The Mutual Influence of Theology and Philosophy," *Independent Journal of Philosophy* (1979): 113. Cf. Ze'ev Levy, *Baruch or Benedict: On Some Jewish Aspects of Spinoza's Philosophy* (New York, 1989), 54.

[12] "But the means that serve for the attainment of security and physical wellbeing ... mainly depend on the operation of external causes of which we are in ignorance ... Nevertheless, much can be effected by human contrivance (*directio*) and vigilance ... To this end (*Ad quod*), reason and experience have taught us ... to organise a society." *TT-P*, chap. 3/p. 90 (= Latin, 2:124). Cf. *Ethics*, i, App./pp. 443–444.

[13] "But surely nature creates individuals, not nations." *TT-P*, chap. 17/p. 267. See also chap. 4/p. 101.

ignorance of ontological causality in the political realm is not
just temporary, something that further research could eventually uncover. Such noetic progress could only be the case in the
actions of certain enlightened individuals.[14] The permanent
ignorance of ontological causality is the very presupposition of
a society truly in keeping with the human condition and its
political contingencies. That is why political knowledge can
never have mathematical certainty.[15] Spinoza seems to be
saying that it would be folly to allow political decisions to wait
for the mathematical demonstration appropriate to the study
of nature. Its very subject does not allow any such precision.[16]

   This also seems to be why Spinoza can be a determinist in
the ontological realm and a democrat in the political realm.
More contemporary determinisms, on the other hand, seem to
entail a much less democratic, if not even antidemocratic
political philosophy. For many of them assume that the hierarchy we can perceive in nature now can soon be paralleled in
human society through scientific advance. They can only make
this assumption, with which Spinoza would seem to disagree
very much, because they believe that human societies are just

---

[14] This distinction between natural, individual action, based on *scientia*, and artificial,
human action, based on teleological imagination, comes out of the following
observation by Spinoza: "Still, it rarely happens that men live according to the
guidance of reason ... They can hardly, however, live a solitary life; hence that
definition which makes man a social animal [e.g., Aristotle, *Politics* 1253a3; Seneca,
De Clementia 1.3.2] has been quite pleasing to most" (*Ethics*, IV, prop. 35, schol./
1:564). Thus the individual morality (*pietas*) of philosophically blessed individuals
like Baruch Spinoza himself, based as it is on apprehension of internal causality, is
essentially different from ordinary political morality, based on the teleological
imagination of political leaders. For these leaders often have to coerce those living
under their authority to obey the law (*obedientia*) because these ordinary people
often do not even understand the teleology of political order, much less true
ontological causality. See *ibid.*, prop. 36, schol. 1 *et seq.*/1:565ff.

[15] *TT-P*, chap. 15/pp. 23–234. Cf. Aristotle, *Nicomachean Ethics* 1094b13ff.; also, John
Rawls, *A Theory of Justice* (Cambridge, Mass., 1971), 136–137.

[16] This sounds somewhat like Saadiah Gaon's decision to practice the commandments
on the *authority* of Jewish tradition *until* he can discover for himself their true
teleological reasons (*Book of Beliefs and Opinions*, intro.). For Saadiah, though, this is
only tentative inasmuch as he believes that there are real final causes in created
nature and that they are simply awaiting discovery. But for Spinoza, since final
causes are not natural but only imagined by humans in their construction of society,
they can never be *discovered* as one would discover natural (i.e., efficient) causes.
Final causes will never admit such certainty. That is why causal ignorance in the
practical–political realm is permanent.

as natural, if not more natural, as human individuals. As such, human societies, and for some of them even all of human history itself, can be understood from the perspective of strict causality of some sort or other.

It is the fundamental confusion of natural causality with human purposiveness that Spinoza sees at the heart of religious thinking stemming from the Bible, thinking that attributes the objects of human choice to the will of God. For Spinoza, this is the great error of anthropomorphism: it is the confusion of God with man. Instead of believing that God *chose* this or that effect to happen, one should attribute to God's inalterable being the primary power that empowered those who brought about beneficial results to human individuals in society.[17] Moreover, although the affirmation of final causality qua human purposiveness is a political requirement, the philosophical recognition of the primacy of what Spinoza insists is *efficient* causality should keep a tight lid on the temptation to project final causality any farther than is minimally required in the ordering of society. There is no ultimate end in history any more than there is an ultimate end in nature. For Spinoza, there is no eschatology. Spinoza is thus highly critical of the Jews, who still see their chosenness as having a divinely intended cosmic purpose rather than as being merely a metaphor for their own unique polity. Chosenness qua distinctiveness is only the effect, not the *telos*, of divine causative action.[18] And the same fascination with final causality, unchecked by a truly critical philosophical perspective, also led the Jews to emphasize miracles, "whose cause cannot be explained on scientific principles known by the natural light of reason."[19]

The most immediate and pervasive purpose of society is to provide its citizens with order and a greater sense of safety than they would have if they lived as lone and isolated individuals. Accordingly, when one is pleased with the function of his or her

---

[17] See *TT-P*, chap. 3/p. 91.

[18] Re efficient causality, see *Ethics*, I, prop. 25. Re the overextension of final causality, see *TT-P*, chap. 6/p. 125.

[19] *TT-P*, chap. 6/p. 127. There is less reliance on miracles by the prophets, the closer they came to philosophical knowledge. See *ibid.*, chap. 11/p. 199.

own society, as the ancient Jews seem to have been with theirs, one retrospectively projects the source of this success back to an original divine plan. This is what Spinoza calls God "acting through hidden external causes."[20] One goes through the particularities of nature as experienced (*natura naturata*) back to nature per se as known directly by the mind (*natura naturans*).[21] What he means by this is that one basically infers from the effect back to the cause. In true ontology, however, one deduces from the cause to its effects. This is the case when one discerns the power of God acting directly within oneself so that one knows oneself to be part of it. At this level, for Spinoza, one is happily knowledgeable and just as happily aware of being part of the divinely determined order of nature. About this Spinoza says "whatever human nature can effect solely by its own power to preserve its own being can rightly be called God's internal help."[22]

It is at the level of external causes that Spinoza understands the first meaning of the idea of election. It is basically seeing one's own way of life that one has chosen for oneself as being consistent with "the predetermined order of nature."[23] In other words, being chosen by God is a metaphor for what human beings have chosen for themselves and believe is part of the eternal cosmic plan of God. One's work, when successfully carried out, retrospectively implies that one is designated for it rather than one's first being chosen establishing the community in which one is to do his or her work. In full retrospect, however, the "choice" could not have been other than it was. That is why it can only be metaphorical to attribute election or special vocation to God. Only man really chooses anything, and those choices are only significant in the political realm.[24]

---

[20] *Ibid.*, chap. 3/p. 91.   [21] See *Ethics*, i, prop. 29.

[22] *TT-P*, chap. 3/pp. 89–90.

[23] *Ibid.*

[24] On this point, Spinoza follows the views of those ancient pagans who found the Jewish (and Christian) idea of a historically active God to be sacrilegious (see, e.g., Origen, *Contra Celsum* 6.23). See also S. S. Gelhaar, *Prophetie und Gesetz bei Jehudah Halevi, Maimonides und Spinoza* (Frankfurt-on-Main, 1987), 167.

THE COVENANT AS SOCIAL CONTRACT

In the classical biblical presentations of election, the event of election is concretized in the covenant. The covenant (*berit*) is not a contract negotiated between two equal parties that can be terminated by mutual consent. It is a relationship offered by God to some of his creatures, and it is one they cannot finally refuse. Sooner or later they are convinced to accept it.[25] Because it is founded by God's promise, it is also interminable. "My covenant of peace shall never depart, says the Lord who loves you" (Isaiah 54:10).

For the reasons discussed above, it is clear why Spinoza cannot accept this idea of covenant as authentic. God does not make agreements with anyone. Only humans make agreements among themselves. The question is just what sort of interhuman agreement the covenant really is. Spinoza defines it as follows:

For if men were by nature bound by the divine law, or if divine law were a law by nature (*ex Natura*), there would have been no need for God to enter into a contract (*contractum*) and to bind them by a covenant (*pacto*) and by oath (*juramento*). Therefore we must concede without qualification that the divine law began from the time when men by express covenant promised to obey God in all things, thereby surrendering, as it were, their natural freedom and transferring their right to God in the manner we described in speaking of the civil state.[26]

Although Spinoza rejects the primary biblical sense of "covenant" precisely because it designates a divinely elected and structured relationship with a particular people, he has, nevertheless, skillfully appropriated the secondary biblical sense of the word. "Covenant" in this sense is an agreement initiated by humans among themselves and placed within the context of the primary covenant between God and his people. For example, "All of the elders of Israel came to the king at Hebron, and David made a covenant with them (*lahem*) in

---

[25] See B. Shabbat 88a–b.
[26] *TT-P*, chap. 16/pp. 24–247 (= Latin, 2:267). See chap. 17/p. 255 re the transfer/ limitation of natural power to a sovereign in the founding of a human polity.

Hebron before (*lifnay*) the Lord" (I Chronicles 11:3). Here it is clear that the covenant between the human parties is only possible because these respective parties have a prior covenantal relationship with God. Accordingly, no human covenant is valid if it contradicts the primary covenant established by God.[27] That is why when it comes to the incorrigibly idolatrous Canaanite nations, the Bible states, "you shall not make a covenant with them" (Deuteronomy 7:2).[28]

This secondary sense of covenant becomes more fully developed in the Talmud's concept of rabbinic law (*de-rabbanan*). (It should not be forgotten that Spinoza not only was a student of the Bible, but also studied the Talmud with the learned Rabbis of Amsterdam.) This law is based on a covenant made between the people and their leaders *before* God.[29] The law of this covenant is made *for the sake of* enhancing the primary covenantal relationship between God and Israel.[30] It is also made *for the sake of* the common good of the people themselves, and it must assume at least their tacit consent.[31] Although itself not directly revealed, it is *sanctioned by* revelation. It is observed *as if* revealed by God, even though directly revealed law (*d'oraita*) retains its normative priority.[32] For this reason, rabbinic law may not directly contradict the primary revealed law.[33]

Spinoza, of course, does not recognize the primary biblical sense of "covenant" because it follows from a literal acceptance of the divine election of Israel. Therefore, for him, it seems that the old secondary meaning of "covenant" becomes its new primary meaning; indeed, its only meaning. This covenant, then, must be *for the sake of* an ultimately noncovenantal, nonhistorical, *natural* relationship between God and any rational person. Nature has now replaced the old primary

---

27 See, e.g., M. Baba Batra 8.5; B. Baba Batra 126b.
28 Cf. Y. Shevi"it 6.1/36c; Maimonides, *Mishneh Torah*: Melakhim, 6.5.
29 See Ezra 10:3 and Neh. 10:1; B. Yevamot 89b; also, pp. 170–177 below.
30 See, e.g., M. Avot 1:1; B. Berakhot 26b.
31 See, e.g., B. Gittin 36a–b; Maimonides, *Mishneh Torah*: Sanhedrin, 24.9; B. Avodah Zarah 36a and parallels; *Mishneh Torah*: Mamrim, 2.6–7.
32 See B. Shabbat 23a re Deut. 17:11 and 32:7; B. Betsah 3b.
33 See, e.g., B. Berakhot 19b re Prov. 21:30; B. Yevamot 90b.

covenant of the Bible and the Rabbis. What has not been replaced, however, is the notion that the stability and permanence of interhuman agreements require a divine referent.

With this biblical and rabbinic background of Spinoza's political theory in mind along with his basic ontology, it is now more evident that Spinoza is not describing a contract in the way we understand that term in our secularized societies. (He was no more a "secularist" in the contemporary sense than he was an "atheist" in the contemporary sense.) God plays no role in our contracts at all. Instead, he is describing a contract between humans, one which is ultimately for the sake of the knowledge of God. Only at this level can God's "laws" be disobeyed, because these laws are only human surmisals of what the divine plan for humans actually is. On the level of strict causality, however, where God's laws are truly operative, nothing can be disobeyed, because disobedience presupposes a nonexistent mutability. Obedience or disobedience presumes a realm of possibility that Spinoza's ontology, as we have seen, cannot admit.[34]

In Spinoza's constitution of the social contract made for the sake of God, two things are accomplished that could not be accomplished in an ordinary interhuman contract.

The first thing is to affirm politically that every citizen is directly related to God.[35] The contract, precisely because it is artificial and not natural, involves no causal series. The individual's relation to God, then, is not mediated by any political structure, because political structure itself is logically subsequent to it: it is not its precondition. Religion, then, begins with the individual citizen, not with any ecclesiastical–political

---

[34] "A law (*lex*) which depends on nature's necessity is one which necessarily follows from the very nature of the things, that is, its definition; a law which depends on human will ... could more properly be termed a statute (*jus*)," *TT-P*, chap. 4/p. 101 (= Latin, 2:134). See also *Tractatus Politicus*, trans. R. H. M. Elwes (New York, 1951), 2.19–22; *Ethics*, III, prop. 2; IV, prop. 37, schol. 2. Cf. *Ethics*, I, prop. 15.

[35] Thus I do not think that Spinoza was speaking altogether pejoratively when he wrote: "Now it is important to note here that the Jews never make mention of intermediate or particular causes nor pay any heed to them, but to serve religion and piety ... they refer everything to God" (*TT-P*, chap. 1/p. 60).

institution, however exalted.[36] Although most ordinary people
do not seem interested in being related to God for its own sake,
Spinoza still insists that "the supreme good" is "the true
knowledge and love of God."[37] The business of divinely
directed law is to make society receptive and supportive of those
individuals who are interested in God as he truly is, that is, as
the *causa sui*, rather than as a personal and selective benefactor.

This end is what characterizes a law as "divine," a point
Spinoza clearly learned from Maimonides.[38] But he also
explicitly asserted that the origin of all law is human, and that
that law is "divine" if concerned with man's relation to God;
"human" if concerned with the relationship between humans
themselves.[39] This is a far more radical notion than Maimonides would allow, since he still affirmed the traditional Jewish
doctrine that all true law comes *from* God (*min ha-shamayim*) as
well as being for the sake of God (*le-shem shamayim*), either
immediately or ultimately.[40] Only rabbinic law is man-made.[41]
For Spinoza, law in the sense of a promulgated statute could
not come directly from God, since God does not speak in words.
Therefore, the words of revelation are human projections,
"statute[s] (*Jus*) which men ordain for themselves."[42] They are
responsible human attempts to promulgate laws that are
intended to be consistent with man's true relation to God. They
are spoken *as if* they were the direct decree of God; in Spinoza's
terms the law is "referred to God."[43] But, in truth, Spinoza is
convinced that "the idea and nature of God [is] not indeed in
words, but in a far superior way and one that agrees excellently
with the nature of mind."[44] In this refusal even to admit

---

[36] In *Tractatus Politicus*, 3.10, when constituting the modern democratic state he
desires, Spinoza built upon this ancient Hebrew political fact and declared religion
to be *quod viri privati officium est* (Latin text, *Opera*, ed. van Vloten and Land, 2:17).
[37] *TT-P*, chap. 4/p. 103.   [38] See *Guide of the Perplexed*, 2.40.
[39] *TT-P*, chap. 4/pp. 102–103.
[40] See *Guide of the Perplexed*, 2.35, 39; also, D. Novak, *The Image of the Non-Jew in
Judaism* (New York and Toronto, 1983), 313, nn. 81–83.
[41] See *Mishneh Torah*: Mamrim, chap. 1.
[42] *TT-P*, chap. 4/p. 101 (= Latin, 2:134).
[43] *Ibid.*, chap. 4/p. 104. See *Ethics*, v, prop. 14.
[44] *TT-P*, chap. 1/p. 60. Note also: "These dictates are revealed to us by God, speaking
as it were, within ourselves (*quasi in nobis ipsis loquente*), or else were revealed to

directed verbal revelation to man, let alone philosophically constitute it, Spinoza was also followed by most modern Jewish thinkers.

By connecting human political equality directly to the human relation to God, Spinoza provides a far more effective ontological orientation for democracy than the totally anthropocentric views of later social-contract theorists.[45] Also, by his reinterpretation of the biblical covenant, which he no doubt believed really did take place in history, Spinoza does not have to invent the fiction of the transition from the "state of nature" to the state of society as the social-contract theorists from Hobbes on had to do.[46] Thus ancient Israel, at least as described in the Bible, becomes for Spinoza a forerunner (although not a literal model) of democracy that is neither theocratic nor atheistic. This was an important political concern of Spinoza's in seventeenth-century Holland, where Calvinistic appropriations of the biblical doctrine of election were used to ground a theocratic polity from which Spinoza and other liberals of the time sharply differed.[47] And, although he was accused of atheism both during his lifetime and after his death, it seems clear that Spinoza would have been opposed to an atheistic society because such a society would demand a total diremption between politics and ontology.[48] It would not allow the individual to pursue his or her true happiness, which is the knowledge and love of God – a point that the atheistic regimes of this century have made all too clearly and painfully. Spinoza would no doubt have perceived their invented mythologies, which inevitably deify the state or its leader, to be idolatrous.

prophets as laws" (*Tractatus Politicus*, 2.22, trans. Elwes, 299 = Latin, 2:12). The word *lex* is only applied to God's decrees "by analogy" (*per translationem*) (*TT-P*, chap. 4/p. 102 = Latin, 2:135). Thus God is the "author" of Scripture only metaphorically. See *TT-P*, chap. 12/pp. 20–211.

[45] See S. Zac, *Spinoza et l'interprétation de l'écriture* (Paris, 1965), 208–209.

[46] See Zac, *Philosophie, théologie, politique dans l'œuvre de Spinoza*, 204.

[47] See *TT-P*, chap. 18/pp. 27–279; also, L. S. Feuer, *Spinoza and the Rise of Liberalism* (Boston, Mass., 1958), 130.

[48] For the sources of the subsequent debate over whether Spinoza was an atheist or not, see M. J. Buckley, *At the Origins of Modern Atheism* (New Haven, Conn., 1987), 11–12.

The second thing that the biblical covenant qua social contract accomplishes is to provide a highly effective means for the end of human law, "whose sole aim (*quae ad*) is to safeguard life and the commonwealth."[49] Now, those who are philosophically astute clearly understand the benefit of social order and tranquillity as ends in themselves. They need no further goad to uphold laws designed for the sake of these ends. For them true knowledge is sufficient. Virtue is its own reward.[50] Such persons do not need any historical revelation. The good is already theirs through what Spinoza calls "natural knowledge."[51] However, Spinoza is convinced that the vast majority of people, acting as they do for the sake of external benefits (and even conceiving God as an external benefactor), require external constraints in order to act in their own best interests. Here again, the biblical teaching of divine reward and punishment helped the citizens of ancient Israel become virtuous in a way that they could not if simply left to their own individual devices. So when communal religion, which is the religion of revelation, performs this function, reason is to "respect" it.[52]

The most immediate purpose of revealed law is to insure the obedience to rightful authority that the virtue of ordinary people requires.[53] That is why revealed law is practical and not theoretical, primarily constraining rather than edifying.[54] In the realm of nature, conversely, being related to God is not an act of obedience inasmuch as God does not command any more

---

49 *TT-P*, chap. 4/p. 103 (= Latin, 2:136).
50 *Ibid.*, chap. 4/p. 105; *Ethics*, v, prop. 42. As such, Spinoza's view of virtue for its own sake is quite close to Aristotle's view of excellent action (*aretē*) being action which is its own inherent end. See *Nicomachean Ethics* 1094a1. The term *energeia*, which Aristotle uses to designate such action, is quite close in meaning to what Spinoza means by *conatus*.
51 *TT-P*, pref./p. 55.   52 *Tractatus Politicus*, 2.22/p. 299.
53 See *ibid.*, 2.20. Spinoza insists that the more rational an individual is, the less submission to external authority his or her morals require. See Zac, *Spinoza et L'interprétation de l'écriture*, 107ff.
54 See *TT-P*, pref. "Thus the Hebrew nation was chosen by God before all others not by reason of its understanding nor of its spiritual qualities, but by reason of its social organisation and the good fortune whereby it achieved supremacy and retained it for so many years" (*ibid.*, chap. 3/p. 91).

than he elects a particular group of people.[55] Yet by referring these constraints directly to God, this system of human law avoids the arbitrary constraints of human authorities, acting only to enhance their own self-conceived political power. As Spinoza put it,

Since the Hebrews did not transfer their right (*suum jus*) to any man, but, as in a democracy, they all surrendered their right on equal terms ... it follows that this covenant (*ab hoc pacto*) left them all completely equal and they had an equal right to consult God ... in government of the state ... Therefore, if one of them transgressed against religion and began to violate individual rights given by God (*jusque divinum*), the others could treat him as an enemy and lawfully subdue him.[56]

By directly relating everything back to God, rather than proceeding through a chain of intermediate causes, the ancient Hebrews could function without the elaborate hierarchy that usually entails tyranny. Israel's choice to covenant with God led to the establishment of a society where the needs of the body for sustenance and safety, as well as the needs of the soul to be related to God by true knowledge and love, were well served.

In this new constitution of the covenant, Spinoza has seemingly retained the classical Jewish distinction between the relationship of man and man (*bein adam le-havero*) and the relationship of man and God (*bein adam le-maqom*).[57] The relationship of man and man is seen as a mutual covenant between free persons, who equally refer this relationship to God and thus insure their own political equality. It is political obedience that is protected from the inequality of tyranny. Thus it is primarily practical.[58] The relationship of man and

---

[55] "For nobody knows by nature that he has any duty. Indeed, this knowledge cannot be attained by any process of reasoning; one can gain it only by revelation confirmed by signs" (*ibid.*, chap. 16/p. 246).

[56] *Ibid.*, chap. 17/pp. 255–256, 263 (= Latin, 2:278, 281). Spinoza means that individual rights are "God given" because they are natural, i.e., coequal with a human being's natural power (*conatus*). See *ibid.*, chap. 16/p. 237. Moreover, by contracting with God rather than with any human potentate, the ancient Hebrews achieved *humani imperii libertas* (*ibid.*, chap. 16/Latin, 2:282).

[57] See M. Yoma 8.9.   [58] See *TT-P*, chap. 3.

God is seen as a perceptive individual's awareness of being part of the *causa sui*.[59] It is the knowledge of the individual's true cosmic status, one that is elevated from the insignificance of mutable history. Thus it is primarily theoretical. And, whereas the practical relationship is explicitly set forth in Scripture, the theoretical relationship is only implicitly alluded to there. Indeed, being based in nature rather than in human society, it cannot be the direct subject of ordinary social discourse. It is a good available only to gifted individuals. Society can only "allow freedom to philosophize (*libertatem philosophandi*) for every individual."[60] Social discourse, on the other hand, is concerned not with eternity but, rather, with the historical good of man, with the "sure dictates of our reason . . . which aim only at the true good of man."[61]

The covenant, then, has both practical and theoretical criteria. Both these sets of criteria are, however, universal. They could apply anywhere at any time. As such, they both preclude that aspect of the covenant most closely connected with the event of Israel's election by God, namely, those laws whose function is commemorative, the "testimonies" (*edot*). These laws, like the commandment to celebrate Passover annually, are designed "that you remember the day you went out from Egypt all the days of your life" (Deuteronomy 16:3). Spinoza calls these laws "ceremonial observances." And, in order to eliminate particular history from being a realm where man is related to God, he sees their sole function as "to strengthen and preserve the Jewish state."[62] In other words, their function is now seen as essentially political in the sense of serving the universal human need for a well-ordered society.

By this reduction of the historical–ritual realm to the political–moral realm, rather than accepting it as the unique celebration of the elect of God in their election, Spinoza has

---

59 Spinoza speaks of man in "the eternal order of nature" as "an atom" (*particula*). *Tractatus Politicus*, 2.8/p. 295 (= Latin, 2:8). Nevertheless, to be an "atom" of eternity is in truth better than to be a transitory historical person, however important one is here and now.

60 *TT-P*, chap. 16/p. 237.   61 *Ibid.*, chap. 16/p. 239.

62 *Ibid.*, chap. 5/p. 112. See also pp. 148–152 below.

inverted the classical Jewish relation of general morality and the singular covenant. For in this relation, as I have argued and marshaled evidence elsewhere, universal morality is seen as the precondition for the historical covenant between God and Israel.[63] The latter, in Maimonides' words, "completes" the former.[64] This universal morality is put forth in the rabbinic doctrine of the Noahide laws, that is, the laws (such as the prohibitions of idolatry, bloodshed, incest, and robbery) that pertain to the descendants of Noah, to humankind per se.[65] However, the historical revelation of God, which is the covenantal context and its normative content, is put forth as the direct relationship between God and humans, for which the indirect Noahide relationship is only preparatory. It is its background, not its ground. Conversely, Spinoza has made historical revelation and its most singular "ceremonial" content a historically contingent means to an essentially moral end.[66] This too was an assumption accepted by most modern Jewish thinkers, most of whom only differed from Spinoza on the degree of contingency and dispensability these ceremonies now had.

In this new elevation of practices that are essentially moral laws over practices that are more immediately "religious" laws, Spinoza was following a lead established by his famous heterodox predecessor in Amsterdam, Uriel da Costa. In his rejection of much of Jewish law as morally and religiously cumbersome, da Costa saw the Noahide laws as not only necessary but sufficient for a fulfilled human life.[67] Furthermore, in a famous critique of Maimonides' connection of full

---

[63] *The Image of the Non-Jew in Judaism*, esp. 407ff.

[64] *Mishneh Torah*: Melakhim, 9.1.

[65] See Novak, *The Image of the Non-Jew in Judaism*, *passim*; also, D. Novak, *Jewish–Christian Dialogue* (New York, 1989), chap. 1.

[66] "If we want to testify, without any prejudgment, to the divinity of Scripture, it must be made evident to us from Scripture alone that it teaches true moral doctrine (*vera documenta moralia*); for it is on this basis alone that its divinity can be proved" (*TT-P*, chap. 7/p. 142 = Latin, 2:173).

[67] Da Costa speaks of the Seven Noahide laws as "qui ante Abrahamum fuerent, hoc illis satis est ad salutem ... secundum rectam rationem, quaes vera norma est illius naturalis legis" (*Exemplar Humanae Vitae*, in *Die Schriften des Uriel da Costa*, ed. G. Gebhardt [Amsterdam, 1922], 117–118).

moral sufficiency with an affirmation of revelation, Spinoza argues that "a true way of life," that is, natural morality, does not depend on specifically "prophetic inspiration."[68] In other words, practical excellence ("virtue") is not at all subordinate to a historical relationship with God. Indeed, morality is the criterion of the validity of revealed law rather than revealed law being the criterion of morality as it is in the classical Jewish sources.[69]

For this reason too, I think, Spinoza frequently invokes Christianity against Judaism in the *Tractatus Theologico-Politicus*. Christianity's practical value seems to be that it stressed the minimal morality required by human flourishing, and it rejected Pharisaic Jewish tradition, with its numerous particularistic accretions to that minimal morality.[70] And despite his usual insistence that philosophy and theology be kept apart each in its own realm, Spinoza makes an important exception when it comes to political philosophy. Being the study of a human artifact, society, as opposed to metaphysics, which is the study of nature in toto (*natura naturans*), it is related to theology. In fact, it determines theology's very validity. He writes that "we can use judgment before we accept with at least moral certainty that which has been revealed."[71] But, even at the level of morality, let alone ontology, the doctrine of election plays no constitutive role. Such a role could only be played by a doctrine that Spinoza could reconstitute as a rational idea in his system. God's election of Israel in the literal, nonmetaphorical sense could never become any such idea.

To many readers, no doubt, Spinoza's subordination of Jewish ceremonial law to Jewish moral law seems to reflect classical Christian teaching about Judaism. Had not Chris-

---

68 *TT-P*, chap. 5/p. 122.
69 This question, of course, is at least as old as Plato. For discussion of it, see D. Novak, *Suicide and Morality* (New York, 1975), 29ff. Cf. Novak, *Jewish–Christian Dialogue*, 151ff.
70 See *TT-P*, chap. 1/p. 64; chap. 3/pp. 97–98; chap. 4/pp. 107–108; chap. 5/p. 113; chap. 11/p. 203; chap. 18/pp. 273–274. That is also why, I think, Spinoza usually has a higher opinion of the Sadducees than he does of the Pharisees. The Sadducees were minimalists, accepting only what was literally in Scripture as normative revelation. See *ibid.*, chap. 12/p. 205; also, B. Horayot 4a.
71 *TT-P*, chap. 15/p. 233.

tianity historically relativized Jewish ceremonial law by insisting that it only applied to the Jewish people before the coming
of Christ, something it had just as strongly insisted was not the
case with the basic precepts of Jewish moral law?[72] Nevertheless, closer reading of the *Tractatus Theologico-Politicus* leads one
to conclude that Spinoza's treatment of Jewish ceremonial law
is much more radical than that of any of the classical Christian
theologians. For they replaced Jewish ceremonial law with the
Christian sacraments, which they saw as now being the true
content of the covenantal relationship with God.[73] As with
Judaism, however, they did not propose a moral justification of
religious practice; rather, they included morality within the
historical covenant between God and his people.[74] Christian
theologians insisted that the ceremonial law pertains to the
true relationship with God, and that it is to be distinguished
from the moral law, which only pertains to human society.[75]
The former is clearly superior to the latter by virtue of its direct
object: God rather than other humans.

The difference between Judaism and Christianity, then, is
what constitutes the full covenant, not *that* the covenant is
foundational. And the covenant, for both Judaism and Christianity, is initiated by God's election of Israel. Jews and Christians differ – and the difference is crucial – as to the extent of
that initiating election. Christians affirm that this election
begins with Israel and extends to the incarnation, God's
coming to dwell within the body of the Jew Jesus of Nazareth
as the Christ. Jews refuse to accept this. Hence, for Christians,
Judaism is deficient; for Jews, Christianity is excessive.

With all of this in mind, Spinoza cannot be taken as simply
an elaboration of the old Christian critique of Jewish "cere-
monialism." Spinoza has gone beyond that critique radically;
for he has deconstructed Christianity every bit as much as he

---

[72] See, e.g., Thomas Aquinas, *Summa Theologiae*, 2/1, q. 100, a. 8; John Calvin,
Institutes of the Christian Religion, trans. F. L. Battles (2 vols., Philadelphia, 1960),
2.7.13.
[73] See, e.g., *Summa Theologiae*, 2/1, q. 102, a. 2 and q. 103, a. 3 and a. 4; *Institutes*, 2.7.1.
[74] See, e.g., *Summa Theologiae*, 2/1, q. 101, a. 1; *Institutes*, 2.7.10 and 4.20.16.
[75] See *Summa Theologiae*, 2/1, q. 101, a. 1; *Institutes*, 2.8.11.

has deconstructed Judaism. In this sense, both Jews and Christians have more in common with each other than either of them has in common with Spinoza.

THE TERMINATION OF THE COVENANT

Because Spinoza sees the covenant presented in the Bible as an essentially human device designed by the Jews to relate their society properly to God and to each other, it cannot be eternal.[76] Hence it is not the object of truth, whose proper object is nature as a whole and in its parts. The covenant is something created within time, and it is thus subject to historical judgment, whose criteria are evaluative rather than veridical.[77] At this level, Spinoza's question about the covenant is whether its original purpose is still being served. If it is, then the covenant is still valuable because, as we have just seen, Spinoza approves of the covenant, including what he considers the historical myth of its origin in divine election. If this is the case, the covenanted society is something that ought to be preserved. However, if that original purpose is not still being served, the covenant is not still valuable. Hence it is something that ought not to be preserved. And, if it is still being preserved by the Jews anyway, then it can only be preserved in some perverted form. That the latter is Spinoza's historical judgment we shall soon see.

As a former rabbinical student, Spinoza knew quite well that in the traditional Jewish understanding of the covenant the law is its primary content. However, he added to that traditional understanding the modern notion that law is essentially the rule for a sovereign state living in its own land functioning as a "social body."[78] Thus he writes that

the Hebrews were called God's chosen people ... for no other reason than that God chose for them a certain territory where they might live in security and wellbeing ... the law of the Hebrew state ... was therefore binding on none but the Hebrews, and not even on them except while their state stood.[79]

[76] See *TT-P*, chap. 3/p. 100.   [77] See *Tractatus Politicus*, 4.6.
[78] *TT-P*, chap. 3/p. 100.
[79] *Ibid.*, pref./p. 54.

Along these lines, of course, the loss of their own sovereign state in their own land should have convinced the Jews that their election had come to an end and that they should assimilate into whatever sovereign states they happened to find themselves living in. Indeed, Spinoza saw the covenant being annulled already during the Babylonian exile, when the Jews had to recognize the king of Babylon rather than God as their sovereign.[80] The very reality of the covenant and not just its subsequent confirmation depended on the transfer of individual natural powers qua rights to one's present sovereign. Thus no human contract, even a covenant with God, is in principle everlasting or nonnegotiable.

Surely the separate existence of the Jews no longer served a positive purpose any more. Even their ceremonial law, which for the most part could be observed by individual Jews anywhere at any time, seemed to Spinoza still to be so communal in its character that its cogency too was ultimately connected with the question of statehood.[81] Revealed religion and its morality only have meaning within a polity.[82] Rational apprehension of God and the natural world alone is a proper individual concern. In contrast to the Rabbis, he did not see ceremonial law as a personal obligation (*hovat ha-guf*), something that relates individual Jews to God in such a way as to remain cogent with or without a state of their own.[83] For him, a stateless society and its cultural–religious practices could only be some sort of historical perversion in which the individual pursuit of truth and virtue would have to be thwarted. Spinoza was convinced that the perpetuation of these ceremonies after the loss of statehood was separation for separation's sake. It is a negation serving no positive purpose, something that could not be related to God, who is the positive foundation of existence itself. Accordingly, Spinoza is very harsh with the Jews' insistence on perpetuating their unique ceremonial practices, and he accuses them of profaning what

---

[80] *Ibid.*, chap. 19/p. 282.   [81] See *Ibid.*, chap. 5/p. 115.
[82] See *Ibid.*, chap. 3/p. 94.
[83] See, e.g., B. Kiddushin 37a; also, Maimonides, *Mishneh Torah*: Berakhot, 11.2. Cf. Nahmanides, *Commentary on the Torah*: Deut. 8:10.

was originally sacred, thus severing it from any relation to God at all.[84]

For Spinoza, then, a stateless society can only justify its continued existence on negative grounds. Instead of its difference being for the sake of its unique sovereignty, which is a positive historical reality, its difference becomes an end in itself. In Spinoza's opinion, such a stateless society determined to persist anyway inevitably incurs "the hatred of all . . . [and] that they are preserved largely through the hatred of other nations is demonstrated by historical fact."[85] In other words, whereas the members of one sovereign nation-state can well understand and respect the desire of the members of another sovereign nation-state to remain separate and independent of others, they cannot very well understand, much less respect, the refusal of a stateless community to remain separated from others. That they inevitably attribute to the Jews' xenophobic hatred, a hatred they return in kind. So it seems from Spinoza's analysis of the reasons for Jewish survival that Jewish separatism as an end in itself led to the hatred of the Jews by the nations among which they lived, and that it is this very hatred that now keeps the Jews in their unhealthy isolation. At the bottom of all this, then, the fault clearly lies with the Jews themselves. It is they who originally "vaunted themselves above all men – indeed, despising all men."[86]

THE FUTURE OF ISRAEL

After his discussion of how hatred of the Jews has actually led to their survival long after their loss of political sovereignty, Spinoza makes a remark, seemingly *en passant*, that has nevertheless had a profound effect on many modern Jewish thinkers who came after him. He writes,

Indeed, were it not that the fundamental principles of their religion discourage manliness (*effoeminarent*), I would not hesitate to believe that they will one day – given the opportunity – such is the mutability

---

[84] *TT-P*, chap. 12/p. 206.　　　[85] *Ibid,.*, chap. 3/p. 99.

[86] *Ibid.*, chap. 1/p. 70. Here Spinoza is following the views of those ancient pagans who attributed Jewish religious separatism to xenophobia per se (see, e.g., Tacitus,

of human affairs – establish once more their independent state (*imperium*), and that God will again (*de novo*) choose them.[87]

The reason for the subsequent Jewish interest in this rather cryptic passage, I think, is that it seemed to offer a way to resolve the great ambivalence many modern Jewish thinkers felt towards Spinoza. On the one hand, they very much admired what we might now call Spinoza's "demythologization" of Jewish tradition. Spinoza showed them how the tradition could be still appreciated even when severed from the supernaturalist theology that had previously undergirded it in what was for them the by now irretrievably lost prescientific age. But, on the other hand, they could not identify with the fact that Spinoza had clearly separated himself from the Jewish people and not just from what they too regarded as antiquated Jewish theology. Therefore, what this passage suggested to many of them was that Spinoza had not totally or irrevocably separated himself from his own people after all.[88] He seemed to be suggesting here that were the state of Jewish belief different, were it made to be consistent with what Spinoza thought was the by now irrefutable new physics (the science of *natura naturata*) and metaphysics (the science of *natura naturans*), an ontology and epistemology in which there was surely no place for a transcendent God, then he too could perhaps return home.

Spinoza seemed, therefore, to be offering the Jews what might be termed a "naturalist" solution to their problem of homelessness.[89] And, although he thought that many aspects of

---

Histories 5.5). See also Y. Yovel, *Spinoza and Other Heretics* (2 vols., Princeton, 1989), 1:181.

[87] *TT-P*, chap. 3/p. 100 (= Latin, 2:133).

[88] For the modern Jewish attempt to reclaim Spinoza for Judaism, however conceived, see, e.g., the collection of of essays by Joseph Klausner, Nahum Sokolow, David Ben Gurion, *et al.* in *Spinoza: Dreihundert Jahre Ewigkeit*, ed. S. Hessing, 2nd enlarged ed. (The Hague, 1962).

[89] "Spinoza is writing only a few years after the upheaval fomented by Sabbetai Zevi, the false Messiah ... Since all human affairs are transient, Spinoza says, the renewal of the Jewish kingdom is not inevitable; but if the return to Zion should take place, it will be because of the immanent laws of nature and not by providential, divine revelation, or messianism" (Yovel, *Spinoza and Other Heretics*, 1:191). For the deep messianic longings connected with *l'affaire* Shabbtai Zvi in the Amsterdam of

the ancient covenant (as he had reconstituted its meaning, of course) were "quite profitable to imitate," he was explicit in his judgment that the covenant itself could not be reinstated in the modern world.[90] By reason of factors both spiritual and historical, Spinoza concluded that any such reinstitution was by now impossible. For even in the ancient world, it was basically the Jews who had elected God rather than being elected by God. And in the modern world that election could only be the business of private individuals, not the state. All the state should now do is to respect such individual human choices, as long as they are not disruptive of "the peace and welfare (*paci et utilitati*) of the commonwealth."[91]

Spinoza thought that the external event of the founding of the covenant between God and man could presently be better seen as the internal awareness of rational persons. Here he invoked the New Testament's great emphasis on inwardness in the relationship with God.[92] But it is clear from his use of the New Testament that he was not advocating conversion to Christianity as a solution to the political problems of the Jews – or anyone else, for that matter. Instead, he saw Christianity as a step away from Judaism towards the rational religion he called "religion universal" or "catholic religion."[93] The latter term, of course, does not designate the Catholic Church (or any religious body), which Spinoza regarded as irrational and oppressive.[94] Instead, the term "catholic" is being used in its original Greek meaning of universal (*kata holos*), a universal religion of reason, one which would be a *novum* in human history, to be sure. The symbiosis of this rational religion – maintained privately by the philosophically perceptive – and the liberal state – maintained publicly by every citizen – can be

Spinoza's youth, see Gershom Scholem, *Sabbatai Sevi: The Mystical Messiah*, trans. R. J. Z. Werblowsky (Princeton, 1973), 518ff.

[90] *TT-P*, chap. 18/p. 272.   [91] *Ibid.*, chap. 19/p. 280.

[92] See *ibid.*, chap. 11.

[93] *Ibid.*, pref./p. 54; chap. 12/pp. 208–209. See Leo Strauss, *Spinoza's Critique of Religion*, trans. E. M. Sinclair (New York, 1965), 258.

[94] See, e.g., *TT-P*, chap. 19/pp. 28off. For the significance of Spinoza making Jesus a paradigmatic philosopher, see S. Pines, "Spinoza's *Tractatus Theologico-Politicus*," *Scripta Hierosolymitana* (1968), 20:22.

seen as Spinoza's combining what he saw as the political
strengths of Judaism with the spiritual strengths of Christianity. This combination is meant to herald a new entity in
human history. As Leo Strauss so well put it, Spinoza "was
both a Jew and a Christian and hence neither."[95]

Spinoza thought too that the ancient covenant was only
suited to a society separated from the rest of the world, living in
splendid isolation.[96] But in the world in which he lived,
especially the Netherlands, whose very survival and prosperity
depended on international commerce, Spinoza concluded that
the reinstitution of such an ancient covenantal polity was not
only highly improbable but also highly undesirable.[97]

The willingness of many modern Jewish thinkers to accept
Spinoza's general premises, even if they would not accept his
own particular religio-political conclusion from them, meant
that they had to alter radically the classical Jewish doctrines of
creation, election, revelation, and redemption into the ideas of
origin, destiny, insight, and progress. As we shall see, creation
was changed from the founding cosmic event into the perpetual origin of cosmic process; election was changed from
external choice into an intuition of one's own destiny; revelation was changed from the voice of God to man into the insight
of man about God; and redemption was changed from an
apocalyptic event into the culmination of historical progress.
This radical alteration is especially evident when one looks at
modern Jewish transformations of the doctrines of election and
redemption. Indeed, these two classical docrines and the
modern ideas of destiny and progress have the greatest similarity.

It seems most likely that Spinoza himself was only suggesting
this naturalistic solution to the Jews' religious–political
problem as a hypothetical possibility. There is no evidence that

---

[95] *Spinoza's Critique of Religion*, 17. Along these lines, see J. Schwartz, "Liberalism and
the Jewish Connection: A Study of Spinoza and the Young Marx," *Political Theory*
13 (1985), 58ff.
[96] *TT-P*, chap. 18/p. 272.
[97] *Ibid.* See R. J. McShea, *The Political Philosophy of Spinoza* (New York, 1967), 163. Cf.
Schwartz, "Liberalism and the Jewish Connection," 84, n. 88 (conclusion).

he had any more interest in the Jews after his departure from the Sephardic Jewish community of Amsterdam in 1656.[98] But many modern Jewish thinkers saw it as the suggestion of something historically probable for the Jews. To them, Spinoza seemed to be advocating that the Jews once again take charge of their own lives and their own future. And clearly their consciousness of their own historical continuity required that they not totally sever their ties to their own past. Most modern Jewish thinkers accepted this, only differing as to what this transformation of the Jewish people and Judaism was to be. Those Jewish thinkers who saw the future of the Jews and Judaism to be within modern secular Western nation-states generally thought that the Jews had to become a faith community of likeminded individuals and that Judaism had to become a religion like Protestant Christianity – in form, that is, but not in substance. Those thinkers who, conversely, saw the future of the Jews within their own nation-state generally thought that the Jews had to become a modern ethnic entity and that Judaism had to become a national culture. Some thinkers tried to combine both perspectives in one way or another. But for all of them, if there was to be any election in the real, nonmetaphorical sense, it was going to have to be the election of the Jews by themselves and of their God by themselves. In other words, these modern Jewish thinkers followed Spinoza's philosophical reconstitution of the covenant, while simultaneously rejecting his permanent relegation of it to the irretrievable past. At the deepest philosophical level, then, they accepted his general premises, and actually built upon them, while at the same time refusing to draw his own particular historical conclusions from them.[99]

The loss of the classical doctrine of election, which Spinoza so powerfully advocated, entailed a considerable lowering of the eschatological horizon. By abandoning the hope for the heretofore elusive Messiah and world-to-come, many modern

---

[98] See J. M. Lucas, *The Oldest Biography of Spinoza*, ed. A. Wolf (New York, 1927), 52; also, Strauss, *Spinoza's Critique of Religion*, 164ff.

[99] For the cogency of such a hermeneutical move, see Novak, *Jewish–Christian Dialogue*, 68ff.

Jews felt that they could now at long last gain control of their own destiny. The loss of the transcendent mystery of their beginning brought with it the loss of the transcendent mystery of their end. This, more than anything else, appears to be Spinoza's legacy to modern Jewish thought hitherto. Yet I believe that it must be overcome if the classical doctrine of election is to be philosophically recovered. But that recovery cannot be truly effective until we see the varied fruit that grew out of the seeds Spinoza planted at the very beginnings of Jewish modernity.

CHAPTER 2

Hermann Cohen's concept of election

It is hard to imagine any philosopher having a greater aversion to any other philosopher than Hermann Cohen to Spinoza. This aversion stemmed from the two most important aspects of Cohen's life: his being a Jew, and his being a philosopher. He believed that Spinoza had done great and almost irrevocable harm to the two cultural institutions Cohen loved most: Judaism and philosophy.

As a Jew, Cohen was outraged at what he considered Spinoza's slander of Judaism. That slander consisted primarily of Spinoza's contention that Judaism is devoid of any genuine theoretical content, the type of content in which philosophy is truly interested. For Spinoza, as we have already seen, Judaism only has value as a political phenomenon, and even that value is by now largely passé. At best it could only function as a somewhat remote historical analogy to the modern democratic state Spinoza envisioned for his time and place. Cohen was well aware that this characterization of Judaism had been enormously influential on subsequent thinkers, even on Cohen's own philosophical inspiration: Immanuel Kant.[1] Because of this, Cohen devoted considerable effort to refuting Spinoza's claims in order to rescue Judaism for serious philo-

---

[1] See Kant, *Religion Within the Limits of Reason Alone*, trans. T. M. Greene and H. H. Hudson (New York, 1960), 116ff.

sophical interest once again, just as Cohen was convinced that Maimonides (who was his Jewish inspiration) had done in an earlier age. Thus, whereas Spinoza had made an absolute distinction (at least in Cohen's mind) between theory and *praxis*, seeing philosophy as the epitome of the former and Judaism as a mere example of the latter, Cohen insisted that "the theory of praxis alone is, however, philosophy."[2] And Judaism's practical character, its moral teaching, has direct and indispensable value for ethical theory, which, following Kant, Cohen assumed to be the highest form of philosophy.

As a Kantian philosopher, Cohen was almost equally outraged by Spinoza's pantheism and determinism. By identifying God within the same natural system that includes man as well as all physical phenomena, Spinoza had made morality – according to the Kantian definition, that is – impossible. For Cohen, morality requires both that God and man transcend the predetermined order of the physical world and that they be correlated in a noumenal realm outside that world. Only through such transcendence can freedom and teleology, the two indispensable ingredients of any authentic morality, possibly function.[3] Thus it was not only that Spinoza had removed Judaism from having any real interest for philosophy, but even more that he deprived philosophy of its highest function by precluding the construction of an authentically independent ethical system. Indeed, whereas a number of modern Jewish thinkers wished that Spinoza had never left Judaism and that a modern Judaism could be constructed which would again include him – at least posthumously – Hermann Cohen considered him to be "this great enemy" ("dieser grosse Feind").[4] Therefore, it was not that Judaism should be reconstructed to accommodate Spinoza; rather, Judaism should be constituted with such philosophical rigor as to demonstrate conclusively just why Spinoza could never be considered a Jewish thinker

---

[2] "Spinoza über Staat und Religion, Judentum und Christentum" (1915), in *Jüdische Schriften*, ed. B. Strauss (3 vols., Berlin, 1924), 3:302.

[3] See *Ethik des reinen Willens*, 4th ed. (Berlin, 1923), 317ff.

[4] "Spinoza über Staat, etc.," in *Jüdische Schriften*, 3:371. See also "Die Bedeutung des Judentums fur den religiösen Fortschritt der Menschheit" (1910), *ibid.*, 1:55.

again. Throughout his writings Cohen made this basic point over and over again about Spinoza's unacceptability on both Jewish and philosophical grounds.

So it would seem that considering Cohen's absolute distancing of himself from anything even resembling Spinoza's ontology, one would find Cohen having a view of the election of Israel essentially different from that of Spinoza. After all, since election denotes a relationship between God and Israel, surely a paradigm shift in ontology, wherein the being of God is constituted, will necessarily entail a commensurate paradigm shift in the way God's historical relationships are constituted. Yet, as we shall soon discover, that is not the case at all. Instead, the difference between Spinoza's view of election and that of Cohen is one of degree rather than one of kind. This is the case, in fact, because the God Cohen conceives philosophically does not function all that differently from the God of Spinoza in the lives of human subjects and their communities.

For Cohen, as for Spinoza, God functions in two ways: (1), in the way religious traditions experience God; (2), in the way philosophers conceive of God. Moreover, the way philosophers conceive of God is not a conceptualization of the experience of religious traditions. Such conceptualization would be the work of theologians, not philosophers, at least not those whom either Spinoza or Cohen would designate as philosophers. Instead, philosophers conceive of God in terms of the function God performs in the philosophical systems they have constructed. The inclusion of a concept of God in any philosophical system necessarily makes it an ontology, that is, a way of thinking about what Aristotle called "first things."[5]

Now if a philosopher (that is, one who is a philosopher on the above criteria) still wants to use the word "God," then he or she is somehow going to have to connect the use of that word in his or her philosophical system with the use of that word in ordinary discourse, discourse which is inevitably derived from the experience of which religious traditions speak. Otherwise, the use of the word "God" per se is pointless, and it would be

[5] *Metaphysics* 981b27.

far less confusing simply to use a philosophical word like "Being" or "the Absolute" consistently.[6]

One can assume that any philosopher who intentionally uses the word "God" and does not totally substitute some philosophically constructed word for it also has some connection with a community whose discourse and practice is determined by a religious tradition. In Spinoza's case, as we have seen, this connection is essentially one of deconstruction, that is, his connection with the Jewish community had already been severed (and a connection with the Christian community had never been initiated). Thus whatever he could salvage from that connection had to be reconstructed within a totally new context. In the case of the doctrine of the election of Israel, as we have seen, what he salvaged were the democratic implications of the election of God as their sovereign by the ancient Israelites.

In the case of Cohen, on the other hand, his connection with a community and its religious tradition was a persistent reality. Hermann Cohen was born a Jew and chose to remain a member of the Jewish community for his entire life. He lived by many of its traditions and honestly spoke its religious language in worship and discourse. However, even though the doctrine of the election of Israel is not something he intended to deconstruct, but rather something he intended to constitute philosophically as a living reality, he nevertheless had to connect it with his philosophically constructed God idea. In so doing, as we shall see, he agrees with Spinoza's main theological point, which is that in essence it is Israel who chooses God, not God who chooses Israel. But the latter is the main thrust of the doctrine of election's original presentation in Scripture and the teachings of the Rabbis, as we shall examine in much greater detail in later chapters. Thus, as we shall see later on in this chapter, the difference between Spinoza and

---

[6] This is a problem faced by all theologians who are also philosophers, and even by all philosophers who are also theologians. See, e.g., Gregory of Nyssa, *Against Eunomius*, in *Nicene and Post-Nicene Fathers*, 2nd series (Grand Rapids, Mich., 1983), 5:50–51. (I thank my colleague Prof. Robert L. Wilken for this reference.) See also Thomas Aquinas, *Summa Theologiae*, 1, q. 2, a. 3.

Cohen on this point has much less to do with their philosophical differences about God and has much more to do with their theological–political differences about the status of the Jewish people.

COHEN'S PHILOSOPHICAL GOD

Although students of the history of philosophy tend to think of Hermann Cohen as a Kantian (indeed, *the* restorer of Kant to the center of philosophical attention in Germany in the middle of the nineteenth century), his philosophical following of Kant was certainly not slavish. His relation to Kant comes closest, it seems to me, to Aquinas' relation to Aristotle. That is, Cohen revived and transformed Kant's philosophy much the same as Aquinas revived and transformed Aristotle's philosophy. This is important to bear in mind because Cohen's God idea is where he makes his most fundamental break with Kant.

Kant had banished the idea of God altogether from his theoretical philosophy, that is, from the philosophy interested in our experience of sense objects qua phenomena, and he confined any meaningful use of the idea to the realm of practical philosophy, that is, to ethics. In ethics God functions as a postulate of what Kant calls "pure practical reason." The postulate of God's existence is required to assure moral agents who still live in the morally indifferent phenomenal world that their adherence to the maxims formulated by the categorical imperative will ultimately bear real results for them. Without such results, the intentionality of moral reasoning would be absurdly ineffectual. These real desired results are subsumed under the term "happiness" (*Gluckseligkeit*).[7]

The problem with this idea of God, for Cohen, is that it compromises the primacy of God by reducing God to functioning as the means to the end of human happiness. Such a "God" hardly satisfies the affirmation of the primacy of God insisted on by both traditional religions – Judaism in particular – and

---

[7] See *Critique of Practical Reason*, trans. L. W. Beck (Indianapolis, 1956), 114ff.

classical ontology.[8] So, as far as Cohen is concerned, only a God who functions as a true "origin" (*Ursprung*) is worthy of the name "God" at all.[9] And by "origin" Cohen does not mean a historical beginning (*Anfang*), but rather a noetic starting point, like a premise in a logical inference, or what Spinoza called *causa sui*, namely, causality by definition.[10] The question is just how God does function as *the origin* in Cohen's philosophical system. This question must be answered before we can better understand how Cohen sees election as a relation involving this *originating* God.

Cohen's break with Kant over the role of God in practical reason stems from his break with Kant over the origin of theoretical reason. In his constitution of theoretical reason (*Erkenntnis*), Cohen removes Kant's notion of the "thing-in-itself" (*Ding an sich*), that is, Kant's insistence that there is some transexperiential reality which lies behind all of the phenomena we experience, and that it is a reality which grounds the objects of experience somehow or other. In Cohen's eyes, such an insistence is a stumbling block to the true understanding of the role reason plays in theoretical reason, especially in the natural sciences.[11] There is little doubt that this break with Kant was made plausible by the advances in science and especially mathematics in the nineteenth century, advances by which Cohen was heavily influenced.[12] These advances showed that the role of reason is much more constructive than had been thought before. Furthermore, the notion of the "thing-in-itself" seemed to be too much of a concession to the

---

[8] See "Innere Beziehungen der Kantischen Philosophie zum Judentum" (1910), in *Jüdische Schriften*, 1:293; also, *Der Begriff der Religion im System der Philosophie* (Giessen, 1915), 51.

[9] See *Religion of Reason Out of the Sources of Judaism*, trans. S. Kaplan (New York, 1972), 63–64, where Cohen constitutes *creatio ex nihilo* as the theological expression of God as *Ursprung*.

[10] See *Logik der reinen Erkenntnis*, 3rd ed. (Berlin, 1922), 79, where Cohen defines *Ursprung* as what the Greek philosophers called *archē*. Note, also, *ibid.*, 36: "Denken ist Denken des Ursprungs. Dem Ursprung darf nichts gegeben sein ... Der Grund muss Ursprung werden." See *Religion of Reason*, 69.

[11] See *Logik*, 376–377; and note 271: "Die Bedingung ist die Be Dingung ... Die Bedingung ist die Ding-Erzeugung." See also *Ethik*, 25.

[12] This is especially evident in Cohen's *Das Prinzip der Infinitesimal-Methode und seine Geschichte* (Frankfurt-on-Main, 1968), e.g., sec. 100.

type of empiricism that Cohen thought had been so thoroughly discredited in his time by Idealism.[13] (Even though Cohen was very much of an anti-Hegelian, on this latter point at least he and Hegel were quite close.[14]) In empiricism, reason's basic function is to be a description *of* experience and ultimately subordinate to it, therefore.

By removing the "thing-in-itself" from consideration in theoretical reason, Cohen shifted the locale of theoretical reason more fully from the object to the thinking subject than Kant had been able to do. Accordingly, "data" are no longer what are *given to* reason, but rather what reason selects from experience using its own criteria and thus what reason gives *by itself to itself*.[15] Even the objects of reason, let alone reason itself, are no longer taken as having their origin (*Ursprung*) in external "reality," but rather in reason's most basic idea, the idea of truth (*Wahrheit*).[16] Truth itself, then, is the origin of all we know, indeed all that we can know. It grounds its own objects. Within its own range, it is beholden to nothing outside itself. Logic, which is truth's full methodology, is at work throughout the sciences. It gives them their rational validity.

Following Kant, in order to constitute the priority of ethics over theoretical reason in his philosophical system, Cohen cannot take the idea of truth as being absolutely originating. If that were the case, then ethics, which is concerned with the good, would have to be subordinate to theoretical reason as it is in virtually all the pre-Kantian philosophies, going back to Plato and Aristotle and up to all those whom they influenced. So, what Cohen does is to show that the interest in truth must be correlated with a commitment to truthfulness (*Wahrhaftig-keit*), which is, of course, a moral virtue. Without a fundamental commitment to truthfulness, no one would make the sustained effort that the interest in truth requires to be intellectually productive. Only truthfulness makes truth worthy of respect. On the other hand, without the rigor of truth, truthful-

[13] See *Logik*, 596.
[14] See Walter Kaufmann, *Hegel* (Garden City, N.Y., 1966), 182–83; also, R. Plant, *Hegel* (Bloomington and London, 1973), 81–82.
[15] *Logik*, 81–82, 587.   [16] See *Ethik*, 88ff.

ness would remain a merely virtuous instinct, but it would be one without any connection to reason.[17] Thus truth and truthfulness are interdependent. As Cohen succinctly put it, "without scientific truth no truthfulness; and without truthfulness no truth."[18]

The superiority of ethics over science, however, comes in with the idea of autonomy. Although science is not dependent on the objects of experience inasmuch as they are not grounded in the external reality of the thing-in-itself but are constituted by scientific reason itself, scientific reason must still select *from* what is *found* in experience (*Empfindung*).[19] Without this condition, the role of experimentation in modern scientific reason would be totally lost. Clearly, no one would take scientific reason seriously if it did not include experimentation in its overall program. Being so influenced by technology and its result-oriented validation, modern science must *do* something in order to be noticed by the culture in which it operates. That "doing," however "creative," is not a *creatio ex nihilo*; it must still work with objects that are already there for everybody. In that sense, then, science does not create its objects but only constitutes them.

Ethics, on the other hand, does create its own objects.[20] The objects of ethics, ultimately subsumed under the idea of the good, are the projections of reason creating its own ideal world. That ideal creation originates in the autonomy of the moral subject, an autonomy that the knowing subject, however constructive, does not and can never have.[21] Both science and ethics are now located in the subject. It is no longer the case that the ground of science is the external thing-in-itself (only the conditions of experience being internal) whereas the ground of ethics is internal (in the moral subject as *causa noumenon*). Both are now internal; their difference is thus one of degree rather than one of kind. The practical reason of ethics

---

[17] See *ibid.*, 507ff.
[18] *Logik*, 604. See Sylvain Zac, *La Philosophie religieuse de Hermann Cohen* (Paris, 1984), 27.
[19] See *Logik*, 67, 145, 401, 418ff., 472; also, *Ethik*, 399.   [20] See *Ethik*, 179ff.
[21] See *ibid.*, 429.

seems to be absolutely creative, whereas the theoretical reason of science seems to be only relatively creative. Nevertheless, for Cohen, this is not the entire story.

In the realm of ethics, Cohen is quite literal in his acceptance of Kant's notion of autonomy.[22] The only moral rules that are rationally valid are those which the moral subject has willed for himself or herself along with every other possible moral subject. Autonomy, then, is not "self-rule" in the sense of practical subjectivism ("doing my own thing," in today's popular parlance); rather, it is the self giving voice to the idea of rational law itself by creating an ideal world through its pure will – a "kingdom of ends," in Kant's words.[23] This ideal realm is constructed with the assumption of the primary dignity of moral subjects, who by the criterion of universal consistency determine a system of rules made by themselves and for themselves alone.[24] Thus autonomy functions as the origin (*Ursprung*) of ethics in the same way that logic functions as the origin of science. But the advantage of the ethical origin is that it is less encumbered than the scientific origin; it is less conditioned (*unbedingt*).[25]

Since Cohen follows Kant in removing God from the construction of his system of theoretical reason, and since he eliminates Kant's postulated God ("the dispenser of happiness") from his system of ethics, it would seem that there is no place at all for God in his systematic philosophy. Yet, as it were, Cohen saves the best for last. This is accomplished by invoking the idea of God as an answer to the question of the correlation of science and ethics.[26] The question's essential weight is from the side of ethics.

Ethics, although positing the most ideally creative origin in

---

[22] See *ibid.*, 321ff.

[23] See *Groundwork of the Metaphysic of Morals*, trans. H. J. Paton (New York, 1964), 100ff.

[24] See *Ethik*, 341. The second formulation of the categorical imperative by Kant, namely, the moral subject as *Zweck an sich selbst*, is for Cohen "der tiefste und machtigste Sinn" (*ibid.*, 322).

[25] See *ibid.*, 425. Note, also, *ibid.*, 14, where Cohen sees ethical idealism as "von der Tyrannei der Erfahrung sich frei macht."

[26] See *ibid.*, 425.

the idea of autonomy, still cannot itself answer the question of efficacy, that is, is it in the end anything more than an elaborate body of good intentions? Ethics does not seem to explain anything in the phenomenal world, ruled as it is by a totally deterministic causality.[27] In this world, freedom and teleology, the two indispensable elements for any ethics, simply do not exist in any meaningful sense.[28] As such, in the end is not ethics simply a form of ethereal inwardness? Is not ethics ultimately absurd if it cannot will what is realizable?

Kant too deals with this question and attempts to answer it by postulating God as the ultimate dispenser of happiness for moral subjects. Cohen, as we have seen, rejects this answer to the question of moral efficacy because it entails the assumption that an experience is the final cause of the very human capacity that is supposed to transcend experience and its limits. Cohen sees this an an unacceptable return to the type of eudaimonism that Kant's whole practical philosophy is intended to get us beyond. Therefore, for Cohen, God is not the dispenser of happiness postulated *within* ethics; rather, God is the origin of all origins, the prime idea that enables ethics to be really efficacious, that is, ultimately rule all phenomena.[29] In this way, then, God does transcend the moral realm – taken as human activity, that is – and not just the physical realm, although Cohen does not seem to see any meaning of divine being that is not correlated with human morality.[30] Thus the

---

27 See Kant, *Critique of Practical Reason*, 117ff.

28 See Kant, *Critique of Pure Reason*, B395 and note thereon; *Critique of Judgment*, trans. J. H. Bernard (New York, 1951), sec. 68.

29 "Der Gott, welcher die Wahrheit ist; welcher die Harmonie der Naturerkenntnis und der Sittlichen Erkenntnis bedeutet" (*Ethik*, 455).

30 See *ibid.*, 470, where Cohen argues that God transcends nature and morality when *each* is taken *separately*. However, God is conceived at the point when "die Transzendenz zwischen Natur und Sittlichkeit aufgehoben wird." The question remains, though, whether Cohen could possibly posit that there is *more* than this regarding God, even if he cannot constitute it – like Kant's positing of the *Ding an sich*, which he could not constitute (see *Critique of Pure Reason*, B306). In one passage in *Religion of Reason*, Cohen says about the attributes of action predicated of God by Scripture, "these norms are contained in the essence of God, but it is impossible to imagine (*nicht auszudenken*) that they could exhaust (*erschöpfen*) this essence: they could have been only conceived for man, could be valid for the actions of man only" (95 = *Religion der Vernunft aus den Quellen des Judentums*, 2nd ed. [Darmstadt, 1966], 110). Furthermore, Cohen's endnote to this passage (n. 16, p. 464) quotes Maimonides,

prime ontological causality is noumenal, it creates its own purposes, but it is not any one of those purposes itself.[31] As the infinite ideal of all ideals, God is beyond teleological attainment by any finite entity. There can never be any unification of the finite and the infinite, even in the Messianic Age. God is ever transcendent, both in the beginning qua idea and in the end qua ideal. Hence God is that which makes the complete correlation of the world of ethics and the world of science ultimately possible.[32] By so doing, Cohen is convinced that he has saved the absolute status of God, without in any way compromising the more specifically originating function of autonomy in ethics and logic in science.

Through this type of systematic philosophical construction, Cohen has saved God as the absolute. He can therefore reintroduce the classical ontological distinction between being and becoming. For Cohen, God is *Being*, that which is perfect in and of itself and by which everything less is measured. Everything less, then, is in a state of development, that is, it is *becoming* what it aspires to be.[33] Therefore, even though God's Being grounds the realms of both science and ethics, it has the most direct effect on ethics. For it is here that teleological striving, the conscious aspiration of becoming *to be* its perfection, is located. This striving is seen as the move from the particular and contingent to the universal and necessary.

By adopting the classical ontological designation of God as Being, Cohen has removed from the realm of the divine the three ontological elements, which, as we saw in the previous chapter, are needed in any philosophical constitution of the classical theological doctrine of election. These elements are: possibility, mutual relationship, and purpose.

Guide of the Perplexed, 1.54, where Maimonides clearly states that God transcends his attributes of action. Although the meaning of the above passage in Cohen seems clear, it is certainly atypical of Hermann Cohen. Much more typical of his theology is a statement like this: "nicht Gott allein und an sich, sondern immer nur in Korrelation zum Menschen" (*Der Begriff der Religion*, 32). Cf., also, *Ethik*, 591: "Innere Beziehungen der Kantischen Philosophie zum Judentum," *Jüdische Schriften*, 1:294.

[31] For the distinction between *Zweck* qua "end" and *Absicht* qua "purpose" in Kant's philosophy, see D. Novak, *Suicide and Morality* (New York, 1975), 91–92.

[32] See *Ethik*, 466ff.   [33] See *Der Begriff der Religion*, 47ff.; *Religion of Reason*, 59ff.

In his adoption of the classical ontological distinction between being and becoming, Cohen's ontology is different from that of Spinoza. To constitute an ontological relation between being and becoming is to constitute a relation that is in essence teleological. Being functions as the *telos* or ideal for becoming. On this point, Cohen is very much in the tradition of Platonism.[34] Spinoza, on the other hand, who is very much in the monistic tradition of Parmenides, does not constitute any such relation on the ontological level.[35] Everything is what it is, that is, *sub specie aeternitatis*, from the perspective of nature per se (*natura naturans*). Change, conversely, is only the modalities of appearance that we experience *sub specie durationis*.[36] Furthermore, beings (*natura naturata*) do not aspire to be what they are not now; rather, they only follow their own innate course of action (*conatus*) that has always been determined as such.[37]

In a relation of being and becoming, there is a place for the element of possibility. For if becoming on the moral level, which is the level in which Cohen's ontology most fully functions, involves choices, then the objects of choice function as possibilities. These possibilities are conscious options of which moral subjects are aware in advance of their actual choices. Moral subjects are faced with possible alternatives which they must judge in order to act rationally. However, it must be remembered that there can be no possibilities for God as Being per se. Possibility, in this way of thinking anyway, functions within becoming alone. (In chapter 4, I shall attempt to constitute divine possibility, relationality, and purposefulness without the assumption of divine Becoming it seems to involve for Cohen and the adherents of this type of ontology.)

Being per se, as it were, cannot step out of itself to be

---

[34] See *Religion of Reason*, 67. The identification of God and Being first enters Judaism with the LXX translation of Exod. 3:14 ("I am who I am") as *eimi ho ōn*, "I am Being." For a full discussion of the theological ramifications of identifying the God of Abraham, Isaac and Jacob with the God of the philosophers, see D. Novak, "Buber and Tillich," *Journal of Ecumenical Studies* (1992), 29:159ff.

[35] For Cohen's location of a line of pantheism from Parmenides to Spinoza, see *Religion of Reason*, 59ff.

[36] See *Ethics*, v, prop. 7.   [37] See *ibid.*, iii, prop. 7.

something else, something which it is not already, something other than itself. Being the ideal of all self-perfecting becoming, God functions as the inspiration behind all authentic moral choices, but God himself does not make any such choices. Accordingly, God is not a moral subject. God grounds ethics, but he is not within the system of ethics itself. To assume that God is a moral subject, that is, a person, would compromise God's perfect, ideal Being. Only an idea, but not a person, can be transcendent.[38] So, it is true that Cohen constitutes nondivine becoming – especially conscious and free human becoming – in his ontology, and this gives election an ontological grounding it does not have for Spinoza. Nevertheless, Cohen's God is very much like Spinoza's inasmuch as this God is a God who is just as incapable himself of choosing anything, let alone any people. In short, God is not free in Cohen's view because he cannot be free. Freedom can only be attributed to those who are the subjects of rational moral becoming. Accordingly, God's creatorhood, which is the expression of God's most radical freedom, is reduced by Cohen to the necessary correlate of creation. Thus the creator is to creation what being is to becoming. But being cannot be anything else but a point in such a correlation. So for Cohen as for Spinoza, God is totally defined.[39] Just as Spinoza insisted that God cannot be anything but *causa sui*, so Cohen insists that God cannot be anything but *originating principle*.

Like Spinoza's God, too, Cohen's God does not engage in any mutual relationships. Even though Cohen speaks of "I–thou" relationships in a way that suggests to many contemporary readers Martin Buber's better-known use of this key concept, it should be emphasized that Cohen, most unlike Buber, does not see this type of relationship pertaining to what

---

[38] *Ethik*, 457.

[39] "If God is recognized through the attribute of being not inert, then he becomes recognizable as creator; *thus*, the idea of *creation is taken into the concept (Begriff) of God*. The riddle of creation is thus resolved through the definition of God. For now creation rather means God's being, which is the being of the originative principle (*Ursprungs*). And becoming now has its basis (*Grund*) in this being as the originative principle" (*Religion of Reason*, 65 = German, 75).

he takes to be the reality between man and God.[40] It is limited to the realm of the human other with whom the moral subject lives in this world (*Mitmensch*).[41] For this reason, then, one should not confuse the correlation Cohen constitutes between man and God with an actual, direct relationship between them as persons. Man loves God as an ideal rather than as a presence; and the notion of God loving man is only metaphorical, that is, God is retrospectively posited as the source for the love humans are to have for each other. Thus Cohen asks: "Does God first love man, or does man first love the unique God?"[42] And he answers his question by asserting, "Only now, after (*nachdem*) man has learned to love man as fellowman, is his thought turned (*zurückbezogen*) to God, and only now (*Jetzt erst*) does he understand that God loves man."[43] In essence, just as this philosophically conceived God prepares the correlation between the noumenal world of ethics and the phenomenal world of science, so does this religiously conceived God prepare the human subject to be ready for the rational autonomy of moral action. This is done by conceiving God as the One who forgives us for sensual lapses into sin.[44]

Finally, like Spinoza's God Cohen's God cannot have any purposes outside himself. For any such divine purpose would immediately imply, indeed presuppose, that God is not perfect, that he has some lack which must be overcome, some need which must be subsequently fulfilled.[45] However, purposefulness is at the very heart of the human state of becoming. The purposefulness of human moral action directs this becoming. And since, for Cohen, this human becoming taken collectively is historical process, human purposefulness is teleological. Its collective *telos* is the culmination of history in a truly united humankind.[46] This united humankind itself is not, of course, God. God, being wholly transcendent, can never be united

[40] See *ibid.*, 250ff., 132ff.
[41] See *ibid.*, 113ff.; also, Zac, *La Philosophie religieuse de Hermann Cohen*, 101, 127.
[42] *Religion of Reason*, 146.   [43] *Ibid.*, 147 (= German, 171).
[44] See *ibid.*, 186ff.
[45] "For he himself is not in need of man as fellowman" (*ibid.*, 148).
[46] See *Ethik*, 499ff.; *Religion of Reason*, esp. 255.

with anything less transcendent, even that most exalted human ideal: a united humankind.[47] Nevertheless, the closest correlation possible between God and man is the correlation of God and messianically unified humankind. And although that unification of humankind is an unlimited developmental process (*Entwicklung*), it can still be gauged by determining how much progress (*Fortschritt*) has been made in the historical movement from particularism to universalism, especially in the realm of politics.[48] Within the correlation of God and humankind at this ideal level we can see the deepest meaning of Cohen's philosophical presentation of the doctrine of election.

THE UNIQUENESS OF ISRAEL IN THE DIVINE–HUMAN CORRELATION

One can best understand Hermann Cohen's philosophical constitution of the classical Jewish doctrine of the election of Israel if one remembers that in his theology the Torah is prior in importance to the people of Israel. Election is consistently subordinate to revelation. The essence of the Torah, for Cohen, is the primordial moral law of the cosmos, a rational law which is now ideal, but which God in the Messianic Age will make fully effective.

The true Torah, then, is universal moral law. As Cohen clearly states, "The Law (*das Gesetz*), therefore, is preeminently called teaching (*Lehre*) ... the only goal of the law is his moral perfection, his fulfillment as man."[49] Nevertheless, what does one do with the greater bulk of the Torah which is so clearly particularistic, pertaining to the unique life of the Jewish people? In order to be closer to much of the thrust of Jewish tradition, should not a Jewish theologian-philosopher constitute the particular as prior to the universal, or to put it in the most originally ontological terms, should not he or she consti-

---

[47] See *Religion of Reason*, 105.   [48] *Ibid.*, 250 (= German, 292).

[49] *Religion of Reason*, 338 = German, 393–394. There Cohen makes the liberal Jewish distinction between the divine origin of the Torah along with the human specification of its actual duties. "Es ist ... eine theoretische Unterweisung, die daher dem Menschen zur Pflicht gemacht werden kann." See also pp. 85–94 below.

tute existence prior to essence?[50] This, however, is a move that is too radical for Cohen the philosopher to make. For his ontology is derived from Kant – and most originally from Plato – and then subsequently applied to Judaism. In this ontology, essence is prior to existence, thus grounding an epistemology in which the universal is prior to the particular. Therefore, the question that Hermann Cohen faced as a Jewish theologian is how the particularism of the Jewish people, which is endemic to the doctrine of the election of Israel, could be justified by the universalistic criteria he has as a philosopher accepted from Plato through Kant. Without such justification, Cohen could not cogently bring his systematic philosophy to bear on his reinterpretation of the historical sources of Jewish theology. And in the background, to be sure, was Spinoza's challenge that the continued existence of Judaism is antithetical to the construction of a rational society worthy of rational persons.

On purely Kantian grounds, the particularism of the doctrine of the election of Israel seems to be an embarrassment.[51] Cohen faces the issue honestly and directly.

Thus the question remains how could this thought of a unique God (*ein einzigen Gottes*) become manifest uniquely and alone (*einzig und allein*) to the spirit of this people? ... does not this universalism call into question not only Israel but every people in its particularity (*seiner Sonderheit*)? ... How incomprehensible the origin of Messianism in the midst of a national consciousness must appear to us, inasmuch as it had to think and feel the "election" (*Erwählung*) of Israel as a singling out (*Auserwählung*) for the worship of God.[52]

To understand this passage properly, one has to be aware of the significance of the categories of "singularity" (*Einzigkeit*) and "unity" (*Einheit*) in Cohen's philosophy.

---

[50] On this point, see D. Novak, *Jewish–Christian Dialogue* (New York, 1989), 115ff. Cf. Franz Rosenzweig, *The Star of Redemption*, trans. W. W. Hallo (New York, 1970), 12ff.

[51] For the difficulty that the early Reform (mostly German) liturgists had with the classical doctrine, see Jakob J. Petuchowski, *Prayerbook Reform in Europe* (New York, 1968), chaps. 9, 11, 12.

[52] *Religion of Reason*, 243 (= German, 284). For the type of perennial critique of Jewish particularism that Cohen was attempting to answer (in this case, by anticipation), see Eric Voegelin, *Order and History* (Baton Rouge, La., 1957), 1:327. For a perceptive treatment of how the embarrassment with the singularity of historical

For Cohen, the designation of God as "one" (*ehad*) does not mean that God is "one" among many like the number one, nor does it mean that God is one entity composed of various parts. If God were simply one among many, he would be less than the absolute, and monotheism (Cohen's continual designation of true religion, of which Judaism is the epitome) would ultimately be a trivial henotheism. And, if God were a unity of several parts, the distinction between God and nature would be dissolved in some sort of pantheism, which is the point Cohen never tired of using to philosophically condemn Spinoza. God is, therefore, *einzig*, namely, the only totally transcendent singularity. God alone is Being per se.[53] Human becoming, which is posited as the infinite task of moral perfection, is to lead to the unification (*Einheit*) of humankind in correlation with God's Being as the singular but unattainable ideal of all ideals.

Following this line of thought, then, it would seem that any individual people claiming for itself true *Einzigkeit* (singularity) would, in effect, be radically confusing human becoming with divine Being. *Einheit* (universal unity) is the ultimate human goal towards which every people is to progress and from which no people should ever detour. But does it not seem to be the case that the Jewish people, by its continued self-isolation, is moving in the opposite direction? Are not the modern anti-Semites, with whom Cohen was all too familiar, right in charging that the Jews are not only out of the progressive and universal tendency of history but, even worse, a major impediment to it?[54] Nevertheless, despite the gravity of this charge and its wide acceptance by non-Jews and assimilationist Jews (whom he detested), Cohen believed that he had an answer to this charge of antiprogressive particularism. In presenting his answer, he called upon the full force of his philosophical creativity and his wide and deep knowledge of the Jewish

---

events in the God–man relationship came to full force in eighteenth-century Deism, see Charles Taylor, *Sources of the Self* (Cambridge, Mass., 1989), 273–274.

[53] See "Einheit oder Einzigkeit Gottes" (1917), in *Jüdische Schriften*, 3:87ff.; also, *Logik*, 169–170, 474.

[54] See, e.g., "Ein Bekenntnis in der Judenfrage" (1880), in *Jüdische Schriften*, 2:73ff.

tradition. His answer is a significant *tour de force* in modern Jewish thought.

With scholarly thoroughness, using both classical sources and modern historical methodology, Cohen demonstrates that authentic monotheism, which is for him the only sufficient ontological ground for universalizable morality, first arose in ancient Israel.[55] Nevertheless, such a conclusion alone would only indicate that the new universal order Cohen saw emerging in Europe, and especially in the reunified Germany after 1871, should not forget its historical origin. But, as we have seen, a historical origin (*Anfang*) is not the same as an ontological origin (*Ursprung*). Only on the basis of an ontological origin could there be a sufficient reason to argue philosophically for the moral necessity of the continued separate existence of the Jewish people in the present, let alone for the moral necessity of the Jewish people to live until the envisioned messianic future. And surely, for Cohen, only moral arguments are adequate for authentic human practice.

Cohen argues that the continued separate existence of the Jewish people is necessary *until* true messianic unity (*Einheit*) is achieved.[56] Hence, in the real absence of such human unity to date, the Jewish people has to remain closer to divine singularity (*Einzigkeit*) than to the real state of the world.[57] In the world, in its premessianic present, there is still only national and religious multiplicity (*Mehrheit*), but no true totality (*Allheit*).[58] Any premature surrender to the world-as-it-is would be countermessianic, a charge leveled by Cohen more than once against Christianity.[59] By this logic, Cohen justifies virtually all those Jewish practices, such as the Sabbath and the dietary laws, that keep Jews apart from the general culture around

[55] See *Religion of Reason*, 24ff.
[56] "Das aber ist der Sinn der Religion der Propheten ... dass er den Staatenbund der Menschheit vorbereitet in der messianischen Idee der vereingten Menschheit" (*Ethik*, 500).
[57] See *Religion of Reason*, 254.
[58] "Die Einheit nicht minder Mehrheit gedacht werde ... Die Sonderung muss ebenso sehr und ebenso bestimmt als Vereinigung werden" (*Logik*, 60) ... die Mehrheit nicht lediglich als Gegenwart gedacht, sondern in die Zukunft gehoben wird" (*ibid.*, 63).
[59] See *Religion of Reason*, 240, 249, 264.

them. Israel must be monotheistic messianism's vanguard for the time being.[60]

The task of the nations of the world is to see in Israel, and the task of Israel is to see in herself, a symbolic vision of the Messianic Age, which is the ideal future.[61] Thus Israel's election (*Erwählung*), her being singled out (*Auserwählung*), is to be maintained until there is a true correlation (Cohen's favorite logical term) between the *Einzigkeit* of God and the *Einheit* of humanity. So Cohen writes,

But this people is less for the sake of its own nation than as a symbol of mankind. A unique (*einziges*) symbol for the unique idea (*einzigen Gedanken*); the individual peoples have to strive to the unique unity (*einzigen Einheit*) of mankind.[62]

Israel is not only the historical beginning (*Anfang*) of mono-theistic messianism, but also the keeper of the pure message of this ideal future in present reality (*Wirklichkeit*). Thus Cohen emphasizes the historical necessity of her continued existence into this future. "From the very outset this symbolism presaged (*Vorbedeutung*) Israel's messianic call, its *elevation* (*Aufhebung*) *into one mankind* (*Menschheit*)."[63] Israel's uncompleted, hence still warranted, task is "the messianic realization (*Durchführung*) of monotheism."[64] Israel's ever-present responsibility is to disseminate the knowledge of God that "makes Messianism capable of unlimited expansion (*unbeschränkte Ausdehnung*)."[65] Here we have what is undoubtedly the most astute philosophical presentation of the distinctly modern Jewish notion of the "Mission of Israel."[66]

---

[60] See *ibid.*, 359.

[61] For the important role of temporality, esp. futurity (*Zukunft*) in Cohen's philosophy, see *Ethik*, 401ff.

[62] *Religion of Reason*, 253 (= German, 295).   [63] *Ibid.*, 260 (= German, 303).

[64] *Ibid.*, 267 (= German, 312).

[65] *Ibid.*, 254 (= German, 297).

[66] For a critical analysis of this notion, see D. Novak, *Jewish Social Ethics* (New York, 1992), 225ff. For the critique of this notion by the early Zionist theorist Ahad Ha'Am (d. 1927), see his "Kohen Ve-Navi" and "Shinui Ha'Arakhin," in *Kol Kitvei Ahad Ha'Am*, 2nd ed. (Jerusalem, 1949), 92 and 156. Ahad Ha'Am did not deny the distinctive role of the Jewish people. His criticism of the West European Jewish notion of the mission of Israel was that it is too beholden to Western liberal notions of individualism and democracy.

What is important to see here with Cohen, being the true
philosopher he was and who thus formulated his terms with
precise care, is that the term he uses for the ultimate fulfillment
of Israel's historical mission is *Aufhebung*. This term, of course, is
the most significant one in Hegel's theory of the progressive
manifestation of Spirit.[67] Now Cohen was usually quite
opposed to Hegel, especially to what he considered Hegel's
unwarranted merging of the infinite/ideal and the finite/real,
even if that merging does not take place until the end of
history.[68] Indeed, his impressive début in German academic
philosophy in the middle of the nineteenth century was to
begin to turn attention away from Hegel back to Kant.[69] Yet
Kant's eschatology, because it seemed to be so oriented to
individual happiness only, as we have seen, is quite insufficient
for Cohen's messianism. So it seems he borrowed a key term
from Hegel, the philosopher who most strenuously attempted
to fuse the philosophical quest for the absolute finality (*telos*)
with the historical quest for the fulfilled endtime (*eschaton*).[70]
Hegel's key term for this whole process is *Aufhebung*, which
designates the temporal means whereby the now separated
particular and universal ultimately merge together within
history as some new future totality. The elements of that which
is *aufgehoben* are wrenched from their original separation from
each other and are then radically reconstructed in a totality
unlike anything theretofore experienced. But Cohen's fundamental difference with Hegel is that in his constitution of

---

[67] See Kaufmann, *Hegel*, 144; also, S. Avineri, *The Social and Political Thought of Karl
Marx* (Cambridge, 1968), 37.

[68] See, e.g., his critique of Hegel's synthesis of *Idee* (infinite) and *Begriff* (finite) in
Logik, 314; also, *Ethik*, 254. Cf. Franz Rosenzweig, *Briefe*, ed. E. Rosenzweig (Berlin,
1935), no. 221, p. 299.

[69] This can be seen in first major work (in 1871), *Kants Theorie der Erfahrung*. See, esp.,
4th ed. (Berlin, 1925), 526ff.

[70] This meaning of *telos* and *eschaton* is clearly expressed by Hegel at the conclusion of
Phänomenologie des Geistes, ed. J. Hoffmeister (Hamburg, 1952), 564: "*Das Ziel*, das
absolute Wissen ... in der Form der Zufälligkeit erscheinenden Daseins, ist die
Geschichte, nach der Seite des begriffenen Organisation aber die *Wissenschaft* des
erscheiden Wissens, beide zusammen, die begriffene Geschichte bilden ... die Wirklichkeit, Wahrheit und Gewissheit." Cf. Martin Heidegger, *An Introduction to
Metaphysics*, trans. R. Manheim (Garden City, N.Y., 1961), 49–50.

Aufhebung it is ideal and will, therefore, never be located within history, even within its culmination. As such, the *Aufhebung* of Israel into humanity could not be a historical event. This being the case, then, Jewish uniqueness can *never really* be sacrificed for anything more general found in the world.

Indeed, by impressive philosophical means Cohen foreclosed the most prevalent modern intellectual justification of Jewish assimilation, namely, that Jewish particularism should be overcome (*aufgehoben*) by the more universal forms of modern society and culture. One can see the more individualistic forms of this justification for assimilation stemming from the liberalism of Spinoza; and one can see the more collectivist forms stemming from Marx (who, of course, derived much of his view of the developmental character of human history from Hegel). Each had many modern Jewish followers. But along philosophical lines, Hermann Cohen was no doubt convinced that he had a valid retort to both of these renegades from Judaism and the Jewish people, and to all whom they respectively influenced. So Cohen surely believed that he alone had saved the classical Jewish doctrine of the election of Israel by philosophical means. Nevertheless, this philosophical feat did not come without considerable tensions.

Occasionally, Cohen did succumb to the progressivist *Zeitgeist* of his own time and place and was wont to make statements in more popular forums that suggested that he too thought that messianism is historically realizable, even imminently so.[71] This tendency was especially exacerbated by his German patriotism, which he justified by universalistic logic more Hegelian than Kantian. When he indulged this tendency, especially as he did during the First World War, the very unification of humankind was seen as capable of

---

[71] Note, e.g., "Kann die Sittlichkeit Wirklichkeit werden auf Erden? So muss die Sittlichkeit fragen. Und die Propheten haben diese Frage in messianischen Idee bejaht. Diese messianische Idee hat die gebildete Menschheit angenommen" ("Die Bedeutung des Judentums für den religiosen Fortschritt der Menschheit," in *Jüdische Schriften*, 1:32–33). See also Franz Rosenzweig's reminiscence of Cohen's messianic impatience quoted in Nahum N. Galtzer, *Franz Rosenzweig: His Life and Thought*, 2nd rev. ed. (New York, 1961), 351.

accomplishment by the expanding German state.[72] The Jewish people was to find its role within this expanding Germanness (*Deutschtum*), a point Cohen even tried to demonstrate to the Jews of America in 1915, when America was being tempted to join the enemies of Germany in the First World War.[73] Yet all the same it must be emphasized that his more rigorous philosophical principles more often than not led him to reject any such subordination of Judaism and the Jewish people to any other historical entity, even one on the historical horizon. (Indeed, despite his acerbic anti-Zionism, one could just as easily develop a theory of Zionist messianism from some of the very principles Cohen himself proposed.[74]) Looked at in the light of Cohen's philosophy and its theological application, both Israel and the nations of the world – in that order – will only be truly and satisfactorily elevated-and-transformed (*aufgehoben*) into that new humanity in the *ever-ideal* Messianic Age. Only here and now in the real world of history, the universalizable moral law of the Torah, which Cohen posits as its primary content, must justify a correlation of Jews and non-Jews in a secular state.[75] Here equality among all citizens is the basic political norm. Yet this does not imply that religio-cultural particularities are to be prematurely – that is, premessianically – suppressed.[76]

---

[72] Unfortunately, Cohen's two First World War essays, "Deutschtum und Judentum" (1915–1916), in *Jüdische Schriften*, 3:237ff., 302ff., in which he like many other German intellectuals was engaged in wartime propaganda, are too often taken as necessary conclusions from his philosophical principles. But they are not. Different political points could be drawn from them. (On this hermeneutical possibility, see Novak, *Jewish–Christian Dialogue*, 68ff.) The move from philosophical or theological reflection to practical historical judgment is done by application, not by univocal logical conclusion. Hence a rejection of Cohen's philosophical or theological principles must be done philosophically or theologically and not by means of historical hindsight. It cannot be done with conviction simply on the basis of a retrospective reading of these essays after the Holocaust – even though they are surely painful for any Jew today to read, even retrospectively. See Novak, *Jewish Social Ethics*, 242, n. 42.

[73] See his "Du sollst nicht einhergehen als ein Verleumder – Ein Appell an die Juden Amerikas," in *Jüdische Schriften*, 2:229ff.

[74] See Jacob Klatzkin, *Hermann Cohen* (Berlin and London, 1923), 46–47.

[75] See *Religion of Reason*, 123; also, "Die Nächstenliebe im Talmud," in *Jüdische Schriften*, 1:159–160.

[76] Cf. Spinoza, *Tractatus Politicus*, 3.10.

All of this must be emphasized in order to remove the canard that reduces Cohen to a caricature of a politically blind, modern German Jew, who ultimately offers nothing more than an intricate rationalization for assimilation.[77] As I hope to have shown by now, he was so much more than that.

THE PROBLEM OF COHEN'S THEOLOGICAL ADEQUACY

It is Cohen's Kantianism that forces him to make what must be considered a basic distortion of classical Jewish doctrine. For Cohen never rejects, or even criticizes, the fundamental Kantian principle that moral law is grounded in the autonomy of the rational will.[78] Unlike both the doctrine of revealed law and the classical idea of natural law, for Kant and for Cohen after him, morality is not one's becoming part of a higher order transcending the moral subject. Instead, morality is one's rational will intending an ideal order, one which is yet-to-be. As such, although God's role in Cohen's philosophical–theological system is far more central than it is in Kant's system, even for Cohen God is introduced into the system *after* the full constitution of rational autonomy.[79] Thus it is moral autonomy's full realization that requires God, but it is never God who is the first to require moral freedom and the last to judge it. "I am the first and I am the last and there is no authority (*elohim*) besides Me" (Isaiah 44:6).[80] Relative moral freedom to respond to *whom* it confronts, but *what* it can never make or postulate, is essentially different from the absolute freedom of the creator of any world, real or ideal.[81] For Cohen, then, the human subject as rational moral agent can only will and

---

77 Along the lines of the accusation of assimilationism, see Klatzkin, *Hermann Cohen*, 109ff.

78 "Die Autonomie bedeutet das Prinzip der Deduktion in der Ethik ... Die deduktive Autonomie schliesst ebenso aber auch die absolute Spontanität aus" (*Logik*, 581–582). See *Religion of Reason*, 339.

79 See *Ethik*, 470.

80 Re *elohim* as authority, immediately human and ultimately divine, see B. Sanhedrin 56b; also, D. Novak, *The Image of the Non-Jew in Judaism* (New York and Toronto, 1983), 96–97.

81 See *Ethik*, 321ff.; also, Hannah Arendt, *The Life of the Mind* (2 vols., New York, 1978), 2:28–29, 89.

choose, he or she can never be chosen by anyone who addresses him or her from above and thus primarily respond to that choice.

For this reason, Cohen's fundamentally liberal Jewish subordination of the so-called "ritual" commandments – that is, those which pertain to the direct relationship between man and God (*bein adam le-maqom*) – to the so-called "moral" commandments – that is, those which pertain to the direct relationship between man and man (*bein adam le-havero*) – is an inversion of the content of the revelation in Scripture and of the teaching of the Rabbis.[82] In terms of the source of the commandments, both types are equally from God.[83] In terms of the subjects of the commandments, both types are equally addressed to humans.[84] The difference comes in in terms of the objects of the respective types of commandments, however. With commandments between man and God, God is the direct object; with commandments between man and man, man is the direct object.[85] But in the case of the latter type of commandments, God is the indirect object. Thus both types of commandments ultimately intend God. And the epitome of the God–human relationship in this world is the covenant between God and Israel, the covenant that is ever initiated by God's election of Israel. Thus interhuman commandments are included in the realm of divine–human, covenantal commandments, but the reverse is not the case. The best example of this, it seems to me, is that one guilty of a sin against another human is also guilty of a sin against God, but one guilty of a sin against God is not also guilty of a sin against other humans.[86]

This does not mean, of course, that one cannot see evident

---

[82] See Novak, *Jewish Social Ethics*, 6.

[83] See B. Hagigah 3b re Exod. 20:1 and Eccl. 12:11.

[84] See B. Kiddushin 54a and parallels.

[85] That is why, it seems to me, Maimonides limited the recitation of blessings before commandments (*birkhot mitsvah*) to commandments in which God is the direct object of the act, acts we now (unfortunately) call "ritual" as opposed to those we now call "moral." See *Mishneh Torah*: Berakhot, 11.2 and Karo, *Kesef Mishneh* thereto. Cf. R. Solomon ibn Adret, *Teshuvot Ha-Rashba*, 1, no. 1.

[86] See, e.g., *Sifra*: Vayiqra, ed. Weiss, 27d re Lev. 5:21; T. Sanhedrin 9.7 re Deut. 21:23; M. Yoma 8.9 and B. Yoma 87a re I Sam. 2:25; B. Yevamot 6b re Lev. 19:3 and Tos., s.v. "kulkhem."

interhuman goods being intended by many of the commandments that pertain to interhuman relationships. However, as
Maimonides pointed out in his critique of Saadiah and Jewish
Kalam in general, the ultimate intelligibility of all the commandments must be seen in the primacy of the human relationship with God, which, transcending as it does the bounds of the
specifically moral realm, is therefore irreducible to it.[87]
Cohen's moral universalism, on the other hand, is thus not
sufficient to constitute properly the religiously experienced
(and not just philosophically constituted) primacy of God. And
this is the indispensable ground of both the revelation of the
Torah and the election of Israel.

What Cohen has done in his theology is to reduce the
doctrine of the election of Israel to the doctrine of the revelation of the Torah, that is, the Torah primarily conceived in
terms of its moral content, the Torah as *mishpatim* (rational
laws). It would seem that for him, only those who morally
merit being of Israel – the symbol of ideal humanity – are in
fact the elect of God. For only they have truly elected God
themselves. Yet Jewish tradition has continually affirmed that
even those Jews whose apostasy might remove them from
communication with normative Jews in this world and the
world-to-come, even they are still part of Israel, God's elect
people, as long as they are alive.[88] Hence they cannot be
considered as already dead – no matter how evil their denial of
the covenant has been – and they are never beyond God's call
to them to return (*teshuvah*).[89] Individual Jews, even groups of
Jews, can deny their election in the most audacious ways, but
from God's point of view as presented in Scriptural revelation
and rabbinic tradition, they cannot annul a covenant they
themselves neither initiated nor are ever capable of terminat-
ing.[90] The covenant is real. It has already been established by
election and given its content in revelation. Only its redemptive fulfillment is ideal, namely, that which has-not-yet-come-

---

[87] See *Shemonah Peraqim*, chap. 6; *Mishneh Torah*: Melakhim, 8.11; also, Novak, *The Image of the Non-Jew in Judaism*, 276ff.

[88] See B. Sanhedrin 44a re Josh. 7:11; B. Yevamot 47b; see also pp. 189–199 below.

[89] See pp. 193–194 below.   [90] See Novak, *Jewish Social Ethics*, 27ff.

to-be. But even that ideal is a new divine creation whose realization is promised to man rather than a human projection intended for God.[91]

Even those who desire to convert to Judaism must cast their lot in with the Jewish people in the present, real historical situation at least as much as they must accept the ideal of practicing all the commandments of the Written Torah and the Oral Tradition.[92] And like the people of Israel herself, converts do not become part of Israel because of their own choice. Their choice is only a precondition inasmuch as no one can be truly converted without his or her voluntary compliance.[93] Instead, like Israel herself they must become elect because they have *been elected*.[94] The members of the Jewish tribunal who accept them, functioning as agents of the divine court, always have the option not to accept them. Their choice is free; they are not functioning out of any necessity. Although, not being God, their choices do have to be justified by some objective criteria.[95]

The specific inadequacy of Cohen's theology of election can be seen in his use of the Noahide laws. They play a central role in Cohen's constitution of morality out of the sources of Judaism. For Cohen, the Noahide laws, pertaining as they do to humanity per se, are the essential content of the Torah precisely because they are exclusively moral (in his view anyway) and the essence of the Torah is morality.[96] Yet he cannot constitute the whole thrust of rabbinic teaching that emphasizes that the revelation to Israel is higher and more complete than the revelation to the world at large, that the Torah is concerned with much more than just morality.

The doctrine of the Noahide laws indicates that the normative content of the Torah is twofold: the major part pertaining to the relationship between God and Israel; the minor part

---

[91] See, e.g., B. Berakhot 34b re Isa. 64:3.   [92] B. Yevamot 47a.

[93] B. Ketubot 11a. See p. 181 below.

[94] See B. Yevamot 22a; see also p. 184 below; cf. B. Kiddushin 70b, Rashi, s.v. "yisra'el ketiv."

[95] See B. Yevamot 24b.

[96] See Novak, *The Image of the Non-Jew in Judaism*, 385ff.

pertaining to more general human relationships. The major part of the Torah consists of the 613 commandments; the minor part consists of the seven Noahide commandments. Elsewhere I have argued at length that the best way to constitute the relation of these two parts is to see the Noahide Torah as the precondition that makes the acceptance of the complete Mosaic Torah possible by rational persons.[97] The acceptance of the highest law presupposes that those accepting it are already living according to divine law and that their law is open to a higher and more complete realization of its full intent.

This preconditional law is incorporated intact into that higher law. It functions as the moral condition – but not the moral ground as it does for Cohen – of that higher law.[98] It is the norm for creation, one mediated by the natural order. This norm emerges when human persons accept their creaturely limitations, both individually and collectively, as being instituted by their creator.[99] Accordingly, they formally order their lives *by* these limitations taken as nature, and the content that is *within* these limitations they develop as history. What is natural is general; what is historical is singular. And the singular is not *a* particularity subsumed by *the* general qua universal, as it is for Cohen, following as he does Kant and ultimately Plato. It is not merely an example.

Finally, this law connects Israel with her pre-Sinaitic past, and it also connects her with her non-Jewish neighbors. It is the only basis of a morally significant relationship with them.[100] However, it is a relationship that recognizes that its formal similarities are far outweighed by those substantial differences that cannot be included in it. For Cohen, this general law is now the universal moral law which is to be the content, the very substance of messianically elevated-and-transformed (*aufgehoben*) humanity. It is humanity in which no differentiating historical singularities are retained. In the more classical Jewish view, conversely, this general law will retain its

[97] *Ibid.*, 407ff.   [98] See Novak, *Jewish–Christian Dialogue*, 129ff.
[99] See D. Novak, *Law and Theology in Judaism* (2 vols., New York, 1974, 1976), 2:15ff.
[100] See Novak, *Jewish–Christian Dialogue*, 141ff.

formal function, no more and no less. But Jewish singularity will never be *aufgehoben* into something more universal, not even ideally. In the end of days the nations of the world will for all intents and purposes become one with Israel in all her singularity.[101] The content of their life will become Jewish. Israel's singularity, not theirs, will alone endure and be redeemed. Therefore, the election of Israel – which most of the commandments of the revealed Torah celebrate in one way or another – is always central to the relationship of God and man. Even in relation to the final redemption, it is not provisional as it turns out to be for Cohen.

In addition to arguing for the greater correspondence to the classical Jewish sources, an alternative to Cohen's theology of election must also be more philosophically coherent. For, as Cohen himself so well recognized, method and data cannot be permanently separated.[102] Only such an alternative can hope to counter the theology of a thinker who was such a master of both the data of Jewish tradition and philosophical method. Only such an alternative can properly respect Hermann Cohen by effectively differing with him on a level of rationality worthy of his true greatness.[103]

---

[101] See *ibid.*, 175, n. 41; see also pp. 158–162 below.   [102] See *Religion of Reason*, 4.

[103] Such an attempt was made by Mordecai Kaplan in his *The Purpose and Meaning of Jewish Existence* (Philadelphia, 1964). But Kaplan's constitution of Judaism is far less convincing than Cohen's, both in terms of correspondence with the data of Jewish tradition and philosophical coherence and rigor.

CHAPTER 3

Franz Rosenzweig's return to the doctrine

THE PHILOSOPHICAL PREPARATION

In its classical form, the doctrine of the election of Israel clearly designates a direct relationship between God and Israel: God *elects* Israel. Everything else within the content of that relationship gets its meaning from that foundational reality. Accordingly, election is not a symbolic rendition of something essentially prior to it. God's act of electing is not a metaphor for the act of someone else; Israel's being elected is not a provisional state for the sake of someone else. Thus any attempt to return to the doctrine in its classical form, as enunciated in Scripture and by the Rabbis, must undo the whole modern project of making God's election of Israel an essentially indirect relationship, so indirect that in the end it is not really God who elects and it is not really Israel who is elected. Because of the predominance of this modern view of election, originating as we have seen in Spinoza's powerful inversion, only the most profoundly philosophical effort can retrieve it for us. Any attempt to achieve this retrieval by simply reasserting the ancient doctrine will inevitably present it as some form of tribalism or chauvinism. When this has been the case, the modern view of election can easily re-present itself as being more compelling by far than the ancient doctrine – so crudely presented, that is. For the modern inversion seems to be able to explain by its own categories the classical data more cogently than the ancient doctrine could ever do alone.

For a number of reasons, Franz Rosenzweig (1886–1929) can be seen as the turning point, the pivotal figure, in modern Jewish thought. And, if the doctrine of the election of Israel ultimately lies at the very core of anyone's view of Judaism, then Rosenzweig's insistence on the truth of the original doctrine of the direct election of Israel by God is his greatest significance for contemporary Jewish thought.[1] That this insistence was the persistent *leitmotif* of his thought, and that he pursued it with dazzling philosophical ability, means that our reflection on the doctrine and its historical trajectory, which is for the sake of retrieving its own truth for our time, can go no further without a thorough analysis and judgment of what Rosenzweig attempted to teach us.

For Rosenzweig, the heart of the modern inability to understand, let alone appreciate, the ancient doctrine of the election of Israel is due to the modern rejection of revelation. Since election is essentially the self-revelation of God, there is simply no context within which to talk about election intelligibly for those who have accepted post-Enlightenment modernity as permanent. So that context must be opened up before the theological constitution of the doctrine can reoccur in the world. The impediments to the experience of revelation must be removed if the context for revelation is to be made available to us again.

The impediments to that constitution are twofold. First, God is seen as having an absolute nature that precludes anything as personal as direct revelation to human recipients. Second, humans are seen as having a universalist ethos that precludes anything as particularistic as direct revelation from God being truly foundational for them. To overcome these impediments, one must see the possibility of going beyond the "nature" of God and of going beyond the "ethos" of human life and culture. Only after this has been done can one constitute again the direct relationship of God and man which is authentic election. In his masterwork, *The Star of Redemption*, a work

[1] Rosenzweig's insistence on this point comes out in his very first essay in Jewish theology, "Atheistische Theologie" (1914), in *Kleinere Schriften*, ed. E. Rosenzweig (Berlin, 1937), 281–282. See also *ibid.*, 31–32.

whose principles he subsequently developed but never rejected, Rosenzweig sees the freeing of God for the relationship as a "metaphysic" and the freeing of man for the relationship as a "metaethic." The meaning of these two key terms must be grasped before we can get to Rosenzweig's specific constitution of the doctrine of election.

Rosenzweig's readers, who he certainly assumes are quite familiar with the history of philosophy, would normally take a "metaphysic" to mean the intellectual attempt to discover the reality that lies "beyond" (one meaning of the Greek word *meta*) the physical (one meaning of the Greek word *physis*) and from which one can better explain the physical than by principles abstracted from experience alone.[2] These same readers would normally take a "metaethic" to mean the intellectual attempt to discover the reality that lies beyond ethical norms and from which one can better explain ethics than by principles abstracted from normative practice alone.[3] But Rosenzweig is not using these two terms in the normal way. Instead, he returns to the etymological roots of the terms in Greek and derives from them very different meanings than the normal ones we have just seen.

What he means by a "metaphysic" of God is the recognition of God as a person who is not bound by what had been seen as God's *nature* (another meaning of the Greek word *physis*) or essence, what philosophers had seen as God's identification with superpersonal, eternal, immutable Being.[4] Thus God's existence is seen by Rosenzweig as transcending God's essence. By this transcendence God is not bound by anything that he himself cannot change. As such, God can be whenever, wherever and with whomever he chooses. God can descend

---

[2] See Aristotle, *Metaphysics* 981b25–30.

[3] By the term "metaethics," Rosenzweig does not mean the analysis of ethical language that came to be known as "metaethics" in contemporary analytic philosophy. Instead, he meant it in the sense of the ontological grounding of ethical precepts in the way that Kant did in his *Grundlegung zur Metaphysik der Sitten*. (See D. Novak, *Suicide and Morality* [New York, 1975], 83ff.) See *The Star of Redemption*, trans. W. W. Hallo (New York, 1970), 38ff. (hereafter, *Star*); also, N. Rotenstreich, "Rosenzweig's Notion of Metaethics," in *The Philosophy of Franz Rosenzweig*, ed. P. Mendes-Flohr (Hanover and London, 1988), 224, n. 3.

[4] See *Star*, 16–18.

from the aloofness of Being (*Sein*) to the directness of being-there (*da-sein*).[5] Thus God's transcendence is not God's *being away from* the world; rather, it is God's *moving away from* his self-enclosure and *coming towards* the direct object of his choice in the world. And whatever "essential" structures (*Wesen*) we can see within our experience of God's presence-to-us are only partial inferences known *a posteriori*, that is, they are subsequent to the experience itself.[6] They are best taken as "qualities" (*middot*) in the rabbinic sense of that term.[7] These structures emerge *from within* the experienced event itself; they are not primary forms *into which* God must necessarily be fitted. They are not definitions in which God is already bound *a priori*. In other words, we do not possess a class called "Being" (God's essence) by which we then identify the God of Abraham, Isaac, and Jacob as the first member (God's existence). We do not have a name of God before God fundamentally names himself to those whom he confronts, to those to whom God presents himself in the event of revelation.[8] God's "existence" is God's self-presentation as an event (*Ereignis*). God's "essence" is only the configuration (*Gestalt*) impressed in our inner experience (*Erlebnis*) of that revelatory event.[9] We can grasp nothing else.[10]

---

[5] "We experience his existence directly (*sein Dasein erfahren wir unmittelbar*) only by virtue of the fact that he loves us and awakens our dead self to beloved and requiting soul" (*Star*, 381) = *Der Stern der Erlösung* (Frankfurt-on-Main, 1921), 478 (hereafter, *Stern*). See also *Star*, 120; *Jehuda Halevi* (The Hague, 1983), 73. In his Bible translation, written with Martin Buber, Exod. 3:14 is translated as "Ich werde dasein als der dasein werde ... Ich bin da." This use of *Dasein* was formulated before its somewhat similar and subsequently much more famous use by Martin Heidegger in *Sein und Zeit*. For the significance of this translation, see D. Novak, "Buber and Tillich," *Journal of Ecumenical Studies* (1992), 29:159ff.; also, J. Tewes, *Zum Existenzbegriff Franz Rosenzweigs* (Meisenheim am Glan, 1970), 85ff.

[6] See *Star*, 386ff.

[7] Thus the Rabbis criticize those who attempt to derive the *middot* of God from preconceived notions of what God ought to be. They insist that revelation is the only standard for inferring these *middot*. See Y. Berakhot 5.3/9c; B. Rosh Hashanah 17b re Exod. 34:6.

[8] See *Jehuda Halevi*, 72, 100–101; also, A. Babolin, "Der Begriff der Erlösung bei Franz Rosenzweig," in *Der Philosoph Franz Rosenzweig*, ed. W. Schmied-Kowarzik (Munich, 1988), 2:609.

[9] See *Star*, 164, 186, 418; *Jehuda Halevi*, 30.

[10] "We move in the orbit in which we found ourselves, and along the route on which we are placed. We no longer reach (*greifen*) beyond this except with the powerless grasp (*Griffen*) of empty concepts (*Begriffe*)" (*Star*, 381 = *Stern*, 478).

What Rosenzweig means by a "metaethic" of man is that modern philosophy (and by that he always means modern Idealistic philosophy, often that of Hegel and sometimes that of Kant via Hermann Cohen) has totally subsumed the individual human person and his or her experiences under the universal class called "humanity." And this ethos of modern life becomes an ethic of universality, which is quintessentially defined by Kant in the categorical imperative: Moral rules are only valid if they are formulated to apply to all rational persons. For all intents and purposes this turns out to be universal humanity. And Hegel extended that universalizability beyond just moral rules into the whole unfolding process of world history.[11] The direct human experience of personal encounter, then, is never primary but only assumes its meaning when wholly placed in this larger universalizing context.

What Rosenzweig means by a "metaethic," however, is not going beyond universal ethical rules to even more universal rational grounds (as does Hegel). Instead, he means that the human person is capable of an experience that can never be subsumed under any prior universal class, an experience that itself can found an altogether different world than that assumed by the modern universalist ethos. Accordingly, going beyond ethics (*meta-ethics*) is not the transcendence of the universality of moral action by the greater universality of world history (as it is for Hegel). It is, rather, the transcendence of both the universality of ethics and the universality of world history in the exact opposite direction. It is the transcendence of the universal by the particularity of human experience.[12]

The questions now to be asked of Rosenzweig's thought are: (1) What human experience cannot be subsumed under a prior universal class? (2) Why can it not be so subsumed? (3) How is the transcendence of this human experience necessarily related to the self-transcendence of God in revelation?

The human experience that cannot be subsumed under a

---

[11] See *Phenomenology of Spirit*, trans. A. V. Miller (Oxford, 1977), 295ff.; *Philosophy of Right*, trans. T. M. Knox (Oxford, 1952), 122ff.

[12] See *Star*, 63ff.

prior universal class is the experience of one's being directly addressed by God. For Rosenzweig this is a possibility when, and only when, the one being so addressed has been prepared for this experience by the deepest awareness of his or her own mortality. For that awareness is something that cannot be explained by the generality of the surrounding world; indeed, that generality can only be used in an attempt to explain it away as epiphenomenal.[13] However, Franz Rosenzweig, like his contemporaries Karl Barth and Martin Heidegger, was awakened to this primal awareness both by the nihilating events of the First World War and by the recently rediscovered writings of Søren Kierkegaard. He now knew that this awareness of the unique significance of *his own* mortality is anything but epiphenomal. It is the necessary condition for the self-presentation of him (God) who is other than oneself. Thus it is that which makes the truly founding human experience possible. One can only be so addressed by God when he or she is fully aware that this event could very well be the last event, so that it cannot be taken as one point within a continuing process.[14] Only the human person, who in and of himself or herself essentially comes from the no-where of *creatio ex nihilo* and is headed to the no-where of his or her own death, only this person is sufficiently open to be directly addressed by God. Only this person has no mediating armor to separate him-self or her-self from God's self-revelation.

With this in mind, it now becomes clearer why the direct experience that Rosenzweig is seeking can only be that of revelation, that is, the revelation of God to man. Revelation must be the founding event which then determines the new

---

[13] See *Star*, 3ff.; also, W. Marx, "Die Bedeutung des Todes im 'Stern der Erlösung,'" in *Der Philosoph Franz Rosenzweig*, ed. Schmied-Kowarzik, 2:611ff.

[14] "God gives man the freedom to make the most significant decision, he gives freedom for just that – only for that. But giving it, he yet retains the powers of realization in his treasure-trove . . . so at the end . . . there is the driving force of the fear roused by God, the fear that perhaps this day will not be followed by a tomorrow. And through this fear the deed is born at last." ("A Note on a Poem by Judah Ha-Levi," quoted in Nahum N. Glatzer, *Franz Rosenzweig*, 2nd rev. ed. [New York, 1961], 291 = *Jehuda Halevi*, 249.) The poignancy of these words, written by a man who was suffering from a terminal disease, cannot go without mention here. See also M. Avot 2.10 and B. Shabbat 153a re Eccl. 9:8.

relationship of the transformed person qua soul (as opposed to the empty "self" finally left by modernity) with both other humans and the surrounding world.[15]

Unlike his close colleague Martin Buber, Rosenzweig did not see the transformation of the human person from universality to particularity beginning in the interhuman I–thou relationship, which moves beyond the impersonal I–it relation and then ascends up to the I–thou relationship between man and God.[16] It would seem that for Rosenzweig, before the trajectory of such a relationship ever reached God it would more probably lapse into the old generality of an ethical (that is, Kantian) universe. And the same would be the case if the transformation of the human person began in the relationship with the world qua sense experience. For here too, before the trajectory of such a relationship ever reached God it would more probably lapse into the generality of a modern scientific universe. In the world of modern science (at least as constituted by Hermann Cohen), God is essentially the transpersonal foundation of the world. In this world God is too remote to reveal himself directly; to do so would compromise the purity of his absolute Being. For Rosenzweig, however, all true relationship (*Beziehung*) begins with God.[17]

Revelation involves a fundamental crossing of borders, a going-beyond, a transcending of which neither the God of modern science nor the God of modern ethics is inherently capable. In the worlds of modern science and modern ethics, God is never there, but only inferred. Only the creator God has the true freedom to be present when and where he alone chooses to be. That is why Rosenzweig, looking retrospectively from the vantage point of revelation, sees the God who reveals himself to man as the creator of the world out of which he selects man for direct address. Transformed man can only begin with God, with no one and nothing else. Without God

---

[15] See *Star*, 176; also, *Jehuda Halevi*, 114.

[16] It is very important to note here that Buber does not get to the relationship between God and man until part 3 of his masterwork *I and Thou*, after he has constituted the I–thou relationship in essence at the level of what is between man and man.

[17] See *Jehuda Halevi*, 49.

present at the very beginning, the totalizing impersonal worlds of either ethics or science will inevitably claim the human person back into their respective totalities. Man's soul can only be awakened by God.[18]

THE ELECTION OF ISRAEL PER SE

For Rosenzweig, the trajectory of election is clearly from God to man. God elects man as the object of his self-revelation; then, and only then, is man able to respond to being so elected. Being an act founded in election from above, revelation is not just a metaphor for discovery of what is ever above by him or her who is now below. For if that were the case, election would be an essentially human act: the choice of concentration on a universal object by a rationally universalizing subject.[19] And since there is no universal memory of an event of revelation to all humankind, revelation can only be an event experienced by some humans. (Indeed, for Rosenzweig, such a truly universal *event* would have to be nothing less than the final redemption of the world.[20]) But so far, there is nothing in Rosenzweig's theology that indicates he is talking about God's revelation to the people of Israel specifically.

The connection between revelation to individuals and revelation to a plural community is an especially difficult problem both for Rosenzweig and for his colleague and best theological interlocutor, Martin Buber. For both of them saw the impediment to the experience of revelation as being the self-enclosure of human consciousness in a totalizing universality. Therefore, both of them constituted a realm of individual experience that fundamentally transcends this enclosure. However, if revelation is to be taken as a *Jewish* event, then the communal factor of this revelation is essential. Jewish revelation is covenantal and collectively normative. Although more than law per se, it certainly entails law necessarily. If this entailment is not constituted, it is hard to see how an experiential theory of revelation can be used in the process of Jewish self-understanding.

[18] See *Star*, 175ff.   [19] See pp. 64–68 above.   [20] See *Star*, 219.

Rosenzweig was very much aware of this theological problem and strove mightily to solve it.

Rosenzweig's problem is how does one go from the event of revelation experienced by the individual soul to the content of revelation that functions as the norm for communal life? Indeed, is there any content of revelation at all other than the event of God's presence itself?

Both Rosenzweig and Buber seem to be saying that revelation is just that, revelation and nothing else.[21] God's presence alone is the true content of the event of God's self-revelation. Thus God elects whomever, whenever, and wherever to reveal himself. Nevertheless, Rosenzweig and Buber come to almost opposite conclusions concerning the relation of traditional Jewish law (Halakhah) to this foundational revelation, the law through which the separateness of the Jewish people that their election involves is concretized by specific, repeatable acts. Buber insists that the dichotomy between the direct divine commandment (*Gebot*) to individuals – or even to a community in one particular event – and the continuing, transmitted law of a community (*Gesetz*) is unbridgeable. The former belongs to the world of I–Thou; the latter belongs to the world of I–it – and never the twain shall meet.[22] Rosenzweig, on the other hand, insists that the dichotomy is bridgeable, that law can become commandment. The question is how is this done. Rosenzweig himself was not all that clear about it.[23] Nevertheless, I think that a plausible answer to this question can be drawn out of several statements of Rosenzweig, and this will, I hope, bring us to the heart of his view of the election of Israel.

---

[21] "That which reveals is that which reveals. That which has being is there (*Das Seiende ist da*), nothing more (*nichts weiter*)" (*I and Thou*, trans. W. Kaufmann [New York, 1970], 157–158 = *Ich und Du*, 2nd ed. [Heidelberg, 1962], 110–111). Cf. *Stern*, 205 (= *Star*, 161), where Rosenzweig too speaks of *einer Offenbarung die nichts weiter als Offenbarung*. But, whereas Buber stuck to this definition with total consistency, Rosenzweig (happily) altered it in his subsequent thought.

[22] See *I and Thou*, 156–157; also, *Two Types of Faith*, trans. N. P. Goldhawk (New York, 1962), 57. Cf. *Franz Rosenzweig: On Jewish Learning*, trans. W. Wolf, ed. Nahum N. Glatzer (New York, 1955), 115. (This is the full English translation of the exchange of letters between Rosenzweig and Buber on the question of normativity called *Die Bauleute*. See *Kleinere Scriften*, 106ff.)

[23] See appendix 2.

In *The Star of Redemption* Rosenzweig writes,

> Thus blood kinship (*Blutsverwandtschaft*), brotherhood, nationhood, marriage, in sum all human relationships (*Beziehungen*) are established in creation ... All have their prototypes in the animal kingdom, and through the rebirth of the soul in revelation, all are first animated with a soul (*beseelt*) in redemption. All are rooted in the community of blood (*Blutsgemeinschaft*) which in turn is the nearest creation (*Schöpfungsnachste*) among them ... man ... knows that he is to love, and to love always the nearest and the neighbor. And as for the world, it grows in itself, apparently according to its own law (*eignem Gesetz*).[24]

Rosenzweig understands revelation to be an event that carries with it considerable consequences. For revelation is to be the central event of history, that which draws from creation and intends the full redemption of the world.[25] In drawing from creation, revelation incorporates the two aspects of election that have been indispensable for its preservation by the Jewish people: the bodily transmission of basic Jewish identity ("blood kinship"), and the legal institutions that give that identity definition and active content ("its own law").

Rosenzweig is able to see this, in a way most unlike Buber, because he does not constitute revelation *de novo*. Instead, he sees the human object of God's electing revelation as already one who is a social being through creation. As such, this human object is not a lone individual. This does not mean that one comes to revelation *through* social structures. If that were the case, we would be back to a Kantian kind of ethical universalism. What it does mean, however, is that the human object of revelation hears the voice of God *together with* the other members of his or her kinship community.[26] Since for Rosenzweig, there is only one kinship community that has constituted itself by an event of the communal experience of revelation, and that community is the Jewish people, it follows that any

---

[24] *Star*, 241 = *Stern*, 306–307.   [25] See *Star*, 258.

[26] Following the aural character of revelation, Rosenzweig emphasizes the primal form of response of the revelation-instituted community as being "archetypal chant (*Urgesang*), which is always the chant of several parties. It is not a solo (*de Einzelne singt nicht*)" (*Star*, 231 = *Stern*, 294–295).

appreciation of this historical reality must recognize that revelation and the Jews are in essence inseparable. And Rosenzweig insists, as we shall examine in more detail later, that the
only non-Jewish religious tradition that is able to affirm this
truth is Christianity.

What is important to see from the quote from the *Star* above
is that in one aspect at least, the Jewish people have a law even
before they are given the prime commandments of love of God
and neighbor in revelation. What the prime commandments
do (the first pertaining to the relationship with God; the second
to the relationship with other humans) is to recontextualize the
old laws of the people as a natural entity. What had formerly
been laws that merely intended social cohesion and harmony
in a natural way are now elements of the covenant between
God and Israel, the covenant that is to be the vehicle for the
redemption of the world. And although Rosenzweig does not
mention the rabbinic concept of Noahide law (possibly assuming that it only lent itself to Hermann Cohen's Kantian reconstitution of it), his reasoning here is very similar to the Rabbis'
view of how the Noahide law was transformed by the Sinaitic
covenant in terms of its ultimate context, but with its specific
content being preserved intact.[27] This seems to be Rosenzweig's meaning, although I am surprised that he himself did
not quote this passage from the *Star* when he was debating the
question of law and commandment with Buber later.

The second passage that shows Rosenzweig's complete view
of election and law is found in a letter he wrote to his close
friend Rudolf Hallo in March of 1922. There Rosenzweig
writes, "Judaism *is not* law; it creates (*schafft*) law. But it [the
law] is not an 'it' (*es nicht*); it *is* Jewish-*being* (*Judesein*). So have
I described it in the *Star*, and I know that it is right."[28] Now,
how does Judaism – which for Rosenzweig is synonymous with
revelation – "create" law? And how is this law-creation connected with the elected status of the Jewish people?

27 Thus the Noahide law is the subject of *Erhebung* rather than *Aufhebung*. See D.
   Novak, *The Image of the Non-Jew in Judaism* (New York and Toronto, 1983), 385ff.,
   407ff.
28 *Briefe*, ed. E. Rosenzweig (Berlin, 1935), no. 342, p. 425.

It would seem that the best way to answer this question, which can only be speculative because Rosenzweig himself is often opaque about it (which shows, I think, that he was continually struggling with it), is to appreciate the difference between post-Sinaitic and pre-Sinaitic law. Pre-Sinaitic law is the type of "natural" law that Rosenzweig saw coming from creation itself. Post-Sinaitic law, on the other hand, is that body of Jewish practice which is the celebration of the events of revelation, specifically Exodus–Sinai.[29] A further difference between the two types of law is that the law from creation is immanent in intent, that is, its end is one already known and experienced: social cohesion and harmony. The law that celebrates the events of revelation, however, is transcendent in intent, that is, its end is not one already known and experienced. Its end is nothing less than the universal redemption that so far "no eye has seen but God's."[30]

The question that this second category of law raises is whether it is to be considered human or divine. That is, is it the specific concretization of the general divine commandment of love by human means, or is it the dialectic of the general and the specific within the divine commandment itself? This question is very much to the point for our analysis of Rosenzweig's teaching on election inasmuch as it is in this area of law-structured Jewish practice that election is celebrated.

There is much in Rosenzweig's own thought that would suggest that he thought the former, that law is the specifically human judgment of just what are the appropriate means to the general end of the commandment of love. In fact, Rosenzweig's disciple Nahum Glatzer drew this conclusion in 1924, and Rosenzweig himself agreed that it was quite reasonable considering his own statements on the question up to that point.

For Rosenzweig, the essential commandment to love God is in direct response to God's election of Israel. When Israel truly experiences the event of divine election, she cannot but love God.[31] Thus only the election of Israel by God would seem to

---

[29] See D. Novak, *The Theology of Nahmanides Systematically Presented* (Atlanta, 1992), 4–8.
[30] See B. Berakhot 34b re Isa. 64:3.   [31] See *Star*, 176–177.

be divine, that is, the only thing that can be experienced as divine is God's direct revelation of his love. However, when Glatzer's version of what he no doubt saw as his teacher's view reached Rosenzweig himself, who was by that time a homebound invalid, Rosenzweig had second thoughts.

Rosenzweig's response to this great problem in his thought is contained in an extraordinary letter he wrote to the faculty of Das Freie Jüdisches Lehrhaus, the adult education center he had founded in Frankfurt-on-Main, but in whose direct operations his illness prevented him from participating by 1924. (Nevertheless, as this letter indicates, Rosenzweig was still very much the leader of the *Lehrhaus* in spirit even if not actually there in body.) A careful analysis of this letter will bring out newer aspects of Rosenzweig's view of election–revelation than were available in the *Star* itself.

First of all, we must look carefully at what Glatzer thought Rosenzweig thought on the matter. It could very well be that Glatzer, who at the age of twenty-one in 1924 was already an experienced Talmudist, saw the logic of Rosenzweig's position as being analogous to the classical rabbinic position on the relation of Scriptural and rabbinic commandments. In this view, the 613 commandments the Rabbis judged to be pre-scribed in the Written Torah are supplemented by the commandments enacted by the Rabbis themselves, a prodecure for which general warrant is found in the Written Torah itself. It was assumed that the essential justification and criterion of each of these specific rabbinic commandments is teleological, that is, they are enacted for the sake of enhancing or protecting the Scriptural commandments. The essential justification for the Scriptural commandments themselves, on the other hand, is revelation itself. The best example of this is the additional decrees the Rabbis enacted (*shevut*) in order to enhance the sanctity of the Sabbath, the Sabbath itself being originally prescribed in the Written Torah.[32]

What Glatzer has done, it seems to me, is to transpose this

---

[32] See M. Avot 1.1; B. Shabbat 23a re Deut. 17:11 and 32:7; M. Betsah 5.2 and B. Betsah 36b–37a.

basic division. In his view, the only revealed commandment is to respond to God's loving election with love. Everything else within the Torah itself is enacted *for the sake of* that founding commandment. In other words, the function of all the other Scriptural commandments is what the Rabbis saw as the function of the rabbinic commandments. So, why can Rosenzweig no longer accept this division proposed by his disciple?

Although Rosenzweig does not use the term "covenant," it does seem that he thinks that Glatzer has missed what we would term the covenantal reality *within which* all of the commandments of the Torah do participate. Thus the relation between the specific commandments and what might be termed the primary commandment (*Ur-Gebot*) is one of whole and parts. The whole – the direct response to God's direct revelation – requires that it be specified in various acts that are to be done. These acts are determined by the human explication (*midrash*) of the revealed commandments, and the line between explication and what is being explicated (*nidrash*) is often hazy. Thus Rosenzweig wrote to Buber in June of 1925, "But where does this 'interpretation' stop being legitimate? That I would never venture to assert in a general proposition."[33] And to the Orthodox Jewish leader Jakob Rosenheim, Rosenzweig emphasized in a letter written in March of 1927 that the Oral Torah is the "fulfilling" (*Ergänzung*) of the Written Torah much more than being a separate revealed supplement to the Written Torah.[34] He made this point to contrast his position explicitly with that of the founder of the separatist Orthodox movement Samson Raphael Hirsch (d. 1888), a movement of which Rosenheim was a major lay leader. Hirsch's view of the Oral Torah, to which Rosenheim firmly adhered, was developed within the context of his polemics against any "reformation" of Jewish law, no matter how "conservative."[35] In other words, in contrast to Buber on his

---

[33] *Briefe*, no. 435, p. 536.   [34] *Ibid.*, no. 488, pp. 582–583.
[35] For the background of Hirsch's polemics, especially against R. Zechariah Frankel (d. 1875), the founder of the "Positive-Historical School," who emphasized a commitment to the Halakhah *and* a belief that it did and could still develop, see N. H. Rosenbloom, *Tradition in an Age of Reform* (Philadelphia, 1976), 106ff. Actually,

left, Rosenzweig argued for the divine connection of halakhic exegesis; and in contrast to Rosenheim (in the name of Hirsch) on his right, he argued for the active human role in revelation itself.

So, what Rosenzweig seems to be struggling to say is that the essential human aspect of the covenant is not the separate act of judgment of human *means* to a divine *end*. There we have a relation that is unilateral (a → b). Rosenzweig would probably see the institution of specifically man-made rabbinic law, which does just that, as being a subsequent factor, only to be constituted after the constitution of the primary covenantal reality. But, if all the specific commandments took this form, as Glatzer seems to have been suggesting, then all specific authority would be human rather than divine.[36] And would this not quickly lead us right back to the modern inversion of the doctrine of election, initiated by Spinoza, since in every specific act it would be Israel electing God rather than God electing Israel? Would we not then have human autonomy rather than the more partial freedom of response the covenant allows?[37]

The human aspect of the covenant is the concrete Jewish response to God's election of Israel, a response that cannot be really separated from the commandment itself. Here the rela-

although both Hirsch and Rosenzweig are right, i.e., the Oral Torah consists of both separate laws (*halakhot*) taken to be revealed and exegesis by the Rabbis themselves, the emphasis of the Talmud is by far more in the direction of the latter than the former (see, e.g., B. Baba Metsia 33a–b). In addition, the differences between Hirsch and Frankel, and later between Rosenheim and Rosenzweig, cannot be simply reduced to the former being "traditionalists" and the latter "liberals." For someone more traditional than all of them, namely, the nineteenth-century Hasidic theologian R. Judah Aryeh Leib of Gur, following solid kabbalistic and Hasidic teaching, also emphasized the role of Jewish creativity in *torah she-b'al peh* (see *Sefat Emet* [5 vols., Brooklyn, 1985], 5:182).

[36] This has been the problem with much Liberal Jewish appropriation of Rosenzweig's *Gebot/Gesetz* dialectic. See, e.g., Jakob J. Petuchowski, *Ever Since Sinai* (New York, 1961), 69ff.; Emil L. Fackenheim, *Quest for Past and Future* (Bloomington, Ind., 1968), 145–147. The latest and most carefully thought out version of this form of Liberal Jewish theology is by Eugene B. Borowitz in his *Renewing the Covenant* (Philadelphia, 1991), esp. 273. For my critique of this point of view as one that leads right back to the Kantian-type autonomy, as inherited by and through Hermann Cohen, that Buber, Rosenzweig *et al.* attempted so strenuously to overcome, see *SH'MA* (January 24, 1992), 22/426: 45–47.

[37] See *Star*, 214.

tion is bilateral (a ←—→ b), that is, we go back and forth from the parts to the whole and from the whole to the parts. The relation here might be seen as "organic" as opposed to "technical" (in the sense of *a* being enacted for the sake of *b*).[38] Without this specified response, election–revelation could only elicit an emotion – an approach that Rosenzweig would probably have seen as entailing all the subjectivism of the theology of the nineteenth-century liberal Protestant theologian Friedrich Schleiermacher.[39] Indeed, one might characterize Rosenzweig's position by paraphrasing Kant: law without commandment is blind; commandment without law is empty.

The separation of the human element from the divine element of the covenant is only formal; in reality they must function together in tandem. The formal separation of the human element enables one to see and analyze the humanly accessible logic of concrete rabbinic interpretations of the commandments, and even to incorporate the results of modern humanistic scholarship. As Rosenzweig puts it, "Certainly not all of these historical and sociological explanations are false."[40] They are only false when from their application to the specifics of the commandments they infer that the commandments as a whole could not be from God. And here in his phenomenology of the commandments (although he does not designate it by that term) Rosenzweig singles out the reductionism of William James, Freud, Wellhausen, and Max Weber.[41] They miss the forest for the trees, so to speak. Accordingly, he is quick to point out that "in the light of the doing, of the right doing in which we experience the reality of the law (*erfahrenen Wirklichkeit des Gebots*), the explanations are of superficial importance."[42] These explanations are only abstractions because they are

---

[38] See Aristotle, *Nicomachean Ethics* 1094a1 for the distinction between what I have called "organic" (intrinsic) teleology as opposed to "technical" (extrinsic) teleology.

[39] For Rosenzweig's antipathy to Schleiermacher's subjectivism, see *Star*, 100–101; also, *Kleinere Schriften*, 279.

[40] *Briefe*, no. 413, p. 520, translation from Glatzer, *Franz Rosenzweig*, 245. Also, see *Briefe*, no. 63, p. 81.

[41] For a discussion of Rosenzweig's phenomenological method, see B. Caspar, *Das Dialogischen Denken* (Freiburg, 1967), 94ff.

[42] *Briefe*, 520 (= Glatzer, *Franz Rosenzweig*, 245).

already made when one is out of the participational reality of direct election and response. As Rosenzweig stated a little earlier in this letter, "We wholly realize that general (*allgemein-ste*) theological connection (*Zusammenhang*) only when we cause it to come alive by fulfilling the individual commandments, and transpose it from the objectivity of a theological truth to the 'Thou' of the benediction."[43] That theological truth can only be expressed by the stark proposition "God is."

So it would seem that both theology and law are abstractions from the prime covenantal reality, a reality that can only be addressed (*anzusprechen*) and that is not describable (*aussprech-bar*).[44] Theology is abstract talk about God without the presence of man; law is abstract talk about man without the presence of God. Rosenzweig certainly does not rule these abstract disciplines out. After all, he was himself a theologian, and he aspired to be a halakhist.[45] Nevertheless, his opposition to liberal Jewish thought can be seen in his rejection of its tendency to derive the reality of the Jewish covenant with God from philosophical theology; and his opposition to Orthodox Jewish thought can be seen in his rejection of its tendency to derive the reality of the Jewish covenant with God from law. The true election–revelation–commandment includes each and transcends both. It must be directly experienced as a whole before it can be abstractly analyzed in its parts.

THE ELECTION OF ISRAEL AND THE REDEMPTION OF THE WORLD

In the theological system Rosenzweig set forth in the *Star*, revelation is the central point of human history. It is prepared for by creation and fulfilled by redemption. Thus revelation, which is essentially present, draws from a more general pri-

---

[43] *Ibid.*, 519 (= Glatzer, *Franz Rosenzweig*, 244).

[44] *Ibid.*, 520–521 (= Glatzer, 244).

[45] In his letter of March 1924 to the Orthodox Jewish thinker Isaak Breuer, who had been critical of the very minimal treatment of the Halakhah in the *Star*, Rosenzweig accepted the criticism and explained that after about ten years of "learning and living" he hoped to write a book on Jewish law. (See *Briefe*, no. 389, pp. 496–497.)

mordial world, which is essentially past, and it intends a more general eschatological world, which is essentially future.

The question we must now consider is just what Rosenzweig's transition from revelation to redemption means for the doctrine of the election of Israel. This is not only important for our understanding of Rosenzweig himself (always a rewarding task), but is even more important because Rosenzweig is our pivotal figure in turning away from the modern inversion of the doctrine back to the classical presentations of it in Scripture and the tradition of the Rabbis. Does Rosenzweig effect this transition sufficiently for us, or does he constitute election in relation to redemption in such a way that he too must be overcome – at least on this point – before we can philosophically retrieve the classical doctrine? For that retrieval of the classical doctrine must be done in such a way that it adequately corresponds to the classical sources, and in such a way that it presents a coherent approach to the issues involving election that face the Jewish people here and now.

Despite his great originality as a thinker, Franz Rosenzweig's thought must still be seen within the context of the questions that concerned others in his time and place. Certainly, the most important question that directly faced West European Jewry after the Emancipation was what the relationship between Jews and non-Jews is to be considering the radically changed social and political reality in which they were now living together. We must now look at Rosenzweig's concept of redemption, since that is where he deals with this question most intensely.

The relationship between Jews and non-Jews was most radically changed when Jews were granted the rights and obligations of full citizenship in the new modern nation-states. This was not achieved and sustained without considerable effort. For the charge was made by the enemies of political equality for Jews that Judaism prevented Jews from treating non-Jews as their equals.[46] This meant that even if Jews were granted the

---

[46] The renewed interest in Judaism on the part of Rosenzweig's teacher Hermann Cohen came about as the result of a famous trial in 1888 at which Cohen defended Judaism against the by then familiar charge of xenophobia. See Cohen's essay "Die

formal rights and obligations of political equality and accepted them honestly, they could still never be able to participate fully and honestly in the person-to-person relationships that comprise the true human substance of any society. Of course, virtually all West European Jews, of whatever religious belief and practice, vehemently argued against this charge. Since he was a theologian first and foremost, in order to locate Rosenzweig most specifically within the discussion of this question, it is best to examine the most theological version of that discussion.[47]

The most theological version of the discussion of the new relationship, or the possibility of a new relationship, between Jews and non-Jews brought by modernity centers around the exegesis of the biblical verse, "you shall love your neighbor as yourself" (Leviticus 19:18). The question is whether "your neighbor" here is to be interpreted as "fellow Jew" or "fellow human." Both interpretations find their advocates within premodern Jewish exegesis.[48]

In Germany as in the rest of Western Europe, the thrust for the political and social equality of all citizens of the new nation-state came from the three ideals of the French Revolution: *liberté, égalité, fraternité*. The question was whether Jews, remaining as Jews, that is, could still accept these ideals. And the most important ideal, the one having the most positive content and social significance, is *fraternité*. Could Jews really *love* their non-Jewish neighbors with the type of love true brotherhood requires? If this was not the case, then it was assumed – by both Jews and non-Jews – that Jewish emancipation (*liberté*) and political enfranchisement (*égalité*) were insuf-

Nächstenliebe im Talmud," in *Jüdische Schriften*, 1:145ff.; also, Novak, *The Image of the Non-Jew in Judaism*, 387ff. For the political and intellectual background of Rosenzweig's entry into this quintessential modern Jewish question, see Richard A. Cohen, *Elevations* (Chicago, 1994), chap. 8.

47 Even though Rosenzweig considered himself a philosopher (see *Kleinere Schriften*, 374), I call him a theologian because his thinking begins with God, unlike Hermann Cohen, Martin Buber, or Emmanuel Levinas, who begin their thinking with the human condition. By this criterion, Rosenzweig is as throroughly a theologian as was Abraham Joshua Heschel, or Karl Barth.

48 For a number of sources on this exegetical–theological debate, see D. Novak, *Jewish Social Ethics* (New York, 1992), 182, n. 30.

ficient formalities in the face of the authentic human participation in society now required of everyone. Therefore, virtually all Jewish thinkers in this new world emphasized in every way possible that the true intent of the biblical commandment was love of *all* fellow humans. And they did this with the full intention of showing that such equality did not entail the religious assimilation of the Jews. Not surprisingly, the modern Jewish thinker who presented the most philosophically cogent version of this argument was Rosenzweig's teacher Hermann Cohen.[49] Nevertheless, although Cohen and Rosenzweig were part of the overall West European Jewish tendency to interpret the love of neighbor commandment as love of one's fellow human, they did so for very different reasons.

For Cohen, love of the neighbor is what autonomous morality ultimately requires when the rational person knows that he or she and the neighbor are both united in the idea of humanity itself. That is the true locus of the act of love. And the love of God is the love of the ideal that alone makes possible the ability of the love of fellow humans to culminate ultimately in the full universality of the Messianic Age, which for Cohen is the final redemption of the world. The love of God, that is, man's love for God, functions for the sake of the love by human persons of humanity per se. As for God's love for man, we have seen that for Cohen this is in truth a metaphor.[50]

For Rosenzweig, the love of the neighbor is not the primary act of love for which the love of God functions. The love of God has priority. And it has priority because the human love for God is in response to God's love for man, which is revealed in God's election of Israel. Love of the neighbor can only be truly initiated and sustained if it follows after God's love and the human response to that love. Indeed, it is the extension of that human response to God. So Rosenzweig writes at the beginning of his discussion of redemption in the third book of the *Star*,

---

[49] See n. 42 above; also, Hermann Cohen, *Religion of Reason Out of the Sources of Judaism*, trans. S. Kaplan (New York, 1972), 127–128. For a similar concern on the part of Rosenzweig's beloved disciple Ernst Simon, see his "The Neighbor (*Re'a*) whom we shall Love," in *Modern Jewish Ethics*, ed. M. Fox (Columbus, Ohio, 1975), 29ff.

[50] See pp. 62–63 above.

Love thy neighbor. That is, as Jew and Christian assure us, the embodiment (*Inbegriff*) of all commandments. With this command-ment, the soul is declared of age, departs the paternal home of divine love, and sets forth (*wandert hinaus*) into the world ... Now if this too is a commandment to love, how is that to be reconciled with the fact that this "love me!" commands the only kind of love which can be commanded?[51]

Rosenzweig then very powerfully shows that if the soul awakened by God's love in revelation were to remain enrap-tured in this bliss and thus become immovable, the soul would soon lose its configuration (*Gestalt*) and be absorbed into divine Being itself. Here we would have the seclusion of the mystic.[52] However, the seclusion of the mystic presupposes that God is the object of a love that originates in human longing, the longing for absolute Being by an entity that is in the state of becoming. It is the quest for the hidden God (*Deus absconditus*). Yet Rosenzweig has already shown that the love relationship between God and humans is just the opposite. It is God's coming out of God's hiddenness, coming out in revelation (*Deus revelatus*) in order to reach his human creature. Therefore, for Rosenzweig, the direction of the human creature in response to God's love is not facing back to God but, rather, facing out into the world to claim it for God. The human coming out of his or her seclusion with God is the act of *imitatio Dei* that replicates God's coming out of his own seclusion. So, just as creation is for the sake of revelation, so is revelation for the sake of redemp-tion. Accordingly, the love of neighbor is the first step in the revelation-awakened soul's new embrace of the world. It is what bridges revelation and redemption. As Rosenzweig reasons,

Thus the neighbor is, as stated, only a place-holder. Love goes out to whatever is nearest to it as a representative, in the fleeting moment of its presentness (*Gegenwartigkeit*), and thereby in truth to the all-inclusive concept (*Inbegriff Aller*) of all men and all things which could ever assume this place of being its nearest neighbor. In the final analysis (*letzthin*) it goes out to everything, to the world.[53]

[51] *Star*, 205 (= *Stern*, 262).   [52] See *Star*, 207ff.   [53] *Star*, 218 (= *Stern*, 278).

At this point Rosenzweig is faced with considerable diffi-culty as a Jewish theologian. For if the love of the world prefigured in the love of the neighbor is what revelation's full trajectory demands, it would seem that revelation demands a missionary community for its fulfillment. It would seem that the full intent of the election of Israel is that Israel make her raison d'être the inclusion of the whole world in her election. Accordingly, Israel herself becomes the "placeholder" that Rosenzweig spoke about above, that is, the love of one Jew for another (*ahavat yisra'el*) is just the first step in the universalizing process of love for the whole world. But, then, are we not right back to Hermann Cohen's universalistic concept of the election of Israel, a theological concept based on philosophical premises that Rosenzweig strove so hard to reject?

Cohen's concept of the election of Israel as founding the "Mission of Israel" to the world not only is based on philo-sophical premises that cannot accept the primacy of God's election of Israel rather than Israel's election of God, as we have already seen, but also suggests something that the vast majority of Jews, especially religious Jews, would find alto-gether foreign. For even though one could argue for the halak-hic permissibility of a Jewish mission to the gentiles, the fact is that this has not been the historical experience of the Jewish people for many centuries, if ever.[54] The whole ethos of Judaism seems to be quite anti-worldly: not anti-worldly in the sense of being ascetic, but anti-worldly in the sense of being concerned with the preservation of the singular life of the Jewish people itself. And Rosenzweig himself, advocating as he did an experiential approach to Judaism, was certainly keenly aware of this experiential reality of native Jewish life.[55]

Nevertheless, the world is still very much there. It is still very much God's own creation. Thus a Jewish theology that did not somehow or other include the world in its theory would quickly become the theology of a finite god in relation to a tribe that is insignificant for the history of the world (*Weltgeschichte* in

---

[54] Cf. D. Novak, *Jewish–Christian Dialogue* (New York, 1989), 64ff.; see also pp. 158–162 below.

[55] See *Star*, 335ff.

Hegel's sense). At this point, then, it would seem that Rosenzweig's view of election is left with the alternatives of either Cohenian-type idealistic universality or the old-fashioned parochialism of the premodern Ghetto.

Rosenzweig's solution to this problem is to include Christianity in his theology in a way that is very much unlike anything before in the history of Judaism. What Rosenzweig does is to assign to Christianity the task of extending the realm of revelation into the realm of redemption. Thus love of the neighbor on the universal level becomes an integral part of the Christian necessity to proselytize the whole world.[56] And he does this in a way that precludes the usual Christian claim that Christianity's extension of the election of Israel to the world makes the continued existence of Judaism redundant. For the usual Christian claim is that the incarnation as the redemptive event has taken all that Judaism was ever to do for God into itself – that Judaism is by now elevated-and-transformed (*aufgehoben*). Whatever eternal truth Judaism retained has already been taken up by Christianity. And whatever temporal truth Judaim retained is no longer necessary, because it has completed its historical task. Indeed, to retain it now is a denial of the accomplishment of redemption in Christ.[57] Contrary to all that, Rosenzweig insists that Judaism is not elevated-and-transformed into Christianity; rather, there is a continuing dialectic between the two faith-communities precisely because, as Judaism asserts, the world has not yet been redeemed. Accordingly, Judaism's task is to preserve the historical reality of revelation in all its purity and all its concentration; Christianity's task is to gather the whole world into that reality.[58]

Without Judaism Christianity is in danger of being diluted into the paganism of the unredeemed world; without Christianity Judaism is in danger of being marginalized as the religion of an exotic tribe. Only at the time of the final-

---

[56] As Rosenzweig puts it, "Die Christheit muss missionieren" (*Stern*, 429 = *Star*, 341). See *Briefe*, no. 57, pp. 69–70; *Jehuda Halevi*, 183.

[57] So the Church quite early condemned "judaization." See Ignatius, *To the Magnesians*, chap. 10.

[58] See *Star*, 335ff.

redemption-yet-to-be will there be a an *Aufhebung*, but it will be the elevation-and-transformation of *both* Judaism *and* Christianity into the wholly unprecedented kingdom of God.[59] Rosenzweig is convinced that the task of both Jews and Christians is to await that culmination of all history – but to wait for it separately. Thus both Judaism and Christianity are "placeholders" for the endtime in which God will be related to man per se.[60]

Although there is a beautiful symmetry in Rosenzweig's unique constitution of the relation of Judaism and Christianity to each other, it does not correspond to the data of Jewish tradition, nor does it provide us with a truly coherent method for dealing with the real relationship of Jews and Christians in the world here and now. Elsewhere I have argued just why Rosenzweig's model is inadequate to the very new relationship between Jews and Christians, especially after the Holocaust.[61] Here I want to argue why this aspect of Rosenzweig's theory of the election of Israel is so unsatisfying. But this is said with the explicit proviso that I accept with gratitude virtually all of Rosenzweig's phenomenology of revelation as election. Indeed, it seems to me to be the most profound contribution to Jewish theology in this century.[62]

In understanding the very large role Rosenzweig has given to Christianity in his theory of redemption, one can see it emerging out of his own personal experience. He himself

---

[59] See *Star*, 415–416; *Briefe*, no. 59, p. 73; Glatzer, *Franz Rosenzweig*, 342; Novak, *Jewish–Christian Dialogue*, 175, n. 41. So, ultimately, Rosenzweig seems to revert to a Hegelian emphasis on the ontological primacy of futurity even over his anti-Hegelian emphasis on present/presence. Along these lines, see his *Understanding the Sick and the Healthy*, trans. T. Luckman (New York, 1954), 69–71. Of course, one can show many differences between Rosenzweig's emphasis on futurity and Hegel's (and Heidegger's), as does the most astute commentator on the *Star*, Stéphane Mosès in his superb book *System and Revelation*, trans. C. Tihanyi (Detroit, 1992), 267ff., 290ff. However, I still maintain that the future *Aufhebung* of both Judaism and Christianity at the time of redemption that Rosenzweig posits is a reversion to Hegelianism that cannot be explained away. Nevertheless, it should not prevent us from appropriating many of his profound insights into Judaism, especially his incomparable phenomenology of revelation.

[60] See *Kleinere Schriften*, 80–82; *Jehuda Halevi*, 188.

[61] *Jewish–Christian Dialogue*, 108ff.

[62] Rosenzweig himself stressed the centrality of his constitution of revelation in his overall theory (see *Kleinere Schriften*, 386).

almost had to become a Christian before he could retrieve his own Judaism. Indeed, he himself could not have returned to Judaism if it had not been for his close relationship with three Christian thinkers. In my earlier discussion of Rosenzweig's treatment of the Jewish–Christian relationship I have dwelt on the connection between his personal experience and his theology.[63] Here, however, I want to argue with his eschatology and show that it detracts from the power of his theory of election, which emerged from his phenomenology of revelation.

The problem with Rosenzweig's theory of redemption is that it signals a reversion, as it were, to a sort of Hegelianism. How ironic this is considering the fact that in his theories of creation and revelation Rosenzweig strove so mightily to overcome the type of totalizing philosophy that could not allow for a sufficient separation between God, man, and the world. And without this separation of elements there could be no consciousness of the relationship between God and the world which is creation, the relationship between God and man which is revelation, and the relationship between man and the world which is redemption. Although Rosenzweig is very careful to state that God still transcends redemption, when it comes to the relationship between man and the world – and by "the world" he means humanity, not the world of nonhuman phenomena – both elements in the relationship are elevated-and-transformed (*aufgehoben*).[64] Accordingly, finally man and the world will be totally immanent in each other. And here, man as the object of revelation is represented by the Jew, and the world as the object of redemption is represented by the Christian. But in the endtime of redemption there will be neither Jews nor Christians but an altogether transposed reality before God.

But surely the tendency in rabbinic teaching was to emphasize that the redemption of the world would in essence be God's

---

[63] *Jewish–Christian Dialogue*, 97ff.
[64] See, esp., *Star*, 305. Cf. *ibid.*, 415–416; Novak, *Jewish–Christian Dialogue*, 100–101; n. 54 above. Rosenzweig does occasionally speak of physical nature, but he does so in the context of revelation, namely, its capacity to present "nature" to man in a prescientific manifestation. (See *Briefe*, no. 342; also, *Jehuda Halevi*, 65, 82.)

redemption of the Jewish people, which would then include all the rest of humankind.[65] Thus a major effect of redemption would be the judaization of humanity.[66] However, this redemption would not be the result of the extension of revelation by the Jews or by anyone else. Instead, it would be the mysterious act of God.

At the present time, then, Jewish eschatology functions as a negation more than anything else. The hope for redemption functions as an antidote to Utopianism, just as the acknowledgment of creation functions as an antidote to naturalism, and just as the acceptance of revelation functions as an antidote to autonomy. All of these human projects are ultimately idolatrous in their denial of the prime authority of God: naturalism in declaring the self-sufficiency of nature; autonomy in declaring the self-sufficiency of human morality; and Utopianism in declaring the self-sufficiency of history.[67] My argument with Rosenzweig is that he has compromised the transcendence of redemption by making it the culmination of a process, albeit a process unlike that proposed by Idealism.[68] In other words, he did not fully exorcise the tendencies of the Idealism on which he cut his philosophical teeth.

For this reason, Rosenzweig has ultimately seen the election of Israel as the means to a higher end, which is the election of humanity itself. However, there is a fundamental difference between the more classical view, which sees the redemption of the world as its apocalyptic judaization, and Rosenzweig's still liberally influenced view, which sees redemption as the *Aufhebung* of Judaism (and Christianity) into a new humanity. In Rosenzweig's view, election is teleologically derivative, whereas in the classical view it is nonderivative. The covenant intends nothing outside its own reality. The Jewish people as members of the everlasting covenantal community hope for the final inclusion of all humankind into their covenant with God. But that inclusion will be the sole result of an apocalyptic

---

[65] Cf. pp. 152–162 below.   [66] See pp. 159–160 below.

[67] For Rosenzweig's insistence on the presence of idolatry in the modern world, see *Jehuda Halevi*, 64.

[68] See *Star*, 230.

incursion by God into history. It cannot be achieved by human proselytizing efforts, not by Jews and certainly not by any non-Jewish community whatever its connections to Judaism are.[69] (And I would agree with Rosenzweig that Judaism and Christianity have a connection unlike any other two religious communities in the world.) Indeed, any such proselytizing by Jews would lead to the dilution of the Jewish covenantal reality. When converts do come to Judaism, it is assumed that God has sent them as especially graced individuals.[70] As for the vast majority of gentiles who remain outside God's covenant with Israel, the thrust of Jewish tradition has taught that God is accessible through creation and through other histories as well. Moreover, it has done this without denying that the covenant is the most primary, the most direct of any human relationship with God on earth.[71]

I share Rosenzweig's concern, which is the concern of all modern Jews who realize that there is no premodern Ghetto any more (a current Jewish debate is whether that fact is for good or for ill), and that the elect community of Israel constitutes for itself out of its classical sources a *modus vivendi* with the non-Jewish world. Neither the classical sources nor more recent historical experience can allow anyone to think of the Jewish people as some exotic tribe, peripheral to the larger world inside herself. I differ with Rosenzweig, however, in just where the relationship between the elect community and the outside world should be really located and theoretically constituted. He has located it at the juncture of revelation and redemption. I have located it at the juncture of creation and revelation. That is, the Jewish relationship with the outside world is governed by the commonalities Jews can discover with other communities and their traditions on the level of natural

[69] Thus Maimonides' assertion that Christianity – and Islam (contra Rosenzweig) – *somehow* contribute to the coming of the final redemption of this world by their spreading the doctrine of monotheism throughout the world (*Mishneh Torah*: Melakhim, chap. 11, uncensored ed.), which Rosenzweig uses in in the *Star* (336ff.), in no wise defers to either of these "daughter religions" in the way Rosenzweig defers to Christianity. For Maimonides, Judaism is never meant to be as "unworldly" as Rosenzweig makes it out to be in his system.

[70] See p.160 below.   [71] See Novak, *Jewish–Christian Dialogue*, intro.

law, and its function as the precondition for the revelation the respective communities affirm as the locus of their inner life. At the level of natural law's practical norms, we have the immanent content of this relationship; at the level of the precondition for revelation we have the transcendent possibility of creation, realized quite differently by the respective communities. And these differences can be respected with theological integrity, not just pragmatically tolerated.[72]

For this reason, contrary to Rosenzweig and Cohen and their modern predecessors and successors, I would theologically emphasize the tendency of most traditional Jewish exegetes to interpret the "your neighbor" (*re'akha*) in the commandment "you shall love your neighbor as yourself" as referring to one's *fellow Jew*. Linguistically, this can be seen in the meaning of "as yourself" (*kamokha*). Your *self* is your-self as the object of God's love in the covenant. That is why you are able to love your fellow covenant member as you yourself are loved by God. The ground of this love of the neighbor is not one's immanent self-love, which is then extended to a larger circle; rather, it is the existential acceptance of one's elected status *along with* all other members of the covenant and acting on it in a human mutuality transcendently grounded.[73] Indeed, as Rosenzweig himself understood quite well, God's love is not experienced *through* creation as a universal given (that of an "all-loving Father"), but only *in the covenant* as the object of God's election.[74] That is

---

[72] See *ibid.*, 114ff.

[73] Cf. Aristotle, *Nicomachean Ethics* 1166a1, where the love of friends (*philia*) that obtains in the *polis* society derives from self-love (*ek tōn pros heauton*). One is to love his or her own good qualities that he or she subsequently finds in someone else. For Hermann Cohen, on the other hand, the love of self (*Ich*) comes from the love of the other (*Du*). (See *Ethik des reinen Willens*, 4th ed. [Berlin, 1923], 251ff.; also, Robert Gibbs, *Correlations in Rosenzweig and Levinas* [Princeton, 1992], 178ff.) However, for both of them, love of one's fellow is based on common participation in an idea that includes both persons as examples thereof. It is not something that involves persons as fundamentally real presences. And even for Emmanuel Levinas, for whom interpersonal relationships (*Beziehungen*) are more original than the relations (*Verhältnisse*) between ideas and their examples, the relationship is not based on an even more direct and prior relationship with God as it is for Scripture and for Rosenzweig. (Cf. *Totality and Infinity*, trans. A. Lingis [Pittsburgh, 1969], 78ff.)

[74] Indeed, he considers attempts to universalize God's love as essentially "Spinozistic." See *Star*, 199; also, p. 244, n. 8 below.

why the verse in Leviticus 19:18 concludes "I am the Lord," that is, YHWH, who is the God of the covenant.[75]

As for the rest of humankind, to whom Israel is related through creation, the relationship is to be one of justice for all. Let it be remembered that the very first mention of justice (*mishpat*) in Scripture is when Abraham requests God to be just in his dealings with the people of Sodom and Gomorrah so as to be an exemplar of the justice Abraham and his clan are to practice towards all with whom they come into contact (Genesis 18:19).[76] For there is a fundamental difference between the minimal principle of no-harm, which the Talmud presents as something universal, and the maximal commandment of intercovenantal love, a difference Rosenzweig himself explicitly recognizes.[77]

Furthermore, there can even be friendship with some who are outside the covenant: we find examples in both Scripture and the rabbinic writings.[78] However, covenantal love that is commanded is only to be found within the covenanted community itself. It is thus intensive rather than extensive. The inclusion of the non-Jewish world in that covenantal love will be the result of God's bringing them into the covenant at the endtime of redemption – God, and not the Jews or anyone else extending the covenant in a triumphal march out to them from a superior point here and now.

I believe that this constitution of the Jewish–gentile relationship does not fall into the problem of only being able to constitute the Jewish–Christian relationship, as does Rosenzweig's (and even there quite problematically), however privileged it certainly is. It can extend to Islam as another religion of revelation, and it can even extend to those religions and philosophies that, although they do not have revelations, do respect a transcendent horizon of human life. And finally, I

---

[75] See Exod. 5:2 and Nahmanides' comment thereon; also, Novak, *The Theology of Nahmanides*, 31ff.

[76] See Novak, *The Image of the Non-Jew in Judaism*, esp. 53ff.

[77] See B. Shabbat 31a; *Star*, 239.

[78] See, e.g., Job 2:11 (assuming that Job is a Jew and his friends non-Jews – see B. Baba Batra 15b); B. Avodah Zarah 30a.

believe it enables us to constitute the doctrine of the election of Israel in a way that intends the utter originality of the reality it affirms.[79] But I could not possibly move on to the classical sources of the doctrine of election and ever hope to retrieve them philosophically if Franz Rosenzweig had not prepared a good part of the way for me.

[79] On this point of theo-*logy*, I have learned much from Karl Barth's argument against attempts within his tradition to derive the Christian doctrine of election from something prior to it ontologically, namely, a general divine providence (see his *Church Dogmatics*, 2/2, trans. G. W. Bromiley *et al.* [Edinburgh, 1957], 94ff.). Of course, my being a Jew and Barth's being a Christian would cause each of us to differ *theo*-logically as to *who* is the direct object of God's election: the people of Israel or Jesus. Along these lines, see the work of the Jewish theologian most influenced by Barth, namely, Michael Wyschogrod in his *Body of Faith* (New York, 1983), esp. 58ff. For more on Wyschogrod's theology of election, see pp. 241–245 below.

CHAPTER 4

The retrieval of the biblical doctrine

SCRIPTURE AND PHILOSOPHICAL ANALYSIS

More than any other modern Jewish thinker Franz Rosenzweig
has enabled contemporary Jews to retrieve philosophically the
biblical doctrine of the election of Israel. This is because
Rosenzweig has enabled us to retrieve philosophically the
Bible itself, to retrieve it at its most essential level: its presentation of the relationship with God. Thus he began the process
of overcoming Spinoza. That, as we have already seen, is the
historical precondition for our contemporary retrieval of the
doctrine. For although even Spinoza agreed with the Bible that
the relationship with God is the most important human
concern, he rejected the Bible's assumption that its covenantal
reality is the primary locus of that relationship. Instead,
Spinoza insisted that the primary locus of that relationship lies
in nature and only secondarily in anything historical.[1] To be
sure, Rosenzweig did not directly argue against Spinoza
himself, but rather against Spinoza's assumption as it came to
be accepted in Idealist philosophy. In this philosophy, even
God's relationships are all part of a larger system that ultimately includes everything. Consequently, the election of
Israel by God, which is certainly the *leitmotif* in the Bible, had
to be radically deconstructed, as we have already seen. Rosenzweig argued and demonstrated that if there is to be any

[1] See pp. 25–30 above.

authentic relationship with God, the Bible and all that it entails must be its primary locus. The beginning of this retrieval, the ground clearing for it, as it were, can be seen in *The Star of Redemption*.[2] And the continuation of it can be seen in Rosenzweig's project of biblical translation, which he undertook with Martin Buber and to which he devoted himself right up until the time of his death.[3]

The immediate philosophical import of Rosenzweig's achievement can be seen in his radical rejection of Spinoza's most basic premise, namely, that God is Being – and what is not God is in a state of becoming.[4] In this view, the world aspires to be as much like God as it can become; God, conversely, being totally self-contained, aspires to nothing outside himself. Thus all transitive action is on the part of the world; there is no transitive action on the part of God, for that would compromise his status as Being: the One who is eternal and immutable. The world is to relate itself to God, but God does not relate himself to the world. The relation, then, is unilateral. But with such an ontology, one cannot constitute the mutuality of the covenantal relationship with God that begins in God's election of Israel to be his covenantal companion.

Hermann Cohen too accepted this most basic premise of Spinoza. His difference with him was at the level of what actually comprises the world's relation to God. For Spinoza, that nondivine "world" is the realm of human politics. All that we call "nature," however, is part of divine Being itself. Philosophically speaking, nature is the primary object of reflection; politics as a historical phenomenon is clearly secondary. But for Cohen, nature itself is an idea that is a human construct and thus a factor in human becoming. The highest level of human becoming is in the realm of the ethical, which ultimately grounds the political and even the scientific realm.[5] Thus election as an ethical act, an act of human becoming, has a greater significance for him than for Spinoza, since unlike for

---

[2] See pp. 78–85 above.

[3] For an anthology of some of Rosenzweig's biblical studies, see *Die Schrift*, ed. K. Thieme (Königstein, 1984), 9–77.

[4] See Plato, *Timaeus* 28Aff.   [5] See pp. 54–62 above.

Spinoza, here is where the most primary relation to God takes place. Being and becoming are directly correlated by Cohen in a way that makes the realm of the ethical (and the political along with it) assume the importance that Spinoza reserves for ontology per se.

By justifying the election of God by Israel on ethical grounds, Cohen believed he made that act of election perpetually significant and not just historically contingent as it was for Spinoza. He restored to the doctrine the philosophical weight that he believed Spinoza had denied it. But he only did this by denying the minor premise, not the major premise, of Spinoza's argument. The minor premise was that Israel is now superfluous in the human election of God. This Cohen vehemently denied. Nevertheless, he fully accepted the major premise that man, not God, elects. Cohen's deconstruction of the Bible, unlike Spinoza's, was unintentional, to be sure. He thought that he was faithfully interpreting its true teaching. The Bible was always an important part of his life, both as an individual scholar and as a practicing Jew. Nevertheless, he still saw philosophy as being more primary for the relationship with God than biblical teaching and, therefore, biblical teaching had to be ultimately justified by it.[6] Hence as for Spinoza the Bible could not be a direct object of philosophical reflection for Cohen.

Even in the Middle Ages, long before Spinoza, when this basic being–becoming ontology was adopted by rationalist Jewish thinkers like Maimonides and Gersonides and then used to explain biblical doctrines, there was always a significant number of thoughtful Jews who were not convinced that this ontology was adequate to the interpretation of Scripture and the Jewish tradition.[7] However, overcoming it has been no easy task. For the one thing that this ontology has been able to do is to constitute the relation of the world to God as well as that of Israel to God. Calls for a simple return to biblical theology,

---

[6] See *Religion of Reason Out of the Sources of Judaism*, trans. S. Kaplan (New York, 1972), intro.

[7] See, esp., Nahmanides, *Commentary on the Torah*: Exod. 3:13; also, D. Novak, *The Theology of Nahmanides Systematically Presented* (Atlanta, 1992), 31ff.

without the philosophical detour of the rationalists, seem inevitably to lose sight of the factor of the world's relation to God. Yet this is a factor that is hardly ignored in Scripture itself, even though the primary concern is God's relationship with Israel.[8] And, furthermore, without the recognition that the world is related to God even before Israel is related to God, the absolute status of God can become quickly lost. For without the constitution of God's relation to the world, God's relation to Israel can easily become reduced to the relation between a tribe and its local deity. And this type of relation, as we shall soon see, is not one of election but one of necessity.[9] Election itself presupposes the absolute status of God, which is indeed the most ubiquitous factor in all of Scripture. So, once biblical theology has confronted the worldliness of philosophy, it can never restore its authority again until it utilizes philosophy by constituting its own worldliness.

This is the first prerequisite for philosophical retrieval of the Bible: appropriating the worldliness of rationalist philosophy and the theology based on it and then overcoming it by constituting a more theologically cogent worldliness of its own. Such retrieval inevitably requires the astute appropriation of philosophical method. More than anyone else, Rosenzweig was able to initiate us into this approach because he was an extraordinary philosopher. He enabled us to learn again from Scripture by means of philosophical retrieval: being in the world but not of it, rather than simply being apart from it in retreat, a retreat which after exposure to modernity willy-nilly can only be reactionary.

The second prerequisite for the philosophical retrieval of the Bible by contemporary Jews is the overcoming of historicism's separation of the reader from the biblical text itself. At this point what is needed is a reaffirmation of Pharisaism. And here again, the source of that which is to be overcome is Spinoza. For it will be recalled that Spinoza had particular antipathy to

---

[8] See, e.g., Jonah 4:1–11; also, Yehezkel Kaufmann, *Toldot Ha'Emunah Ha-Yisra'elit*, 2.2.12 (4 vols., Jerusalem and Tel Aviv, 1966), 433ff.

[9] See Yehezkel Kaufmann, *The Religion of Israel*, trans. M. Greenberg (Chicago, 1960), 298.

the Pharisaic attempt to extend the authority of the biblical text beyond the confines of its most evident context. His preference was for the more literally confined reading of the Bible by the Sadducees.[10] However, what the literalist reading of the Bible by the Sadducees accomplished was to make the Bible an antiquarian book and thus to leave large areas of human life outside its authority.[11]

By rejecting the continuing and uninterrupted historical connection of the people of Israel with the Bible *by* and *through* tradition, a tradition both theirs and that of the Bible itself, the Sadducees and their modern admirer Baruch Spinoza precluded philosophical reflection on the Bible. For philosophical reflection requires that its prime datum be present, indeed that datum which is most consistently present to us. Only such a datum can be taken with ultimate seriousness. Anything less would make the datum of philosophy finally reducible to something more primary than itself and so inevitably lead the philosopher to reflect on it instead.[12] What is primary to us is always normative inasmuch as it makes immediate and continual claims on our attention and elicits our concern. And what is primary to philosophers is what elicits their reflective concern. The essential seriousness of philosophy requires the normative horizon of its reflection to be in full view. The consistent presence of Scripture and the full range of its normative potential was one of the prime bequests of Pharisaism to its rabbinic (and Christian) heirs. Because of that, some of them have been able to reflect on the Bible philosophically.

To be sure, the understanding we now have of the initial context of the biblical text in time and place supplied for us by historical research cannot be ignored without our becoming totally arbitrary in our scholarly standards. Historical research cannot be rejected out of hand any more than natural science can without the worldly weight of the Bible being simultane-

---

[10] See p. 40 above.

[11] For the overall thrust of the Pharisee project, see my late revered teacher Louis Finkelstein, *The Pharisees* (2 vols., Philadelphia, 1938), 1:261ff.

[12] See D. Novak, *The Image of the Non-Jew in Judaism* (New York and Toronto, 1983), xv–xvi.

ously surrendered and the Jewish readers of the Bible being relegated to the level of obscurantists.[13] The Bible within our tradition, where it is the primary source of truth, is also found in other contexts. This has been demonstrated convincingly by modern historical means. And the doctrine of creation surely implies that there is truth in the wider world, however subordinate it must ultimately be to the truth of revelation.[14] Nevertheless, historical research must always be secondary precisely because the Bible is the book that Jews have never stopped reading. It is a book addressed to them in all their generations. Modern historical research on the Bible, conversely, has been conducted on the assumption that contemporary readers of the Bible are reading about someone other than themselves. Occasionally, the Rabbis too recognized the gap between the historical context of their own generations and the historical context of certain biblical texts. However, the notion that the Torah speaks just to its own time is only rarely mentioned.[15] Much more often it is assumed that the Torah speaks far beyond the time in which it was originally uttered.[16] The tradition of Jewish reading of Scripture as the founding document of Jewish tradition is unbroken. Accordingly, the tradition is always the most immediate and evident link between the reading community and the read text.

This primary traditional context of and for the Scriptural text fulfills a third philosophical prerequisite. That is, the datum for philosophical reflection must be an integral enough unity so that the reflection on it does not irrevocably fragment it, thus leading to the loss of its consistently integral presence and all that this entails. This affirmation can only be made today if we emphasize the role of tradition in the redaction and

---

[13] Along these lines note: "Es gibt nur Eine Wahrheit. Zu einem Gott, den er als wissenschaftlicher Mensch leugnet, kann kein Ehrlicher beten ... Aber Gott hat die Welt, also den Gegenstand der Wissenschaft, geschaffen" (Franz Rosenzweig, *Die Schrift*, 32 – a postscript to a letter written to the Orthodox Jewish leader Jakob Rosenheim in 1927; see pp. 91–92 above). See also Wolfhart Pannenberg, *Systematic Theology*, trans. G. W. Bromiley (Grand Rapids, Mich., 1991), 1:231.

[14] See D. Novak, *Jewish Social Ethics* (New York, 1992), 3–4.

[15] See, e.g., B. Baba Batra 120a–121a.

[16] See B. Kiddushin 29a re Deut. 3:28 and Num. 15:23; also, R. Baruch Halevi Epstein, *Torah Temimah* (5 vols., New York, 1962): Num. 15:23, n. 61.

canonization of the text of Scripture. This means avoiding the extremes of historicism on the one hand and fundamentalism on the other. For, as we have just seen, the error of historicism is to atomize context and thus to suggest a normative fissure between what was written in the past and the reader in the present. In the context of tradition, however, the reader never comes to the text as an outsider in the guise of an archaeologist. He or she is linked to the text by virtue of the community in which he or she participates, even before the text is opened by him or her to be read. And the error of fundamentalism is to assume that the unity the biblical text subsequently assumes *in and from* the tradition is evident even when the text is examined apart from that tradition. It assumes that the unity of the text can be taken as evident in any context whatsoever because it is assumed that is inherent in the text *before* it is related to any context.[17] But in the context of traditional exegetical reading (midrash), it is ultimately futile to demarcate precisely just where the text ends and the readers begin.[18] Read in other contexts, the biblical text assumes other meanings, both as a whole and in each of its parts.

Ironically enough, both the historicist and the fundamentalist come together in their isolation of the biblical text. And they come together in their preclusion of a philosophical reading of the biblical text. The fundamentalist precludes it because philosophical reflection on the text threatens the literal and immediately evident unity that he or she dogmatically posits. It cannot stand the radical suspension of simple certitude that philosophy requires.[19] The historicist precludes it because philosophical reflection assumes that there is an essential intelligible unity of the text to be constantly discovered.[20] As a species of nominalism, however, historicism cannot accept any

---

[17] Along these lines, see George A. Lindbeck, *The Nature of Doctrine* (Philadelphia, 1984), 65ff.
[18] Note Franz Rosenzweig's polemic with modern Jewish Orthodoxy on this point, pp. 91–92 above.
[19] See Paul Ricoeur, *Hermeneutics and the Human Sciences*, ed. and trans. J. B. Thompson (Cambridge, 1981), 112ff.
[20] See, e.g., *Sifra*: Vayiqra, ed. Weiss, 3b (re the thirteenth hermeneutical principle of R. Ishmael); also, B. Baba Kama 41b re Deut. 10:20.

assumption of essential intelligibility outside its own invention. At this juncture of history, fundamentalism entails the notion that we can read Scripture now as if Spinoza and his heirs never existed. Historicism entails the notion that Spinoza and his heirs – at least at the level of biblical scholarship – can never be overcome. The philosophical retrieval of Scripture in general and its doctrine of the election of Israel in particular requires a course that carefully avoids the Scylla of the one and the Charybdis of the other.

CREATION AND ELECTION

In the narrative of Scripture the election of Abraham, the progenitor of the covenanted people of Israel, comes suddenly and without warning. It seems to catch us unprepared.

The Lord said to Abram: "you go away from your land, from your birthplace, from your father's house to the land that I will show you. I will make you a great nation and bless you; I will make your name great and you will be a blessing. I will bless those who bless you and those who curse you I will curse. Through you (*vekha*) all the families of the earth will be blessed. And Abram went as the Lord had spoken to him." (Genesis 12:1–4)

In this elementary text there seems to be no clue as to why God elects Abraham and his progeny or why Abraham obeys the call to respond to being elected by God. Unlike in the case of Noah, who is elected to save humankind and the animal world from the Flood "because (*ki*) I have seen that you are righteous (*tsadiq*) before Me in this generation" (Genesis 7:1), and who obviously responds to God's call because of the biological drive for self-preservation, there is no reason given here for either God's choice or Abraham's positive response to it. Any righteousness attributed to Abraham is seen as subsequent, not prior, to God's election of him.[21] It is thus a result of not a reason for election. And unlike Noah, Abraham does seem to have the alternative of staying where he already dwells. He seems to have a reasonable alternative to obedience to God's

---

[21] See Gen. 26:5; Neh. 9:7–8.

call. From the text of Scripture itself it seems as though Abraham could have stayed home. In his case, there is no destruction like a universal flood on the imminent horizon.

Simply leaving the matter at this mysterious level, is not speculation about the deeper meaning of the covenant established by this election and its acceptance thereby precluded? In the case of God's reason for electing Abraham and the people of Israel his progeny, the answer seems to be yes. At that side of the covenant, Scripture itself seems to imply "My thoughts (*mahshevotai*) are not your thoughts" (Isaiah 55:8) when it states,

For you are a people consecrated to the Lord your God; the Lord your God chose you (*bekha bahar*) to be unto him a treasure people from out of all the peoples on the face of the earth. It was not because you were more numerous than all the other peoples that the Lord desired you (*hashaq bakhem*) and chose you, for you are the least (*ha-me'at*) of all the peoples. It was because of the Lord's love for you (*me'ahavat adonai etkhem*) and his keeping the promise (*ha-shevu'ah*) he made to your ancestors. (Deuteronomy 7:6–8)

Of course, taken by itself this statement is a tautology: God loves you/chooses you/desires you because God loves you/chooses you/desires you. For there is no reason given as to why he made his promises to Abraham, and to Isaac and Jacob in the first place.[22] And the people of Israel themselves cannot claim any inherent qualities that could be seen as reasons for their election by God.[23]

---

22 See R. Judah Loewe (Maharal), *Netsah Yisra'el* (Prague, 1599), chap. 11; *Gevurot Ha-Shem* (Cracow, 1582), chaps. 24, 39, 54.

23 See H. Wildberger, *YHWH's Eigentumsvolk* (Zurich, 1960), 111; N. W. Porteous, "Volk und Gottesvolk in Alten Testament," in *Theologische Aufsätze: Karl Barth zum 50. Geburtstag* (Munich, 1936), 163. Cf. H. H. Rowley, *The Biblical Doctrine of Election* (London, 1950), 38–39, n. 2. Rowley sees Israel's election being based on teleology (35ff.), that is, God chose Israel because she had qualities useful for universal divine purposes. However, Rowley's supercessionist assumptions lie just beneath the surface of his scholarship. For when Israel fails God, then her election is annulled (49ff.) The implication, of course, is that the Church will have better qualities, so that it will replace Israel in and for God's universal plan. Porteous and Wildberger, conversely, being under the influence of Karl Barth (and it seems Calvin too) see God's electing promise and covenant to Israel as unconditional and never annulled or to be annulled. (See Barth, *Church Dogmatics*, 2/2, sec. 34, trans. G. W. Bromiley *et al.* [Edinburgh, 1957], 195ff.; Calvin, *Institutes of the Christian Religion*, 2.10.1ff.,

This is consistent with the logic of creation. In Scripture, unlike other ancient sagas, we are not told about any life of God prior to creation. Indeed, only the God to whom "all the earth is mine" (Exodus 19:5), to whom "the heavens and the highest heavens" (Deuteronomy 10:14) belong, only this God has such absolute freedom from any natural necessity to create a singular relationship like the covenant with Israel. There is nothing that could be considered a divine *a priori* from which one could infer the possibility of a nondivine world, much less the reality of any such world. All of God's relations with the world are, therefore, *a posteriori*. From revelation we learn some of the things God wants to do with the world, most especially what God wants his human creatures to do with the world along with him, but we do not learn why he made the world the way he did in the first place or, indeed, why he made it at all. So, too, we do not learn why God chose the people of Israel or, indeed, why he chose any people at all. All we learn, *a posteriori*, is what God wants to do with this people. "The secret things (*ha-nistarot*) are for the Lord our God; but the revealed things (*ve-ha-niglot*) are for us and our children forever: to practice all the commandments of this Torah" (Deuteronomy 29:28).

However, on the human side of this relationship of election, it is not only Abraham who is to respond to election. Election is primarily generic and only secondarily individual. Abraham is elected as the progenitor of a people. Every member of this people is elected by God and every member of this people is called upon to respond to his or her generic election. So, even if Abraham's individual reasons for accepting God's call could well be left alone as his own private and inscrutable business, speculation about his generic reasons for accepting it is our business as well inasmuch as his response is archetypal for all of

trans. F. L. Battles [2 vols., Philadelphia, 1960], 1:428ff.) Whatever differences Calvinist and Barthian Christians have with Judaism over the ultimate meaning of election – and they are crucial – these Protestants are not offended by the Jewish doctrine of the unconditional election of Israel, which is not the case with most of their more liberal co-religionists. Along these lines, see K. Sonderegger, *That Jesus Christ was Born a Jew* (University Park, Pa., 1992), 161ff.

us who follow after him.[24] For a communal response is a public matter, one whose reasons have to be rooted in continuing common experience before they can enter into personal reflection. This, then, calls for our reflection on our own human situation and what conditions in it enable us to respond to God's electing presence without caprice. Projecting our own reflection on the human conditions for election back to Abraham retrospectively is essential midrashic thinking.[25] Without it, we would lose our singular connection to the text of Scripture. It would become merely *a* datum among other data rather than *the* datum for us.

Of course, at the most original level, the prime reason for obeying God is that God is God. In Scripture, God's original presence is explicitly normative: his first contact with humans in the Garden is set forth in the words: "The Lord God commanded (*vayitsav*) the humans (*al ha'adam*)" (Genesis 2:16).[26] Norms are a necessity for human life because humans are beings who must consciously order the conflicting parts of their experience if they are to survive and cohere. That ordering requires a primary point of authority. (One can only be a moral relativist when looking at someone else's choices from afar, not when one is required to make his or her *own* choices at hand.) A human life without an ordering hierarchy of authority could only be that of an angel: an infallible life without conflict.[27] So it follows that any rejection of God's norms presupposes the substitution of God's authority by the authority of one who is not-God being made into God. The prime authority wherever is always taken to be God. There can be no

---

[24] See Isa. 41:8–10; 51:1–2.

[25] See Isaak Heinemann, *Darkhei Ha'Aggadah*, 2nd ed. (Jerusalem, 1954), 21ff.

[26] See B. Sanhedrin 56b re Gen. 2:16 and Exod. 32:8 (and, esp., the view of R. Judah; see the view of R. Meir on B. Avodah Zarah 64b); also, Maimonides, *Mishneh Torah*: Melakhim, 9.1.

[27] See *Shir Ha-Shirim Rabbah*, 8.13 re Lev. 15:25 and Num. 19:14; B. Kiddushin 54a and parallels. In rabbinic theology, angels are seen as monads with only one function to perform for which they are programmed by God (see *Bere'sheet Rabbah* 50.2). The primary human need for conscious ordering is coeval with the need for communicative community because that ordering finds its locus in the *public* nature of speech. See Gen. 2:18; B. Yevamot 63a re Gen. 2:23; B. Ta'anit 23a. Cf. Aristotle, *Politics* 1254a20.

normative vacuum.[28] That is why the first temptation to disobey God is the temptation that "you will be like God" (Genesis 3:5). You, not God, will become the prime authority. Without absolute authority, the creator would no longer be the creator; he would be forced to abdicate, as it were.

The relationship with God the creator at this original level is essentially negative, however.[29] It only consists of prohibitions that function as divine limitations of human illusions of self-sufficiency and autonomous authority. So far there is nothing positive between humans and God. It is with Abraham's call that we begin to see the establishment of a substantive relationship of humans *with* God. And in order for any such positive relationship to be sustained, there must be the discovery of positive reasons by humans *within* themselves for them to want to accept and maintain this relationship. Thus, whereas resistance to the idolatrous temptation to substitute the authority of not-God (the world or the human person) for God involves the affirmation of truth, the response to the covenant involves the desire for good.[30] By obeying God, what good did Abraham desire? What did his response intend?

The covenant itself must be the object of human desire. This desire for it as good is an essential component of it. Hence in presenting the positive covenantal norms, Moses appeals to the desire of the people for what is their good.[31] "The Lord commanded us to practice (*la'asot*) all these statutes, to fear the Lord our God, which is good for us (*tov lanu*) all times for our vitality (*le-hayyotenu*) as it is today. And it will be right (*tsedaqah*) for us to be careful to do this whole commandment before the Lord our God as he has commanded us" (Deuteronomy 6:25). And shortly before this passage, each one of the people is commanded to "love the Lord your God with all your heart,

---

[28] That is why God's most generic name is *elohim*, "authority," which is first divine and then human. See B. Sanhedrin 56b re Gen. 2:16 and Exod. 22:7; also, D. Novak, "Before Revelation: The Rabbis, Paul, and Karl Barth," *Journal of Religion* (1991), 71:58.

[29] Thus the Noahide laws, stipulating the minimal relation of humankind to God, are essentially prohibitions. See B. Sanhedrin 58b–59a and Rashi, s.v. "ve-ha-dinin" re Lev. 19:15.

[30] See Novak, *Jewish Social Ethics*, 14ff.   [31] See *ibid.*, 27ff.

with all your life, and with all your might" (6:5). But can there be any love without desire? And is not desire experienced, inchoately to be sure, even before its desideratum comes to it?[32] "For you O Lord is my whole desire (*kol ta'avati*)" (Psalms 38:10).[33] And does not desire entail hope, which is essentially an anticipation of something in itself unknown in the present? Moreover, can there be any desire that does not intend good for the one in whom it stirs?[34] Or as the Psalmist puts it, "Who is there for me in heaven, and besides you I desire (*lo hafatsti*) no one on earth . . . As for me, the nearness of God, that is my good (*li tov*) . . ." (Psalms 73:25, 28). Is not God to be served by a "desiring soul" (*nefesh hafetsah*) (I Chronicles 28:9)?

It seems to me that the reasons for Abraham's answering the electing call of God, and thus the paradigm for all subsequent Jewish answering of it, can be seen in the promise made in the initial call itself that Abraham and his progeny will be the source of blessing for all of humankind. Accordingly, Abraham's relationship with God is correlative to his relationship with the world. And the precise presentation of that correlation is found in Abraham's dialogue with God over the judgment of

---

[32] There is an important debate about the role of *eros*, i.e., desire, in the God–human relationship between Christian theologians that I venture to enter here because it helps one gain a better philosophical perspective on the role of desire in the biblical covenant itself (see M. Avot 4.1 re Ps. 119:99 and Maimonides, *Commentary on the Mishnah*: intro., trans. Y. Kafih [3 vols., Jerusalem, 1976], 1:247). The main protagonists are Augustine and Paul Tillich, who emphasize the erotic component, and Karl Barth and Anders Nygren, who deny it. I would say that without the factor of inherent human desire for God, the covenantal relationship between God and humans can only be seen as essentially one of God with himself rather than one between God and his nondivine covenantal partners. So it seems to me that Jewish covenantal theologians have more in common with Augustine and Tillich than they do with Barth and Nygren on this key point. See Augustine, *Confessions*, 7.10; Paul Tillich, *Systematic Theology* (Chicago, 1951), 1:282; Karl Barth, *Church Dogmatics*, 2/2, sec. 37, pp. 555ff.; Anders Nygren, *Eros and Agape*, trans. P. Watson (Chicago, 1982), 160ff.; also, Novak, *Jewish Social Ethics*, 51ff.

[33] Following R. Judah Halevi, "Adonai Negdekha Kol Ta'vati," in *Selected Religious Poems of Jehudah Halevi*, ed. H. Brody (Philadelphia, 1924), 87.

[34] See Aristotle, *Nicomachean Ethics* 1094a1; *Metaphysics* 1072a25. For the recognition of the universal desire for God, see Mal. 1:11 and R. Solomon ibn Gabirol, "Keter Malkhut," in *Selected Religious Poems of Solomon ibn Gabirol*, ed. I. Davidson (Philadelphia, 1924), 86. The kabbalists called human *eros* for God *it'aruta dil-tata* ("awakening from below" – see *Zohar*: Vayetse, 1:164a). But without an adequate theology of revelation, the God so desired becomes trapped as an eternal object like the intransitive god of Aristotle (see *Metaphysics* 1072a20ff.) or something similar to *it*.

the cities of Sodom and Gomorrah. God justifies including Abraham in this dialogue as follows:

How can I conceal what I am doing from Abraham? And Abraham shall surely become a great and important (*atsum*) nation, in whom all the nations of the earth shall be blessed. For I know him, so that (*le-ma'an*) he will command his children and his household after him to keep the way of the Lord to do what is right (*tsedaqah*) and just (*mishpat*). (Genesis 18:17–19)

The question now is to determine the connection of the blessing of the nations of the earth to Abraham and his people keeping the way of the Lord to do what is right and just.

The first thing to note is that God's statement of his knowing does not seem to be a noetic prediction. The text does not say "I know that," but rather "I know him (*yed'ativ*)."[35] Abraham is the direct object of God's knowing, and the result of his being aware of God's knowing him will be that he will be able to keep the way of the Lord. Without God's knowing him and his being aware of it, Abraham would not be able to recognize the way of the Lord and keep it.[36]

---

[35] For this epistemological distinction, see Bertrand Russell, "Knowledge by Acquaintance and Knowledge by Description," in *The Problems of Philosophy* (Oxford, 1959), 46ff. Although there are significant differences between Russell's empiricism and my phenomenology, his essay is still useful for making my point here.

[36] "He [R. Akibah] used to say that man (*ha'adam*) is beloved (*haviv*) being created in the image (*be-tselem*); even more beloved in that it is made known to him that he is created in the image of God ... Israel is beloved being called children of God; even more beloved in that it is made known (*noda'at*) to them" (M. Avot re Gen. 9:6; Deut. 14:1). Thus human knowledge/awareness is subsequent to God's knowledge/care (in the sense of *Sorge* in German, meaning care/concern/attention/interest/involvement, etc.). Revelation, then, brings the truth of being elected to conscious mutual relationality. The creation of humans in the *imago Dei* is also election; hence the Torah is "the book of human history (*toldot ha'adam*)" (Gen. 5:1; see Nahmanides' comment thereon). It brings the meaning of being created in the image of God to human awareness and action. And the *tselem elohim* itself is the human capacity for a relationship with God (see D. Novak, *Law and Theology in Judaism* [2 vols., New York, 1974, 1976], 2:108ff.; *Halakhah in a Theological Dimension* [Chico, Calif., 1985]). It is not a quality humans have any more than the election of Israel is due to any quality she has. For a quality can be discovered through solitary introspection or inferred by ratiocination. Although felt inchoately by desire in advance, the meaning of this capacity only comes to knowledge/experience when her desideratum presently reveals himself to her. For the relation of humankind and Israel indicated in the above *mishnah*, see R. Israel Lipschütz, *Tif'eret Yisra'el* (*Bo'az*) thereon.

Here "knowing" is not a judgment of a state of affairs drawn from the objects of past experience and then projecting from them into the future. This knowing is, rather, a relationship of direct and intimate personal contact. It is presence. Thus in the Garden the "tree of the knowledge (*ets ha-daʿat*) of good and bad" is a symbol for the direct contact with all the experience the world now has to offer and which the first human pair desire.[37] Since they were able "to judge favorably (*va-tere*) that (*ki*) the fruit of this tree is good to eat and delightful in appearance" (Genesis 3:6) even before they ate it, their judgment preceded their experience or "knowledge." Their judgment is in essence a prediction of what they think they will experience. This is why "knowledge" is used to designate the intimacy of sexual contact – "And the man knew (*yada*) Eve his wife and she conceived" (Genesis 4:1) – although it is not limited to sexual contact.[38] It is something that can be judged desirable based on one's desire of it in advance, but it can only be experienced directly in the present.

In connection with the election of Israel, the prophet Amos conveys to Israel God's announcement: "Only you have I known (*raq etkhem yadʿati*) of all the families of the earth" (Amos 3:2). Now, the prophet could not be saying that God is unaware of the other nations inasmuch as he himself has already been called to prophesy about them by God.[39] What the prophet is saying is that God shares a unique intimacy with Israel that is the basis for the unique claims he makes upon her. The claims are because God cares for Israel. Since these claims are made in the context of covenantal intimacy, the prophet then says in the very next verse, "Can two walk together if they have not met each other (*noʿadu*)?"[40] Israel is intimately known by God and is to act based upon her intimate experience of that knowing. The relationship here is not a noetic relation of a

---

[37] See Maimonides, *Guide of the Perplexed*, 1.2.
[38] See Martin Buber, "The Election of Israel: A Biblical Inquiry," trans. M. A. Meyer in *On the Bible*, ed. N. N. Glatzer (New York, 1968), 80–81.
[39] See Amos 1:3ff.
[40] Whether the roots *yod daled ayin* and *yod ayin daled* are etymologically related or not, there seems to be a literary relation between them being made by this juxtaposition. (I thank my colleague Prof. Gary Anderson for pointing this out to me.)

subject and an object. It is the divine I reaching out to embrace a human thou who then chooses to be so embraced.[41] Thus at the very beginning of God's regeneration of the covenant with Israel in Egypt, Scripture states:

And the children of Israel groaned from their toil and cried out, and their cry reached up to God from out of their toil. Then God took notice (*va-yizkor*) of his covenant with Abraham and Isaac and Jacob. And God looked with favor (*va-yar*) at the children of Israel and God cared (*va-yeda*). (Exodus 2:23–25)[42]

As for Abraham's response to God's election, it is initially a response to being in intimate contact with God. That is what he desires. That intimacy is, as we shall soon see, the main characteristic of the covenantal life of the Jewish people in the present. Those commandments of the Torah that specifically celebrate the historical singularity of the covenantal events give that life its rich substance.

What we must now see is how the experience of being known by God leads Abraham and his progeny to practice the way of the Lord. That can be better understood if we remember that the act of election is first a promise. Thus the covenant itself is founded in a promise. But why does Abraham believe the promise of God? Is his response anything more than a "leap of faith"?

In terms of the sequence of the biblical text itself, it is important to remember that the promise of God to Abraham is not the first promise God has made. After the Flood God promises that "I shall uphold my covenant with you ... and there will be no further deluge (*mabul*) to destroy the earth" (Genesis 9:11). The Rabbis were very astute in insisting that

---

[41] See Abraham Joshua Heschel, *Man is Not Alone* (Philadelphia, 1951), 125ff.; *God in Search of Man* (New York, 1955), 136ff.

[42] Note how the Passover Haggadah connects this "knowing" with the sexual "knowing" of the people themselves, the essential connection between the two being the factor of intimacy. See M. M. Kasher, *Haggadah Shlemah*, 3rd ed. (Jerusalem, 1967), pt. 2, p. 41. That is how R. Akibah could see the eroticism of Song of Songs as the holiest intentionality (see *Shir Ha-Shirim Rabbah*, 1.11). And whereas in Song of Songs human sexuality suggests God's love of Israel, here God's love of Israel suggests human sexuality. Along these lines, see Novak, *Jewish Social Ethics*, 94ff.

unconditional divine promises are made as oaths. Any oath made by God could not be annulled by God thereafter inasmuch as the annulment of an oath (*shevu'ah*) can only be done by a higher authority than that of the one who made it. But there could be no higher authority than God to annul it. God must keep his own word, then; if not, his credibility would be totally undermined.[43] Moreover, the connection between the promise made to Noah and the promise made to Abraham is explicitly made by Deutero-Isaiah. "For this is to me like the waters of Noah: just as I promised (*nishba'ti*) that the waters of Noah would never again pass over the earth, so do I promise ... that even if the mountains be moved and the hills be shaken, my kindness shall not be moved and my covenant of peace (*u-vriti shalom*) shall not be shaken – so says the Lord who loves you" (Isaiah 54:9–10). Furthermore, we learn that God's relation to the world is the correlate of his relationship with Israel, and Israel's relationship with the world is the correlate of her relationship with God.

I think that one can see the inner connection of these two promises in the term used to characterize the "way of the Lord" that Abraham is to teach his progeny: "what is right and just" (*tsedaqah u-mishpat*). But this requires that we look upon the two words in the term as denoting two separate but related acts. The usual interpretation of them sees them as denoting one single act, namely, correct justice, which is the standard whereby the distinction between the innocent and the guilty is consistently maintained in adjudication. This interpretation of the term is appropriate to the immediate context of the dialogue between God and Abraham in which Abraham indicates that consistency in judgment is the bare minimum to be expected from God who has chosen to be "the judge of all the earth" (Genesis 18:25). This interpretation concentrates on the ethical issues in the text.[44] However, looking at the even deeper theological issues in the text, one can take *tsedaqah* as one term and *mishpat* as another. Along

---

[43] See, esp., B. Berakhot 10a re Exod. 32:13; also, Novak, *Halakhah in a Theological Dimension*, 116ff.

[44] So I too argued in *Jewish Social Ethics*, 41, n. 48.

these lines, one can interpret *tsedaqah* as the transcendent aspect of God's relation to creation and *mishpat* as the immanent aspect of it. The elect people, then, are to imitate both the transcendent and the immanent aspects of God's relation to the world.

Tsedaqah is the transcendent aspect of God's relation to creation because it is something totally gracious. God's creation of the world is an act of grace; there is nothing that required that there be something created rather than nothing. And after the Flood, the renewal of creation in the covenant with the earth is even more gracious inasmuch as God's human creatures – made in his own image – were so ungrateful for the gift of their existence and that of the world.

God's *tsedaqah* is the ultimate explanation of the contingency of existence. As such, it could only be expressed in a promise, which extends from the present into the future. For the past by itself never guarantees any continuity or permanence. Its immanent order is itself contingent.[45] So, to use a current metaphor, reliance on this order in itself might be nothing more than "arranging deck chairs on the *Titanic*." But a primary promise in and of itself has no antecedents; indeed, if it did, it would be the process of making an inference and then a prediction based upon that inference. It would, then, designate a relation *within* the world already there. A primary promise, conversely, is infinitely more radical, infinitely more originating. Accordingly, it could not come from the world itself, whose real existence (rather than its abstract "Being") is no more necessary than real, mortal, human existence.[46] It could only come from the One who transcends both the world and humankind.

Yet despite its ultimate contingency, worldly existence has structure and continuity. The primal event of creation founds existence as an orderly process. That is because the divine promise is itself covenantal. The structure and continuity of existence, its essential character, is what is meant by *mishpat*. It

---

[45] See David Hume, *A Treatise of Human Nature*, 3.1.2, ed. L. A. Selby-Bigge (Oxford, 1888), 473ff.

[46] See Novak, *Law and Theology in Judaism*, 2:19ff.

is through *mishpat* that existence coheres. Minimally, that coherence is seen in the principle of contradiction, by which things maintain their distinct identities in relation to each other. Abraham's challenge to God that the judge must act justly and consistently distinguish between the innocent and the guilty is the biblical presentation of this basic principle of all reason. *Mishpat*, then, is the standard whereby the boundaries between things and between acts are maintained. *Mishpat* is violated when those boundaries are not respected. That is why *mishpat* is basically negative. It functions as a limit. Indeed, it is not inappropriate here to use Spinoza's formula: *determinatio negatio est.*[47] *Mishpat* is that fundamental *determinatio* that makes an ordered approach to existence possible. Nevertheless, *mishpat*, precisely because it is essentially negative, can never guarantee the facticity of existence; it always presupposes that existence is being maintained by God's *tsedaqah*. Expressions of *mishpat* are always ultimately conditional, namely, *if* there is a world, *then* it must have certain structures to cohere. As Jeremiah puts it, "Without my covenant by day and by night, I would not have put the laws (*huqqot*) of heaven and earth in place (*lo samti*)" (Jeremiah 33:25).[48] Essence in biblical theology follows from existence, but existence is never derived from essence.[49]

That is why truth (*emet*) is God's faithfulness before it is external correspondence and before it is inner coherence. Truth is first God's faithful promise that created existence will abide. "He makes heaven and earth, the sea and all that is in them, keeping faith (*ha-shomer emet*) forever" (Psalms 146:6).[50]

---

[47] *Epistola*, no. 50, in *Opera*, ed. J. van Vloten and J. P. N. Land (The Hague, 1914), 3:173: "Haec ergo determinatio ad rem juxta suum esse non pertinet: sed econtra est ejus non esse ... et determinatio negatio est."

[48] In the Talmud, that covenant is seen as the covenant between God and Israel (B. Pesahim 68b; also *Ruth Rabbah*, petihah, 1 re Ps. 75:4). Indeed, the divine *tsedaqah* that creates the world and maintains its existence is most immediately experienced in the covenant with Israel. See *Mishnat Rabbi Eliezer*, sec. 7, ed. Enelow, 1:138; R. Judah Halevi, *Kuzari*, 1.25 re Exod. 20:2.

[49] See Heschel, *God in Search of Man*, 92.

[50] For two important discussions of truth as faithfulness (*emet v'emunah*), see Martin Buber, *The Knowledge of Man*, ed. M. Friedman (New York and Evanston, 1965), 120; Eliezer Berkovits, *Man and God* (Detroit, 1969), 253ff.

Only when nature is "your faithful seasons (*emunat itekha*)" (Isaiah 33:6) can it function as a standard to which human judgment can truly correspond. And human judgment and action can only cohere fully, can only "do justly and seek fidelity (*emunah*)" (Jeremiah 5:1) when it is aware of the coherence of cosmic *mishpat*. That complete awareness only comes when the Torah functions as the "true witness (*ed emet*)" (Proverbs 14:25) of creation and its order in both nature and history.

The world until the time of Abraham was certainly aware of cosmic *mishpat* and the necessity to practice it in society. Thus after the Flood and the reconstruction of human life on earth, the basic moral law prohibiting bloodshed and establishing its commensurate punishment – "one who sheds human blood shall have his blood shed by humans" (Genesis 9:6) – is directly preceded by the affirmation of the cosmic order: "For as long as the earth endures (*od*), there will be seedtime and harvest, cold and heat, summer and winter, day and night, they shall not cease" (Genesis 8:22). That cosmic order, in which both the human and the nonhuman participate, is its *mishpat*. Thus Jeremiah employs an analogy between human and nonhuman *mishpat* to make the following point: "Even the stork in the sky knows her seasons, and the turtledove, the swift, and the crane keep the time of their coming; but my people do not know the law (*mishpat*) of the Lord" (Jeremiah 8:7). Clearly, the "seasons" (*mo'adeha*) of the stork and the regular cycles (*et bo'anah*) of the other birds are their *mishpat*.

Mishpat, however, is known only as a negative, limiting force. Because of that, the violation of it is considered a denial of the fear of God, which is in effect restraint before the highest authority, the epitome of *mishpat*, the pinnacle of cosmic justice. Thus when Abraham assumes that there is no respect for the boundaries of the marital relation in the Philistine city of Gerar, specifically assuming that his wife Sarah will be abducted into the harem of the city's ruler Abimelech, he justifies his lying about Sarah being his wife by saying, "surely (*raq*) there is no fear of God (*yir'at elohim*) in this place" (Genesis 20:11). In other words, there is no *mishpat* there.[51]

---

[51] See B. Baba Kama 92a. For the distinction between universal *mishpat* and local custom, cf. Gen. 29:26 and 34:7.

What is not recognized, though, until the time of Abraham, is the reality who is the source of this cosmic order, this *mishpat*, the reality who created and sustains the cosmos in which *mishpat* is to be operative as its norm.[52] But the philosophical questions to be asked now are: What difference does it make whether we know or do not know the source of this cosmic order? Indeed, why does it have to have a source at all to be appreciated theoretically and implemented practically by us? And, furthermore, why does this source have to reveal his presence to Abraham, which is simultaneously an act of election, as biblical revelation always is? And if there is such a cosmic source, why can't this source be discovered by ratiocination, which is universal in principle?

Only when the cosmic order is perceived by those who suffer enough philosophical unrest can the most basic existential question be asked authetically: What is my place in the world? That question lies at the heart of Abraham's desire for God's presence.

This question arises from our experience of the phenomenal order of things we immediately and regularly experience around us through our bodily senses. What we soon learn from this order is our own mortal vulnerability, our superfluity in the world. When we "eat of the tree of knowledge of good and bad" (Genesis 2:17) – which is the acquisition of worldly experience – we simultaneously discover the imminence of our own death.[53] "Dust you are and to dust you shall return" (Genesis 3:19). "All is futile (*havel*). What advantage (*yitron*) is there for man in all his accomplishments (*amalo*) under the sun? One generation goes and another comes and the earth remains the same forever" (Ecclesiastes 1:2–4). Therefore, throughout human history, perceptive persons have become aware that their place is not immanently available as an animal-like instinct. As a result of this existential predicament, the transcendent desire that goes beyond immanent need arises.[54]

---

52 See Novak, *Jewish Social Ethics*, 163–164.
53 See Nahmanides' comment thereon.
54 Along these lines, see Hannah Arendt, *Lectures on Kant's Political Philosophy*, ed. R. Beiner (Chicago, 1982), 12–13.

The first possibility is for us to discern with the intellect a higher noumenal order undergirding the phenomenal order initially perceived by the senses. Our motivation is to subordinate ourselves to this order. It alone offers us a transcendent end for our participation.[55] This is the attitude of scientific (understood as *scientia* or *Wissenschaft*, that is) *homo spectator*. The second possibility is for us to despair of ever finding the higher noumenal order "out there" and thus to look within our human selves for an order of our own device with which to use and control as much of the world as we can. This is the attitude of technological *homo faber*. The third possibility is for us to cry out for the person who stands behind this cosmic order to reveal himself to us; since the presence of persons can never be inferred from something nonpersonal, it must always be self-revelation.[56] This is the attitude of *homo revelationis*, the person of faith. For the Bible, Abraham is the first *homo revelationis*.[57]

In the biblical narrative preceding the emergence of Abraham, we find hints of both the first and the second possibilities and their attendant human attitudes. And both are seen as being in essence idolatry.

As for the first possibility, Scripture notes that during the time of Enosh, the grandson of the first couple, "the name (*shem*) of the Lord began (*huhal*) to be invoked" (Genesis 4:26). Rabbinic interpretation notes that the word for "begin" is etymologically similar to the word for "profane" (*hol*).[58] Thus it sees the time of Enosh as the beginning of idolatry, not the worship of the true God. The question here is: If this interpretation is accepted, what did this idolatry consist of?

Maimonides, in introducing his comprehensive treatment of the specifics of Jewish tradition concerning idolatry, speculates that at this time human beings were so impressed with *what* they perceived, namely, the cosmic order, the highest manifestation of which is the astronomic order, that they forgot *who* so

---

[55] See Plato, *Republic* 476Bff.
[56] See D. Novak, "Are Philosophical Proofs of the Existence of God Theologically Meaningful?," in *God in the Teachings of Conservative Judaism*, ed. S. Siegel and E. B. Gertel (New York, 1983), 188ff.
[57] See B. Berakhot 7b re Gen. 15:8.   [58] *Bere'sheet Rabbah* 23.7.

ordered it.[59] Their worship, then, was transferred from the creator to his most impressive creations. In an earlier discussion of the essence of idolatry, Maimonides speculates that the worship of the cosmic order itself inevitably leads to a situation where some people understand this order much better than others by virtue of their greater powers of discovery. As such, they translate their noetic power into political power by convincing the masses that they should be given absolute authority, being the effective conduits of that cosmic power. They alone can channel it for the public weal.[60] Here we have the rule of the philosophical guardian.[61] In Maimonides' reading of Scripture, tyranny is the practical result of theoretical idolatry.

As for the second possibility, Scripture is more explicit. During the time of the Tower of Babel, humankind despaired of ever discovering the cosmic order, much less making peace with it in order to live *within* its limits. The cosmic order is now the enemy to be conquered by technological means. "And each man said to his neighbor, 'come let us make bricks and fire them in a kiln ... come let us build for ourselves a city, and a tower with its head into heaven, and we will make a name (*shem*) for ourselves, lest we be scattered over the face of all the earth" (Genesis 11:3–4). In response to all this, the Lord says, "this they have begun (*hahillam*) to do, and now nothing they are plotting (*yazmu*) to do will be withheld from them" (Genesis 11:6). An important thing to note here is that in the preceding passage, dealing with what we might in modern terms call "heteronomous idolatry," the *name* sought is still something external to humans themselves. Here, however, dealing with what we might in modern terms call "autonomous idolatry," the *name* sought is one of human making.

The connection between this idolatry and political tyranny is even more obvious. Here we have the rule of the techno-

---

59 *Mishneh Torah*: Avodah Zarah, 1.1. See also T. Boman, *Hebrew Thought Compared with Greek*, trans. J. L. Moreau (London and New York, 1970), 117.
60 *Commentary on the Mishnah*: Avodah Zarah, 4.7; also, *Mishneh Torah*: Avodah Zarah, 11.16.
61 See Karl Popper, *The Open Society and its Enemies* (2 vols., Princeton, 1962), 1:138ff.

crat.[62] Here the exercise of power becomes an end in itself. There is no longer even the pretense of a higher justification and purpose for the exercise of human power. Thus in rabbinic interpretation, Nimrod is the true founder of Shinar, the place where the Tower of Babel was built.[63] About Nimrod it is said, "He began (*hehel*) to be a mighty man on earth. He was a mighty warrior (*gibor tsayid*) before the Lord" (Genesis 10:8–9). And in rabbinic tradition, Abraham's quest for God quickly challenged the tyranny of Nimrod and was taken as a mortal threat by Nimrod.[64] And, finally, since I am following rabbinic insights, it should be noted that in the case of Enosh, in the case of the Tower of Babel, and in the case of Nimrod, the word that the Rabbis saw as connoting idolatry (*hallel*) is found.[65]

As for the third possibility, which is the cry for the person behind the cosmic order to reveal himself, we only have our speculation that God's call to Abraham is in truth a response to an existential question. And there is a long tradition of speculation about just what this question is. In this tradition, Abraham begins his career as a philosopher.[66] The error, however, of many in this tradition was to assume that Abraham *found* God through what is called "the argument from design," namely, that the perception of order leads one to *conclude* that there is an orderer who brought it about.[67] But as many philosophers have argued, no such conclusion is necessary. One can take the order itself as ultimate.[68] And if there is such an orderer, then the most one can rationally conclude is that the orderer and the order are essentially identical, and that the orderer cannot be understood as transcending his order in any way, as in Spinoza's view of God as *causa sui*, as we

---

[62] See Jacques Ellul, *The Technological System*, trans. J. Neugroschel (New York, 1980), 145ff.

[63] See Louis Ginzberg, *The Legends of the Jews* (7 vols., Philadelphia, 1909–1938), 5:199ff., nn. 81ff.

[64] See *Pirqei De-Rabbi Eliezer*, chap. 26.   [65] See *Bere'sheet Rabbah* 23.7.

[66] See Ginzberg, *Legends of the Jews*, 5:210, n. 16; also, Maimonides, *Mishneh Torah: Avodah Zarah*, 1.3 and *Guide of the Perplexed*, 3.29.

[67] The first to make this argument was Josephus in *Antiquities*, 1.155–156. Cf. Novak, *Law and Theology in Judaism*, 2:21–22.

[68] See Plato, *Euthyphro* 10E.

have already seen.[69] In other words, the orderer need not be taken as a person, that is, one consciously engaged in transitive acts, let alone mutual relationships.

Abraham's cry for the master of the universe to reveal himself, to follow the speculation of a well-known midrash, is not an exercise in inferential thinking.[70] Without the revelation whereby God personally elects him through a promise and establishes a perpetual covenant with him and his progeny, without that, Abraham's cry would have been the epitome of futility, an unheard cry in the dark, a dangerous gamble, an exercise in wishful thinking. The free choice of God, his liberty to be when he will be, where he will be, with whom he will be, cannot in any way be the necessary conclusion by any inference whatsoever.[71] The most Abraham or any human person can do is to prepare himself or herself for the possibility of revelation, to clear the ground for God, but without any immanent assurance that God will ever come.

One can speculate, from philosophical reflection on the human condition itself, that Abraham could not accept the first and second approaches to the cosmos (that of *homo spectator* and that of *homo faber*) because neither of them could establish the cosmos as the authentic dwelling-place for humans. Abraham the bedouin is looking for his home.[72]

To regard order itself as ultimate, as does *homo spectator*, is to regard humans as souls from another world, souls whose task is to "escape and become like God."[73] And in this view, God is eternal and immutable Being. But there is no relationship *with* Being; there is no mutuality between Being and anything less

---

[69] See pp. 23–26 above; also, H. A. Wolfson, *The Philosophy of Spinoza* (2 vols., Cambridge, Mass., 1934), 2:346, who sees the deity of Spinoza as a return to Aristotle's deity, "an eternal paralytic," in Wolfson's colorful words.

[70] *Bere'sheet Rabbah* 39.1: "Abraham used to say, 'could it be that the world has no leader (*manheeg*)?' God peered out and said to him, 'I am the leader and the lord (*adon*) of all the world.'"

[71] See Exod. 3:13 and the discussion of its philosophical career by D. Novak, "Buber and Tillich," *Journal of Ecumenical Studies* (1992), 29:161ff.

[72] See Rashbam, *Commentary on the Torah* and Hizquni, *Commentary on the Torah*: Gen. 20:13.

[73] Plato, *Theaetetus* 176A–B. See also *Republic* 501B; *Timaeus* 68E–69A; *Philebus* 63E; *Laws* 716C.

than itself. There is only a relation *to* Being. God dwells with himself alone. That is why in this view of things, the highest achievement of humans is to reach the level where they can only silently gaze on that which is eternal. The philosopher, like God, is ultimately beyond human community and beyond the world.[74] And to regard the cosmic order as mere potential, a resource for its own use, as does *homo faber*, something to be ultimately outsmarted, is to regard the cosmos as ultimately disposable. All being is engulfed *by* human *technē*. There is, then, no authentic being-at-home in the world.[75] One is in constant struggle *against* the world. Humans dwell with and among themselves alone, but that brings them no rest. For the struggle against the world is extended into their struggle with each other for mastery.[76] For *homo faber*, there is not enough trust of either the world or one's fellow humans for him to be able to enjoy the vulnerability of a Sabbath.

Only an authentic relationship with the creator God who made both world and humankind enables humans to accept the world as their dwelling-place. Without that, the world becomes either our prison that we are to escape *from*, or our prison *against* whose walls we battle, striving to tear them down. "For so says the Lord, the creator of heaven, he is the God who formed the earth, who made it and established it, who did not create it to be a void (*tohu*), but who formed it to be a dwelling (*la-shevet*)" (Isaiah 45:18). "God brings the lonely homeward (*ha-baitah*)" (Psalms 68:7). All true dwelling-in is a dwelling-with more than ourselves. But it is only the case when we prepare the world from our singular place for God's descent into the world to dwell with us therein in covenantal intimacy. "They shall make for Me a holy place (*miqdash*) and I shall dwell in their midst" (Exodus 25:8). "Surely the Lord is here (*yesh*) in this place (*ba-maqom ha-zeh*) ... it will be the house of God (*bet elohim*)" (Genesis 28:16, 22).[77]

---

[74] See Aristotle, *Nicomachean Ethics* 1177b25ff. For Plato's struggle with this problem, see *Republic* 516cff.; also, D. Novak, *Suicide and Morality* (New York, 1975), 21ff.

[75] See Novak, *Jewish Social Ethics*, 133ff.

[76] See, e.g., Ginzberg, *Legends of the Jews*, 1:179.

[77] See B. Pesahim 88a and Rashi, s.v. "she-qara'o bayit."

Here the propensity for tyranny we noticed in the first and second human approaches to the cosmos (that of scientific *homo spectator* and that of technological *homo faber*) is less. For here is where everyone in the covenant is to be directly and equally related to God. Even the quintessential modern apostate from Judaism, Baruch Spinoza, was impressed by this political aspect of the covenant, as we saw earlier.[78] Here is where the prophet can say, "O were it so (*mi yiten*) that all the people of the Lord would be prophets, that the Lord would place his spirit upon them" (Numbers 11:29).[79]

Thinking along these lines, one can see why Scripture requires the people of Israel, when they are at home in the land of Israel and satiated with an abundant harvest, to remember their bedouin origins by declaring about Abraham (and perhaps the other patriarchs too): "a wandering Aramean was my father" (Deuteronomy 26:5).[80] Indeed, even in the land of Israel, which is at the same time as Abraham's election itself elected to be the homeland, the dwelling-place of his people, this people is reminded in Scripture that "the land is Mine, that you are sojourning tenants (*gerim ve-toshavim*) with Me" (Leviticus 25:23).[81] Indeed, the purpose of a home is to be the location for persons to coexist, a place for authentic *mitsein*. It is not a part of them, and they are not parts of it as is the case with the first two attitudes we have detected above. Although God dwells with the people of Israel wherever they happen to be, the most complete dwelling-together of God and his people is only in the land of Israel.[82] The rest of the earth is created;

---

[78] See pp. 31–38 above.

[79] Cf. Exod. 20:15–18. That is why, it seems to me, the Rabbis had to impugn the motives of Korah's rebellion against the authority of Moses (e.g., *Bemidbar Rabbah* 18.1ff.), namely, the argument "you have taken too much for yourselves, for the entire assembly is holy and the Lord is in their midst. So why do you elevate yourselves above the congregation of the Lord?" (Num. 16:3). The premise of the argument is surely valid *prima facie*. Indeed, there is always a suspicion of too much human authority in the covenantal community (see, e.g., Jud. 8:22–23; I Sam. 8:7ff.).

[80] See the comments of Ibn Ezra and Rashbam thereon.

[81] See Ps. 119:19; I Chron. 29:15.

[82] See Nahmanides, *Commentary on the Torah*: Deut. 8:10; also, Novak, *The Theology of Nahmanides*, 89ff.

the land of Israel like the people of Israel is elected in history. It is selected from among multiple possibilities.

On the basis of this theology, time and space are to be constituted as abstractions from event and place.[83] Time is ordered by the events in which Israel is elected and the covenant with her given its content. These events are the prime point of temporal reference; they are not in time, but all time is related to them. As Scripture puts it in the first creation narrative itself: "And God said, 'let there be lights in the expanse of the sky to divide between day and night, and to be for signs and seasons (*le'otot u-le-mo'adim*), for days and for years'" (Genesis 1:14).[84] And space is ordered by its relation to the land of Israel. It is the *axis mundi*, the prime point of spatial reference.[85] It is not in space, but all space is related to it. As Scripture puts it just before the people of Israel entered the land of Israel: "When the Most High gave nations their homes (*be-hanhel*) and set the divisions of man, he fixed the boundaries (*gevulot*) of peoples in relation to the numbers (*le-mispar*) of the children of Israel" (Deuteronomy 32:8).[86]

Getting back again to Abraham's keeping of "the way of the Lord to do what is right (*tsedaqah*) and just (*u-mishpat*)," we are now in a better position to discern the reason for his – and our – acceptance of God's election. It must be immediately recalled that Abraham's concern with *tsedaqah u-mishpat* is in connection with the nations of the world which are to be blessed through him. Indeed, his concern here is that justice be done to the people of Sodom and Gomorrah, whom Scripture shortly before described as "exceedingly wicked sinners (*ra'im ve-hat'im*) against the Lord" (Genesis 13:13). Abraham is concerned that justice be done to these people as the due process of law that even they deserve, whether the final verdict be guilt or innocence. His response to his being known-and-chosen by God is

---

83 "And even as prayer is not in time but time in prayer, the sacrifice not in space but space in the sacrifice – and whoever reverses the relation annuls the reality" (Martin Buber, *I and Thou*, trans. W. Kaufmann [New York, 1970], 59).

84 See Rashi's comment thereon.

85 See Nahmanides, *Commentary on the Torah*: Gen. 14:18; Deut. 16:20.

86 See *Targum Jonathan ben Uziel* thereon.

to want to imitate in microcosm the way God relates to the whole world in macrocosm. Both God and Abraham are now concerned with the earth and especially with all the peoples in it. Thus Abraham's concern is that *mishpat* be done. That in itself is an act of justice; he acts as their defense attorney seeking some merit in them. And the very fact that he involves himself in their case, when he owes them nothing, is an act of *tsedaqah*. Knowing that he is known by God, Abraham is now in a position to act truly as *imitator Dei*.[87] His being known by God is not only something he enjoys and can celebrate; it is something he can act on.

As *homo revelationis*, Abraham desires to dwell *with* God *in* and *for* the world. Conversely, the desire of *homo spectator* is for absorption *into* God *outside* the world; and the desire of *homo faber* is to be God *against* the world. Only the right relationship with God founds one's rightful place in the world. And only the acceptance of one's rightful human place in the world prevents one from intending either absorption into God or the replacement of God.

Finally, in the covenant, the relation of existential *tsedaqah* and essential *mishpat* is not only one of originating event and subsequent process. Sometimes, *tsedaqah* is subsequent to *mishpat* and not just the origin behind it. *Mishpat*'s world is never so tightly constructed that *tsedaqah* cannot on occasion intrude into it. Indeed, the contingency of created existence would be eclipsed if even God's *mishpat* were to be taken as an impermeable total order, as a system perfect in itself. There always remains the possibility of miracle. *Tsedaqah* can be directly experienced at rare times in history/nature (time/ space). For a miracle is the unpredictable exception to ordinary, normal order, and it is beneficial to those for whom it is performed. In fact, outside the singular experience of the faithful, illuminated by revelation, a miracle can soon be explained by more mundane categories.[88] Thus the splitting of

---

[87] See B. Shabbat 133b re Exod. 15:2 and 34:7; Maimonides, *Guide of the Perplexed*, 3.54 re Jer. 9:23 and D. Novak, "Maimonides' Concept of Practical Reason," in *Rashi 1040–1990: hommage à Ephraim E. Urbach*, ed. G. Sed-Rajna (Paris, 1993), 627ff.

[88] See Nahmanides, *Commentary on the Torah*: Gen. 14:10.

the Red Sea for Israel was seen by them as the "great hand" (Exodus 14:31) of the Lord. But precluding the presence of God, one could see the act as that of "a strong east wind" (Exodus 14:21). Israel's redemption from Egyptian slavery illumined by revelation is because "the Lord took us out of Egypt with a mighty hand" (Deuteronomy 26:8). But precluding the presence of God, one could see it as an escape by fugitives: "It was told to the king of Egypt that the people had escaped (*barah*)" (Exodus 14:5).

The election of Israel is assumed to be the greatest intrusion of divine *tsedaqah* into the usual order of nature and history.

You have but to inquire about bygone ages that came before you, ever since God created humans (*adam*) on earth, from one end of the heavens to the other: has anything as great as this ever existed or has it ever been heard of? Has any people ever heard the voice of God speaking out of fire, and you have and are still alive? Or has God ever so miraculously (*hanissah*) come to take for himself one people out of another? (Deuteronomy 4:32–34)

This notion of intrusive *tsedaqah* – miraculous grace – became the background for explaining how God can mercifully cancel the inevitable consequences of sin by forgiveness and atonement. For the Rabbis, the world could not be sustained if strict justice (*mishpat* as *din*) were always maintained consistently by God.[89] And the covenantal community could not be sustained without periodic infusions of grace by those in legal authority, at times ruling "deeper than the limit of the law (*lifnim me-shurat ha-din*)."[90] The theological import of all of this is enormous.

Also, in terms of our philosophical retrieval of the biblical doctrine of election, no philosophical reflection can ignore the outlook and findings of its contemporary science. At this juncture in history, the outlook and findings of Quantum Theory

[89] See, e.g., *Bere'sheet Rabbah* 12.15 re Gen. 2:4; B. Rosh Hashanah 17b; also, Ephraim E. Urbach, *Hazal* (Jerusalem, 1971), 400ff.

[90] See T. Shekalim 2.3; B. Baba Metsia 30b. For the use of the term *lifnim me-shurat hadin* re God's merciful overriding of his own created *mishpat*, see B. Berakhot 7a; also Y. Makkot 2.6/31d re Ps. 25:8 and R. Moses Margolis, *Penei Mosheh* thereon. Cf. W. Eichrodt, *Theology of the Old Testament*, trans. J. A. Baker (2 vols., Philadelphia, 1961), 1:244.

can be helpful. For unlike earlier modern science, where a totally interconnected universal causal model was required, Quantum Theory only requires a statistical model. Here phenomena in general, but not each phenomenon, have a causal explanation.[91] Furthermore, here the intrinsic role played by scientific observers themselves makes the total abstraction of scientific objects impossible.[92] Thus Quantum Theory constitutes a physical universe in which the unusual and the subjective are not precluded in principle. And it is the unusual datum plus the integral role of the one for whom it is performed that is the ontological *sine qua non* for a philosophical acceptance of the possibility of miracles. It is not that Quantum Theory "proves" any miracle or even engenders the concept of miracle at all. What it does for us, however, is to present a natural science that does not contradict what revelation teaches about miracles. That is enough for our theology.

COVENANTAL OBLIGATION AND FREEDOM

We must now consider the role of human volition in the initiation and reception of the covenant. Here the connection between the covenant and creation is the heart of the matter. The covenant itself is an act of creation; in fact, the thirteenth-century Spanish theologian Nahmanides argued for the etymology of *berit*, the word for "covenant," as coming from the root *bero*, meaning "to create."[93] Moreover, he also recognized the more obvious meaning of *berit* as "agreement" (*haskamah*).[94]

When it comes to human volition, there is a paradox that runs through all the texts that deal with God's electing Israel and establishing the covenant with her. On the one hand, it is quite certain that the whole relationship is initiated by God. In

---

[91] See Bernard Lonergan, *Insight*, 3rd ed. (San Francisco, 1970), 97ff.

[92] See M. Sachs, *Einstein versus Bohr* (La Salle, Ill., 1988), 235ff.

[93] *Commentary on the Torah*: intro., ed. C. B. Chavel (Jerusalem, 1963), 1:4 re *Shir Ha-Shirim Rabbah* 1.29. Cf. Jacques Ellul, *The Theological Foundation of Law*, trans. M. Wieser (Garden City, N.Y., 1960), 50, who sees *berit* coming from *barah*, "to choose." However, creation itself is God's choice, and totally free choice is presupposed by *creatio ex nihilo*. Hence these two views are complementary.

[94] *Commentary on the Torah*: Deut. 9:12.

one particularly striking passage, God declares that he "forced the hand" (*hahaziqi be-yadam*) of Israel to leave Egypt at the time of the Exodus (Jeremiah 31:31).[95] On the other hand, the requirement of Israel's active assent to God's election of her and covenant with her is presented as something just as certain. Thus at the end of his career Joshua exhorts the people, "you are your own witnesses that you yourselves have chosen (*behartem lakhem*) the Lord to serve him" (Joshua 24:22). This element of human volition becomes even more prominent when after the Babylonian Exile the people of Israel – now in effect only the Judeans/Jews – themselves reestablish the covenant. About them it says, "In view of all this, we make (*anahnu kortim*) this pledge (*amanah*)" (Nehemiah 10:1).[96]

So the paradox is: If the covenant is dependent on God, then what difference does Israel's compliance make? Yet, even at Sinai, when God's commanding presence is most powerful, the compliance of the people is still invited. "He [Moses] placed before them all the things that God had commanded him. And the people all of them together answered and said, 'everything that the Lord has spoken, that we will do.' Then Moses brought the words of the people back to God" (Exodus 19:7–8).[97] But if the covenant requires human compliance, why doesn't Israel have any other real option? As the contemporary Jewish Bible scholar Jon Levenson astutely puts it, "for all the language of choice that characterizes covenant texts, the Hebrew Bible never regards the choice to decline covenant as legitimate. The fact that a choice is given does not

---

[95] See B. Shabbat 88a re Exod. 19:17; also, B. Sanhedrin 105a.

[96] See pp. 163–177 below.

[97] Much has been made by contemporary Bible scholars of the similarity between the biblical *berit* and the suzerainty treaties of the ancient Near East, beginning with the Hittites. In these treaties, a greater king took a lesser king under his wing and delegated more authority to him than his actual political or military status called for. The by now classic presentation of this position is by George Mendenhall, *Law and Covenant in Israel and the Ancient Near East* (Pittsburgh, 1955). For the various other opinions, see D. J. McCarthy, *Old Testament Covenant* (Oxford, 1972). Cf. Roland de Vaux, *The Early History of Israel*, trans. D. Smith (Philadelphia, 1978), 443ff., who points out a number of significant differences between the *berit* and the suzerainty treaties as well as questioning any real historical connection between them.

make the alternative good or even acceptable, as a proponent of a purely contractural ethic might wish."[98]

Since we are dealing here with the question of obligation and choice, a comparison with the treatment of the relation of these two concepts to each other on the human level in later Jewish law might be the key to solving this great philosophical paradox of the covenant.

In the Mishnah it is taught that one person may not obligate another person without his or her knowledge and consent, but that one person may benefit another person without his or her knowledge and consent.[99] An example of this would be: I may accept money on your behalf without your knowledge and consent, but I may not pledge money on your behalf without your knowledge and consent.[100] Nevertheless, even in this latter situation, the benefited party may refuse the benefit performed on his or her behalf if he or she judges that what the other person thought was beneficial is in truth detrimental to him or her.[101] This rabbinic formulation utilizes the identical root in Hebrew (*hov*) for both "obligation" and "detriment."[102] The reason behind this formulation is that I have more authority over my life than another individual because I have more knowledge of and concern for what is beneficial to me than another individual has. Even though other individuals can often assume that they know what is benficial to me, that assumption can always be belied by my explicit denial. The converse is equally true, that is, the other individual knows what is beneficial to him or her better than I do, and he or she is more concerned for it. Indeed, this mutual transcendence can be seen as the basis of political equality.[103]

However, I would be very foolish indeed if I assumed that I always know my own situation better than someone else. There

---

[98]   *Creation and the Persistence of Evil* (San Francisco, 1988), 141. See G. von Rad, *Old Testament Theology*, trans. D. M. G. Stalker (2 vols., New York, 1962), 1:129–130.

[99]   M. Eruvin 7.11. See B. Ketubot 11a; also, Novak, *Jewish Social Ethics*, 43, n. 83.

[100] See Maimonides, *Mishneh Torah*: Zekhiyyah U-Mattanah, 4.2.

[101] See B. Kiddushin 23a and Nahmanides, *Hiddushei Ha-Ramban* thereon; also, B. Ketubot 11a.

[102] See, e.g., B. Baba Metsia 19a.

[103] See Novak, *Law and Theology in Judaism*, 2:15ff.

are times I have to trust the judgment of someone else for my own good. Thus I can go to a physician because I desire the good of health, and I can recognize that good when it comes to me. But in terms of the treatment itself, I must assume the superior knowledge of the physician and trust his or her concern for me. During the course of the treatment, I very often do not recognize what is my own good. At times, aspects of the treatment, even the whole treatment itself, might appear to me to be detrimental to me. Nevertheless, even if I resist the treatment prescribed for me, it is still for my good. It is just that at present I am estranged from what is my own good. The wise and benevolent physician – within the limits of human patience, of course – will wait for me to come to my senses. The wise and benevolent physician will be willing to prescribe for me again the same treatment that I may in an impulsive moment have rejected. My active cooperation is required for successful treatment, but the treatment is hardly a point of negotiation. The treatment is there before it is offered to me. And, finally, the extreme situation of punishment for covenantal lapses might be compared to the extreme situation where a patient has to be subdued lest he or she do harm to himself or herself.[104] If the patient recovers from such an extreme situation, with good faith the patient is likely to want to thank the physician for his or her expertise, concern, and patience.

In the human situation described above, the hierarchy between physician and patient is relative. For the physician has authority in his or her area of specialty, but he or she is just as much the subject of someone else's authority in that person's area of speciality. In this model, it is quite possible that A the physician of B is also the client of B, his lawyer. The authority in each of them is relative because neither of them has full knowledge of and full concern for the other. They are only specialists. And even within the physician–patient relationship, the authority of the physician is not absolute. In the case of the ability to bear pain, for example, the patient is the better judge of what can be borne than the physician since pain,

---

[104] See Maimonides, *Mishneh Torah*: Gerushin, 2.20.

unlike visible symptoms, cannot be abstracted from its subject for external examination.[105] Authority, then, is balanced between self and other. Neither is wholly transparent to the other; neither is wholly transparent to itself.

Accordingly, when one human person or group of human persons assumes complete knowledge of the general human situation, in the event they attain power tyranny is the inevitable result of the rule of such "experts." In the case of God the creator, however, such limitations are not present. About God's knowledge and concern, "could you find the limit (*ad takhlit*) of the Self-Sufficient One (*shadday*)" (Job 11:7)? God is the ultimate general practitioner.[106] That is, God knows more than he is known, cares more than he is cared for. Humans, conversely, in relation to God are known more than we know, cared for more than we care. Only God sees the whole.

Therefore, to use familiar modern terms, covenantal obligation is not "heteronomous" and covenantal freedom is not "autonomous."[107] Covenantal obligation is not heteronomous because it does not come from an "other" (*heteros*) as human authority is that of an other: valid when limited and distributed; invalid when unlimited and unilateral. And covenantal freedom is not autonomous because God is closer to us than we are to our-selves (*autos*). His word is "very close" (Deuteronomy 30:14). Our self-vision, conversely, is always the abstraction of a part from the whole and its projection away from ourselves in order that we might subsequently see it. It is "far" (Deuteronomy 30:11). We can never fully transcend ourselves as God transcends us and the world. Covenantal freedom is not autonomous because "He not we made us," therefore we are "his not ours" (Psalms 100:3).[108] The covenant is certainly not

---

105 See B. Yoma 83a re Prov. 14:10.
106 See, e.g., *Mekhilta*: Be-shalah, ed. Horovitz–Rabin, 158, and Rashi, *Commentary on the Torah*: Exod. 16:26.
107 See Levenson, *Creation and the Persistence of Evil*, 144.
108 Here I have combined both the written version (*ketiv*) and the vocalized version (*qrei*) of the Massoretic text. For the legitimacy of using both or either reading for exegesis, see, e.g., B. Sanhedrin 4a.

a contract.[109] There is no autonomous ground *from which* we can choose one specific thing or another and *to which* we can always safely return. God is sovereign of both the self and the other, the individual person and collective society. That is why covenantal freedom is a total existential all or nothing, "life or death" (Deuteronomy 30:19). There is no *tertium quid* either for individual persons or society *from which* the covenant can be judged. "You shall not test the Lord your God" (Deuteronomy 6:16). "There is no wisdom, there is no understanding, there is no counsel over against (*le-neged*) the Lord" (Proverbs 21:30).

THE LIFE OF THE COVENANT

Whereas the origin of the covenant between God and Israel lies in *tsedaqah* as an act of God's grace, and whereas the most evident structure of the covenant is in the standards of *mishpat* as cosmic justice, the life of the covenant itself largely consists of an elaborate system of acts that we today would call "ritual." The word itself is hardly adequate to describe what Jewish tradition has designated as "what is between humans and God" (*bein adam le-maqom*), so it should be discarded after it has performed the most elementary task of introduction. Indeed, in our current parlance, ritual in its adjectival form "ritualistic" most often connotes an obsession with minutiae, something designed to divert our attention from reality. That, of course, is opposite to what the commandments as *mitsvot* are designed to accomplish, as we shall soon see.[110]

This system of acts comprises what most consistently gives the Jewish people its distinct character in its own eyes and in the eyes of the world. Because of this, however, it has been as vexing a problem for modernity as has been the doctrine of God's election of Israel itself. For us, retrieving its meaning philosophically is, therefore, essential for our philosophical

---

[109] See Martin Buber, *Königtum Gottes*, 3rd rev. ed. (Heidelberg, 1956), 98; also, Eichrodt, *Theology of the Old Testament*, 1:65–66; Novak, *Law and Theology in Judaism*, 2:23.

[110] For the admonition not to "ritualize" the commandments, see M. Avot 2.13.

retrieval of the doctrine itself. It lies at the heart of the traditional Jewish relationship with God.

The two modernist thinkers we examined at the beginning of the book, Baruch Spinoza and Hermann Cohen, both deconstructed the classical biblical–rabbinic teaching about what might be termed the "cultic" aspect of Judaism precisely because neither of them could accept the classical teaching about election. Neither of them could accept that these commandments comprise the substance of the relationship between God and his people. Each had to see the function of these commandments as something other than directly religious.

Spinoza saw the function of these commandments as political, that is, they are designed to give a particular people enough of a unique identity to resist assimilation into another people. For him, this was all well and good when that people enjoyed political sovereignty. This is what all national entities do: they develop a uniquely identifiable culture for reasons of political survival. However, such separatism is pure negativism when that people no longer enjoys sovereignty, as has been the case with the Jews since antiquity; and even more so when it was now possible for that people to become part of some other polity without having to adopt someone else's theology, as was to be the case, he had reason to hope, in the emerging modern states (especially in his native Netherlands).[111] For Spinoza, the real relationship with God is located in the contemplation of the natural order.

Cohen saw the function of these commandments as moral, that is, they serve to give the people who have maintained the purest ethical monotheism enough of a distinct identity to hold out until the Messianic Age.[112] To lose their unique identity by assimilating into some other national-cultural entity would be a betrayal of their vision of what universal humanity is yet to be. It would be pseudo-messianism. All that they can do here and now in good faith is to participate as equals in modern secular states (especially in Cohen's native Germany), waiting until culture directs politics to the highest moral reality in

---

[111] See pp. 34–42 above.   [112] See pp. 67–68 above.

which Jews and gentiles can participate both equally and totally. That will be when all humankind become ethical monotheists. Unlike Spinoza, for whom morality could not be abstracted from the political situation, Cohen saw morality as transcending politics and essentially being the province of individuals. Following Kant, Cohen saw truly rational politics as being the domain of individuals who are themselves fully moral in their outlook.[113] For Cohen, the real relationship with God, especially in worship and prayer, itself has to be morally justified. It is what prepares the individual for his or her full autonomy.

Even Franz Rosenzweig, emerging as he was from the Idealism of the Hegelians and later from the Neo-Kantianism of Cohen, as well as from his near conversion to what seems to have been Lutheran Christianity, had his problems with "the law" too.[114] For, although he was able to appreciate positively and beautifully the role of cultic practice in the covenantal life of the Jewish people, he had a tendency to put such an eschatological thrust on every Jewish cultic practice that he often missed the phenomenological significance of their very presence. And, as we saw, he had a similar tendency to explain election as being for the sake of cosmic redemption, and thus the task of Jews and Christians as being to maintain (in the case of the Jews) and extend (in the case of the Christians) until the end of all history.[115]

Whereas in modernist versions of the covenant, the cultic realm had to be ultimately justified within the context of the moral–political realm, in the classical versions of the covenant it is the exact opposite. That is, the moral–political realm is ultimately justified within the covenant. It is the relationship between God and Israel that gives ultimate meaning to the relationships between humans themselves. Without covenantal intimacy, morality loses its ultimate justification.[116] Life

---

[113] See Kant, *Groundwork of the Metaphysic of Morals*, trans. H. J. Paton (New York, 1964), 104ff.

[114] See pp. 86–94 above; 259–261 below.   [115] See pp. 100–104 above.

[116] See R. Joseph Albo, *Sefer Ha'Iqqarim*, 3.28; also, R. Meir Leibush Malbim, *Commentary on the Torah* (2 vols., New York, 1956): Deut. 6:25.

together with God minimally requires respect of the order of
his creation, which is most immediately required in the proper
order of human society. Thus in the Decalogue itself, the first
tablet deals with what is to obtain between God and his people,
and only thereafter, in the second tablet, do we learn what is to
obtain between the people themselves. The first tablet begins
with "I am to be the Lord your God" (Exodus 20:2), and only
after the relationship with God is given substance in the commandment "remember the Sabbath to sanctify it" (Exodus
20:8) do we hear "you shall not murder" (Exodus 20:13),
which begins the second tablet.[117] So, too, all crimes between
humans themselves are ultimately seen as sins against God,
requiring reconciliation first with the wronged human party
and, finally, with the wronged divine party. "When a person
sins and offends (*teheta u-ma'alah ma'al*) the Lord by cheating his
fellow (*ve-khihesh ba'amito*) ... he shall pay it to the owner when
he becomes aware of his guilt (*be-yom ashmato*). Then he shall
bring his guilt offering (*ashamo*) to the Lord" (Leviticus 5:21,
24–25).[118] Along these lines, it should be recalled that Joseph
justifies to Potiphar's wife his refusal to make love to her, first
because it would betray Potiphar's trust in him, and second
because "How can I do this great evil and sin against God
(*ve-hat'ati l'elohim*)?" (Genesis 39:9). Also, Joseph's brothers'
sense of guilt over their selling him into slavery is first seen as
something humanly evil. "We are guilty (*ashemim*) over our
brother" (Genesis 42:21). And immediately thereafter it is said
that "his blood too will surely be avenged (*nidrash*)." This
vengeance undoubtedly refers to God's promise to avenge all
innocent human blood that has been shed and not been
avenged by human justice. "Surely, your lifeblood I [God] will
avenge (*edrosh*)" (Genesis 9:5).

When this centrality of the life of the covenant that is
essentially celebrated in cultic acts is appreciated, it becomes
clear that the numerous prophetic statements that are critical
of the sacrificial cult, and indeed of worship in general, are not

---

[117] See *Midrash Leqah Tov*: Yitro, ed. Buber, 69b; *Zohar*: Yitro, 2:90a–b.
[118] See *Sifra*: Vayiqra, 27d; M. Yoma 8.8 and B. Yoma 87a re I Sam. 2:25; also, Jon D.
Levenson, *Sinai and Zion* (Minneapolis, 1985), 49ff.

rejecting them in principle.[119] What is being condemned is the human tendency to isolate the cult from considerations of human justice (*mishpat*). Without these considerations, the cult deteriorates into a human invention designed to control God rather than a divinely ordained institution designed to bring the whole covenantal community, all of whom have been elected by God, into a more intimate relationship with God their elector. For without considerations of human justice – that is, justice *for* humans *by* humans coming *from* God – the cult becomes a means of human exploitation: those in hierarchal power at the cult shrine (priests, king, and plutocracy) using the cult as an endorsement of their own power. Thus Jeremiah rebukes the people of Israel:

Improve your ways and your actions and I will let you dwell in this place. Do not trust the lying words: 'the Temple of the Lord, the Temple of the Lord, the Temple of the Lord are these precincts (*hemah*)' ... only if you do justice (*mishpat*) between a man and his neighbor ... and you do not go after other gods to do evil for yourselves ... then will I let you dwell in this place. (Jeremiah 7:3–7)

What is seen from this most explicit prophetic rebuke is that the ultimate *telos* for mundane *mishpat* is the cultic center, the Temple. Justice is to be practiced *in order that* the people can dwell *with* the true God in covenantal intimacy in *his* sanctuary, and not enshrine there a god of their own making. The sanctuary is the center of the covenantal life of the people to be sure, but that life is not confined to the sanctuary.[120] Thus the proper ordering of the extracultic relationships *between* the members of the covenantal community themselves must be consistent with the will of the Dweller within the sanctuary, he who is the Lord of all creation, all mundane existence too. Hence all immorality is related to idolatry –the primarily cultic sin of worshiping other gods – because both are lies and both entail bad, not good, for Israel wherever.

Bible scholars both ancient and modern have pointed out

---

[119] See G. Ashby, *Sacrifice* (London, 1969), 45.

[120] That is why the Temple is seen as the desideratum of Jewish religious life but not its *sine qua non*. See A. Büchler, *Studies in Sin and Atonement in the Rabbinic Literature of the First Century* (New York, 1967), 353.

that the Temple is an earthly microcosm of the created cosmos itself.[121] The emphasis on the human need for *mishpat* reminds the worshipers of Israel, especially when they are deeply involved in the singularities of their cultically centered life, that the Lord is the creator God of the whole world. And this is directly connected to election. For only a God who is over the whole world has the options to elect or not to elect, and to elect this people rather than that people. Since the world cannot contain him, his entrance into the world is on his terms alone, not those of the world.[122] God's special interest in the sanctuary – "You shall make for me a sanctuary and I will dwell therein (*be-tokham*)" (Exodus 25:8) – does not nullify his interest in the whole life of his people. And God's interest in the life of his people is not confined to the singularities of their life exemplified by their cult. God is still just as interested in those aspects of their life that pertain to *mishpat*, the order of the cosmos and humankind in general. In fact, when the people of Israel assume that the Lord is bound to them by a natural bond *aside from* the world, a bond over which they have equal control and therefore equal liberty, the Lord reminds them that as God he has not ceased to be involved with his other creatures as well, even with other nations. "To me O Israelites, you are just like the Ethiopians – says the Lord. True, I brought Israel up from the land of Egypt, but also the Philistines from Caphtor and the Arameans from Kir" (Amos 9:7). God's relationship with Israel is indeed special. Thus the prophet continues, "I will restore my people (*ammi*) Israel" (Amos 9:14). But that relationship is not that of an only child. Being "holy unto the Lord, his first (*re'sheet*) produce" (Jeremiah 2:3) implies that there are others for God too. Israel's relationship with God is unique but not symbiotic.

The substance of the life of the covenant is the practice of those commandments known as "testimonies" (*edot*). They testify to the mighty acts of God's grace for Israel. First and foremost among these acts is the Exodus from Egypt, to which

---

[121] See B. Ta'anit 27b; *Midrash Aggadah*: Pequdei, 189; also, Levenson, *Sinai and Zion*, 11ff.

[122] See I Kings 8:27–30; Isa. 66:1–2; II Chron. 2:4–5.

the celebration of Passover is the prescribed response. As the paradigm for all Jewish commemorative celebration, the celebration of Passover is the key to our understanding of the life of the covenant as its most direct level. Thus the Torah states,

When in time to come your son will ask you, "what mean the testimonies (*edot*), rules and regulations (*ve-ha-huqqim ve-ha-mishpatim*) that the Lord our God commanded you?," you tell him, "we were slaves unto Pharaoh in Egypt, but the Lord brought us forth from Egypt with a strong hand ... Then the Lord commanded us to practice all these rules, to fear the Lord our God for our good (*le-tov lanu*)." (Deuteronomy 6:20–21, 24)

The Passover event, then, is the reason given for practicing all the commandments. But how does it function as a reason? The answer to this question is determined by how we see the relation of the past and the present in the life of the covenant.

One could easily see the reason for practicing the commandments as being gratitude. In view of the great good the Lord did for Israel in redeeming her from Egyptian bondage, it seems only fair that Israel owes the Lord a positive expression of gratitude in return.[123] In this view, the present owes a debt to the past. The problem with this view, however, is that it is based on *quid pro quo* logic: God did good for Israel, so Israel must now do good for God. But debts are eventually paid off. When, then, is Israel's debt to God paid off? And if a debt is to be paid *off*, then it would seem that the purpose of the covenant is finally to terminate itself. Moreover, since the Holocaust especially (although not originally), we might ask the question with great poignancy: What is our relationship with God, based on the *quid pro quo* model, when by all humanly known standards there are times when God has been bad and not good to Israel? Are there not times when "the Lord has become like an enemy" (Lamentations 2:5)? Finally, if Israel is to do good to God in return, that means that God and Israel have commensurate needs. We know what Israel's needs are. Certainly the need to be free from human bondage is such a need. But

[123] For the notion of repayment of a debt (*hov*) as the basis of the obligation of children to honor their parents (Exod. 20:12), see Y. Kiddushin 1.7/61b.

what are God's needs? Indeed, if God has needs by nature as humans have needs by nature, then does that not imply that nature is a reality in which both God and humans are participants and to which, therefore, they are both subordinate?[124] All of these theologically troubling problems follow when we probe the gratitude model carefully.

But, on the other hand, what if we assume that the past is for the sake of the present in the covenant? So, let us interpret the relation between the Passover event in the past and its celebration in the present as follows:

The experience of what is good for us can only be in the present. If one is miserable in the present, remembering past good is not only not compensatory in any way, but actually makes matters worse by reminding the now miserable person what he or she has lost.[125] A past good can only be appreciated when one is experiencing good in the present. One then wants to relate the past good to the present good, as well as project future good from the present good, so that the present good is not to be taken as peripheral or ephemeral. "Be thankful (*hodu*) to the Lord, for that is good, for his mercy endures forever" (Psalms 118:1). According to the Torah's teaching, the prime good experienced in the present is active, not passive. More than what God has done for us, the good is what God enables us to do with him here and now, namely, practice the commandments. Thus it is not that Jews are to observe the commandments in return for what God did when he "took us out of the land of Egypt, out of the house of slavery" (Exodus 20:2), but rather God's taking Israel out of Egypt is the beginning of the good we now experience in keeping his commandments.[126] Unlike a debt, the command-

---

124 See Eichrodt, *Theology of the Old Testament*, 1:42ff.

125 In Aristotle, *Nicomachean Ethics* 1100a1ff. the famous maxim of Solon, "look to the end," is presented as a paradox, namely, only after one is dead does one know whether or not he or she was happy. One of the implications of this paradox is that even if one lived a happy life for the majority of his or her years, misery in the last years is not alleviated by pleasant memories. Quite the contrary: the misery of the present is exacerbated by remembering how different the good of the past is from the misery of the present.

126 See *Sifre*: Devarim, no. 33 re Deut. 6:6, ed. Finkelstein, 59; also, Levenson, *Sinai and Zion*, 43.

ments are to be observed for their own sake, not for their elimination.[127]

Remembering the events of the past, in which God's saving power manifested itself to Israel, indicates to us what first occasioned the commandments to be kept. The event is for the sake of the practice, not vice versa. This can be seen in the interpretation of the following verse discussing the observance of Passover: "You shall remember that you were a slave in Egypt and the Lord freed you from there; therefore (*al ken*) I command you to practice this commandment" (Deuteronomy 24:18). The eleventh-century French commentator Rashi stresses that this is the logic of the verse: "For the sake of this (*al menat ken*) I freed you, in order to keep my laws, even if there is cost involved."[128] In other words, the celebration of past redemption is because it has enabled present observance. And an essential part of this present good is that it can only be experienced by free beings, those who chose to be redeemed, whatever the cost. Thus the Passover Haggadah notes that the one who considers the observance of Passover to be a burden rather than a boon in the present would not have been redeemed had he been in Egypt. "If he had been there (*ilu hayah sham*), he would not have been redeemed." It is only those who regard themselves "as if" (*k'ilu*) they went out from Egypt themselves in the present who fulfill the commandment of "telling" (*haggadah*) the Passover event.[129] Moreover, it is important to recall that the first Passover was observed in anticipation of redemption, not because of it.[130] In other words, redemption is retroactive from the present back into the past or projective from the present into the future. Passover is as much a celebration of the past as it is an anticipation of the

---

[127] See Aristotle, *Nicomachean Ethics* 1094a1–5 for the distinction between integral and instrumental teleology. While not denying that the commandments have their good consequences, the emphasis of rabbinic teaching is that they are ends in themselves as responses to God's commanding presence (see M. Avot 1.3; *Avot De-Rabbi Nathan*, A, chap. 5, ed. Schechter, 13b).

[128] Nahmanides' comment thereon, however, stresses remembrance itself as the reason of the commandment. For Nahmanides, the *edot* are participations in the archetypal events of the past. See Novak, *The Theology of Nahmanides*, 8ff.; 116ff.

[129] See Kasher, *Haggadah Shlemah*, pt. 2, pp. 23–24; 63–64 re Exod. 13:8.

[130] See Exod. 12:11–14.

future. As such, its meaning is essentially present before it is either past or future. This too might be the reason why the elements of Passover observance have symbolic significance in the present but are not fundamentally representational of the past. They are not reenactments. Not every detail of the past is to be repeated in the present.[131] In this way, the remembered past makes room for the lived present, providing points of reference for it but not subsuming it by making it a clone.

This explains the joy that traditional Jews have known in the observance of the commandments, especially the commemorative commandments, whose main points of reference are so experiential. Even though we are fully aware of the fact that we will frequently sin – "There is no human who only does good and does not sin" (Ecclesiastes 7:20) – that is a chance worth taking for the good of being able to observe the commandments and live the life of the covenant. "Even a live dog is better than a dead lion" (Ecclesiastes 9:4) is interpreted by the Rabbis as follows: "*the live dog* is the wicked person still alive in this world; if he repents God accepts him. But the righteous person [*the dead lion*] once dead can never again increase benefit (*zekhut*) for himself anymore."[132] The earlier rabbinic text in the Mishnah that inspired this interpretation is the statement of the sage Hillel, "If not now (*im lo akhshav*), when?"[133]

THE FUTURE OF THE COVENANT

In looking at the question of the future of the covenant at this point in our attempted philosophical retrieval of the doctrine of election, once again Franz Rosenzweig is the best transitional thinker between us and the modernity that essentially lost the doctrine's truth by deconstructing it for another meaning. And what Rosenzweig more perceptively discerned is that the covenant in the present is still incomplete.[134] Not only is it incomplete because Israel's relationship with God is

---

[131] See M. Pesahim 9.5; B. Pesahim 96a–b.
[132] *Avot De-Rabbi Nathan*, A, chap. 27, p. 27b.
[133] M. Avot 1.14.
[134] See *The Star of Redemption*, trans. W. W. Hallo (New York, 1970), 383ff.

often so ambivalent, and not only is it incomplete because Israel is still so vulnerable to other forces in the world. Ultimately, it is incomplete because the Lord is not yet "king of the whole world," not yet "intimately unique (*ehad*)" (Zechariah 14:9) for the world as he already is for Israel and Israel already is for him.[135] "Kingship (*ha-melukhah*)" is still not yet "the Lord's" (Obadiah 1:21). To the world God is related as creator to his creatures; with Israel God is related in the covenant. With Israel God's relationship is intense but still isolated as regards the world. The world is related to God and God to the world, but the relation is still remote. The covenant's full intent, its true purpose, calls for a future in which its reality is both deeper and wider. The most immediate philosophical question, however, is just how the covenantal present and the covenantal future are related.

In reading the various prophetic texts concerning the "end of days" (*ahareet ha-yamim*), what is now commonly called "biblical eschatology," two basic positions have arisen within Jewish tradition. I would term the first position "extensive" and the second "apocalyptic." Philosophically, they can be distinguished by the way they constitute the relation of present and future, respectively.

In the first position, the extensive one, the future is an extension *from* the covenantal present *into* its fulfilled future. That is, the covenant is essentially intact here and now. The future of the covenant is that the political conditions now absent for the full normative authority of the covenant, the Torah, will be finally made present. Most immediately, Israel will at long last dwell in security in her land. As for the rest of the world, they will either be subordinate to Israel or become part of the people through their conversion to Israel and its Torah. Israel's extension will bring them into the covenant one way or another. Here the future is essentially immanent. Accordingly, the Torah already revealed will remain intact.[136]

---

[135] For the background of this translation of *ehad*, see B. Berakhot 6a re Deut. 6:4 and I Chron. 17:21.

[136] The leading proponent of this view has been Maimonides. See *Mishneh Torah*: Melakhim, chaps. 11–12. However, it is important to remember that for Maimo-

In the second position, the apocalyptic one, the future is far more radical. It is the transcendent interruption *into* the present *from* somewhere else. As such, it will radically alter the relationship between Israel and God, including that which has been codified in the Torah already revealed. It assumes that the future will bring an ontological change much more radical than the mere improvement – even vast improvement – of political conditions for the Jews.

In terms of biblical texts themselves, the apocalyptic position has greater support by far. On theological grounds, it is convincing because it helps mitigate the error that Israel often assumes from her covenental experience, namely, that she possesses within herself the power to carry the covenant from the present into its future completion. And on philosophical grounds, it enables us to appreciate the finite fragility of the present through the affirmation of the future that transcends it.

The final and future redemption will radically change Israel's relationship with God and with the world, especially with the nations of the world.

Israel's relationship with God will be one without the need for any external coercion; the heteronomous aspect of the covenant of the present will be absent from the covenant of the future. The future, then, will be much more than the extension of the authority found in the present, even the authority of the Torah and its sages.

Behold the time is coming – says the Lord – when I will make a new covenant (*brit hadashah*) with the House of Israel and the House of Judah ... For this is the covenant I will make with the House of Israel after these days – says the Lord. I will place my Torah within them (*be-qirbam*) and write it on their heart ... No longer will someone have to teach his neighbor or his brother saying, "know the Lord!" For all of them shall know me from the smallest to the greatest. (Jeremiah 31:30, 32–33)[137]

---

nides, the truly transcendent realm is not the Messianic Age but the world-to-come. See *Mishneh Torah*: Teshuvah, 3.7–8 re B. Berakhot 34b; also, Gershom Scholem, "Toward an Understanding of the Messianic Idea in Judaism," in *The Messianic Idea in Judaism*, trans. M. A. Meyer (New York, 1971), 30ff.

[137] See Isa. 29:1–14.

Furthermore, the fundamental point of reference for the commandments that pertain to the relationship between humans and God will be changed in the future. As we have seen, that point of reference is the Exodus. "Assuredly, a time is coming – says the Lord – when they will no longer say, 'as the Lord lives who brought the children of Israel up out of the land of Egypt,' but rather, 'as the Lord lives who brought the offspring of the House of Israel from the land of the north and from all the lands whereto I have dispresed them'" (Jeremiah 23:7–8). There is an early rabbinic debate as to whether the Exodus will be no longer a point of reference at all, or whether it will remain as a secondary point of reference (*tafel*).[138] The majority view is the more conservative opinion, the one that still sees some connection between the life of the present covenant and that of the future. Yet even for this latter more conservative view, there would still have to be many cultic commandments that would no longer be within the range of Jewish observance because of the absence of their necessary preconditions. The Torah of the redeemed future (*l'atid la-vo*) might not be totally different from the one at present.[139] But even in this view, it will be radically changed.

Needless to say, however, even the proponents of this apocalyptic view were on guard against any pseudo-messianism that declared the kingdom of God to be now with us and that much of the present Torah, therefore, is to be presently abrogated.[140]

---

[138] T. Berakhot 1.10; B. Berakhot 12b. Cf. Kasher, *Haggadah Shlemah*, pt. 1, pp. 118–119. See also *Vayiqra Rabbah*, 3.13; *Midrash Mishlei*, 9, ed. Buber, 31a; R. Solomon ibn Adret, *Teshuvot Ha-Rashba*, 1, no. 93; Ginzberg, *Legends of the Jews*, 5:47–48, n. 139. Maimonides, consistently with his "extensive" eschatology, rejected this whole line of rabbinic thought and opted for the opposite rabbinic view (see n. 140 below). Indeed, he posited the nonabrogation of *any* commandment *ever* as a dogma of Judaism (see *Commentary on the Mishnah*: Sanhedrin, chap. 10/Heleq, principle 9). On this point he was challenged by R. Joseph Albo (see, esp., *Iqqarim*, 3.16) and defended by R. Isaac Abrabanel (see *Rosh Amanah*, chap. 13).

[139] See appendix 3.

[140] The earlier rabbinic teaching that many, if not all, the commemorative commandments would be would be abrogated in the messianic future (*mitsvot betelot l'atid la-vo*), having fulfilled their function (see n. 138 above), was reinterpreted in later rabbinic teaching to mean: "the commandments do not obtain when an individual person is dead" (Niddah 61b re Ps. 88:6; see Tos., s.v. "amar R. Joseph" and R. Zvi Hirsch Chajes, *Hiddushei Maharats Chajes* thereon). It seems to me that this

For them, the redeemed future must be an event so messianically self-evident that it would not entail the type of dispute
that led to the schism of the Christian community.[141]
Moreover, there was explicit prophetic evidence for believing
that whatever changes would take place in the redeemed
future, whatever "new covenant" there would then be, that
future would still be for the same people of Israel, past and
present. "Thus says the Lord who made the sun as daylight,
the laws (*huqqot*) of the moon and the stars as nightlight ... If
these laws should ever be removed from before me, only then
will the offspring of Israel cease to be a people for all time"
(Jeremiah 31:34–35). "Just as the new heavens and the new
earth that I make stand before me – says the Lord – so will your
offspring and your name stand" (Isaiah 66:22). Even in that
new world, Israel, like God himself, will retain her identity.[142]

As for Israel's relationship with the world, here meaning the
physical world, there has always been debate among traditional Jewish exegetes as to how literally or figuratively to
interpret prophetic verses such as, "For behold I create (*vore*)
new heavens and a new earth. The earlier things shall not be
remembered, not even considered. Be glad then and rejoice
forever in what I create. For I create Jerusalem as a joy and her
people as a delight" (Isaiah 65:17–18).[143] However, the tendency more often than not has been to interpret them quite
literally precisely so that the redeemed future should not be
seen as part of some continuum with the unredeemed past,
something that the conclusion of a process rooted in the present
could include.

might well have been part of a counter-Christian polemic, namely, not only is Jesus
of Nazareth not the Messiah, but even were he the Messiah, he would not have had
the authority to abrogate any of the commandments (cf. Matt. 12:8; Rom. 10:4).
This rabbinic prophylactic against Christian antinomian claims found a renewed
polemical function in countering the antinomian claims of the followers of the false
Messiah Shabbtai Zvi from 1666 on. See Gershom Scholem, *Sabbatai Sevi: The
Mystical Messiah*, trans. R. J. Z. Werblowsky (Princeton, 1973), 802ff.

[141] See Nahmanides' "Disputation," in *Kitvei Ha-Ramban*, ed. C. B. Chavel (2 vols.,
Jerusalem, 1963), 1:315–316; also, R. Chazan, *Barcelona and Beyond* (Berkeley,
Calif., 1992), 172ff.

[142] See, e.g., Exod. 32:9ff

[143] See Rashi's comment thereon; cf. comment of R. David Kimhi (Radaq) thereon.

The best example, I think, of this literalness is the interpretation of Ezekiel's vision of the dry dead bones coming to life. "And he said to me, O mortal (*ben adam*), these bones are the whole House of Israel. They say 'our bones are dried up, our hope is lost, we are doomed!' . . . thus says the Lord God, I will open your graves and bring you, my people, up out of your graves" (Ezekiel 37:11–12). Of course, one could interpret this as a metaphor for the national restoration of the Jewish people promised to take place after the Babylonian Exile in which Ezekiel and the people were then living. Indeed, the Zionist movement's anthem *Ha-Tiqvah*, which later became the national anthem of the State of Israel, is built on the theme that the hope the Jewish people claim to have lost (*ve'avdah tiqvatenu*) has never really been lost, and that it is soon to be restored through the historical restoration of Jewish national sovereignty in the land of Israel. One can certainly accept – even enthusiastically accept – the legitimacy of the Zionist hope, but realize, nevertheless, that these passages have more often than not been interpreted to refer to the future resurrection of the dead, something for which there is no real analogue in the ordinary present world.[144] Israel's future redemption will have literal cosmic effects. It will be an invasion from the future into the present, not a transition from the present into the future. This doctrine is the very antithesis of any idea of "progress" – ancient, medieval, or modern.[145]

Finally, as for Israel's relationship with the nations of the world, there is a crucial difference between "extensive" and "apocalyptic" Jewish eschatology. This comes out in the interpretation of the following passage:

Thus says the Lord of Hosts, Creator of the heavens who spreads out the earth and what comes out of it, who gives breath to the people on it and spirit to those who walk in it. I the Lord in my grace (*ve-tsedeq*) have called you and I have grasped you by the hand. I have formed you; I have made you a covenant people (*le-vrit am*), a light of nations (*or goyyim*). Opening (*lifqoah*) blind eyes, bringing the bound out of prison, they who dwell in darkness. (Isaiah 42:5–7)

---

[144] See B. Sanhedrin 92b.   [145] See Scholem, *The Messianic Idea in Judaism*, 10.

The extensive view of eschatology usually reads the phrase "light of nations" (*or goyyim*) as if it were written "light to the nations" (*or la-goyyim*), and the phrase "opening blind eyes" (*lifqoah aynayim ivrot*) to mean what it is that Israel as the light of the nations is to do here and now for the sake of redemption.[146] In this view, Israel's vocation, or at least part of Israel's vocation, *is to be* "a light to the nations." Israel has a mission.[147] And in some way or other, when the logic of this view is followed through, there is some sense of a proselytizing imperative. Whether that proselytizing is done through the monotheism of Christianity and Islam as Maimonides believed, or through Christianity alone as Rosenzweig believed, or through a universalist ethical monotheism as Cohen believed, the implication is that it is Israel's task to be the vehicle for the revelation first given to her to be ultimately brought to all the nations.[148] In some versions of the extensive view, the implication seems to be that Israel will dominate the nations of the world either politically or spiritually.[149] In what I think are more philosophically sensitive versions of this view, it will be persuasion or inspiration, not force, that ultimately reconciles Israel and the world under God.[150]

Of course, the suggestion that there is a proselytizing agenda in Judaism will strike most non-Jews and even more Jews as bizarre. It simply does not correspond to the experience of Jews and Judaism by outsiders or by Jews themselves. However, despite its absence from years of Jewish history, it is not an

---

[146] Cf. T. Sotah 8.6 and B. Sotah 35b re Deut. 27:8.

[147] For a discussion of this idea, especially among liberal Jews, see Novak, *Jewish Social Ethics*, 225ff. For its use by liberal Christians, see Rowley, *The Biblical Doctrine of Election*, 59ff.; 93, 164, who argues the supercessionist view that Israel did not fulfill her mission (see n. 23 above).

[148] Re Cohen, see pp. 64–72 above; re Rosenzweig, see pp. 94–102 above; re Maimonides, see D. Novak, *Jewish–Christian Dialogue* (New York, 1989), 57ff.

[149] See, e.g., *Bere'sheet Rabbah* 44.23 re Gen. 15:19–21; R. Saadia Gaon, *Emunot Ve-De'ot*, 8.6.

[150] Thus Maimonides emphasizes the theological persuasion to be exercised by Jews on gentiles for the sake of the messianic future (see Novak, *Jewish–Christian Dialogue*, 61ff.). For discussion of the various views of the status and role of gentiles in the Messianic Age, see Menachem Kellner, *Maimonides on Judaism and the Jewish People* (Albany, N.Y., 1991), 33ff.

impossibility in Normative Judaism.[151] In fact, its absence might well be because Judaism lost the struggle for pagan proselytes with Christianity (and Islam) and because the interests of immediate Jewish survival in the face of the severe prohibition of proselytizing by the Church forced Jews to abandon what was by the early centuries of the Common Era already a dangerous pursuit.[152] But still, there is no actual halakhic prohibition against it, something Maimonides especially was well aware of in his seeming suggestion of a proselytizing role for Jews. The imperative to proselytize, when possible, was one he included under the general commandment to "sanctify God's name" (*kiddush ha-shem*).[153] Although there was virtually nobody after him who followed him in seeing any such halakhic imperative (Cohen and Rosenzweig did so theologically rather than in formal halakhic terms), there is, nevertheless, no compelling halakhic argument that one can raise against it.

Although there is no halakhic argument that can be raised against the proselytizing agenda implicit in the extensive view of eschatology, there is a theological argument against it, however. And that theological argument is, I think, implicit in the apocalyptic view of eschatology. This can best be seen if we return to the verses of Isaiah 42:5–7 we examined above. For there it is not that Israel herself *is to be* a light to the nations. In fact, in the Talmud *kiddush ha-shem* (and, especially, its antonym *hillul ha-shem* – "profaning God's name") more modestly means that Jews are not to behave in a way that would cast moral aspersions on the Torah.[154] Instead, it is what God *will do for* Israel in the future that will so impress the gentiles that they will be drawn by God's work to the Temple

---

[151] Thus the prohibition of teaching Torah to gentiles (B. Sanhedrin 59a; B. Avodah Zarah 3a) would not apply if done for purposes of preparing a candidate for conversion to Judaism (see B. Yevamot 47a). The extent of that preparation and when it can actually begin are certainly subject to a latitude of interpretation.

[152] See B. Blumenkranz, *Juifs et chrétiens dans le monde occidental* (Paris, 1960), 320.

[153] *Sefer Ha-Mitsvot*, pos. no. 9. Nevertheless, the more usual Jewish practice was to distinguish between accepting converts (*meqablei gerim*) and active proselytizing per se (*masi'in otan le-hitgayyer*). See, e.g., B. Yevamot 109b and Tos., s.v. "ra'ah."

[154] See, e.g., B. Baba Kama 113b; Y. Baba Metsia 2.5/8c; also, Novak, *The Image of the Non-Jew in Judaism*, 90ff.

in Jerusalem, which will then be "a house of prayer for all peoples" (Isaiah 56:7). A most plausible interpretation of this verse is that it predicts mass conversions to Judaism at the end of days.[155] But it is not Israel's light but God's light on Israel that will be an integral part of her redemption. It is not that Israel's task is to bring *her* light to the nations but, rather, that God will bring them to *his* light that is to shine on Israel as a beacon. "For your light has come and the glory of the Lord will shine on you ... nations will go towards your light" (Isaiah 60:1, 3).[156] That light will be universally irresistible in the future. In the present, God's incomplete light on Israel is only capable of attracting random individuals.[157]

The affirmation of this truly transcendent future that apocalytic eschatology entails accomplishes two important things for the Jewish people here and now. First, it enables us to see all of our normative decisions as tentative, that the human interpretation of the Torah is only for as long as this present unredeemed world remains. This comes out in the role that the prophet Elijah, the herald of the Messiah, plays in the halakhic system itself. The truly hard decisions, those based on incomplete knowledge, might very well all be overturned by Elijah's eschatological judgment.[158] It reminds us once again that redemption, like creation and revelation before it is the act of

---

155 See comment of R. David Kimhi (Radaq) thereon. For rabbinic precedent, see B. Avodah Zarah 24a re Isa. 60:7 and Zeph. 3:9; also, R. Nissim Gerondi, *Derashot*, no. 7, ed. Feldman, 120–121. Cf. B. Yevamot 24b, where it states that "converts will not be accepted in the Messianic Age." Nevertheless, it is important to note that Maimonides does not codify this ruling in the *Mishneh Torah*.

156 See Ahad Ha'Am, "Shinui He'Arakhin," in *Kol Kitvei Ahad Ha'Am*, 2nd ed. (Jerusalem, 1949), 156–157.

157 See Zevahim 116a re Exod. 18:1 (the view of R. Eleazar Ha-Moda'i); Y. Berakhot 2.8/5b re Cant. 6:2; also, B. J. Bamberger, *Proselytism in the Talmudic Period* (New York, 1968), esp. 174ff. Cf. B. Kiddushin 31a re Ps. 138:4.

158 See M. Eduyot 8.7; Menahot 45a; Bemidbar Rabbah 3.13. Even the celebrated text in B. Baba Metsia 59b re Deut. 30:12, where the heavenly court follows the earthly court, only refers to a premessianic time. Also, re the tentativeness of human judgment here and now, see Y. Sanhedrin 1.1/18a and R. Moses Margolis, *Penei Mosheh*, s.v. "ve'atiyya," quoting B. Sanhedrin 6b re I Chron. 19:6. Cf. Hullin 5a and Tos., s.v. "al-pi ha-dibbur" as interpreted by R. Zvi Hirsch Chajes, *Hiddushei Maharats Chajes* for a more conservative view of the halakhic role of Elijah; also, his *Torat Ha-Nevi'im*, chap. 2: "Beirur Eliyahu," in *Kol Kitvei Maharats Chajes* (2 vols., B'nai B'rak, 1958), 1:17ff.

God's "righteousness to be manifest" (*ve-tsidqati le-higgalot*) (Isaiah 56:1). Israel is to "do rightly" (*va'asu tsedaqah*) in imitation of God's righteousness, but she herself has no righteousness in the face of God's. "The righteousness is yours O Lord; we have only our own evident shame (*boshet panim*)" (Daniel 9:7). Like Abraham before her, Israel is not righteous because she has faith; rather, "he had faith in the Lord and considered the righteousness that is His (*lo tsedaqah*)" (Genesis 15:6).[159] And when it comes to what God will actually do in the future, "Never before in the time of the world (*u-me'olam*) did anyone ever hear or note; no eye but yours O God will see what you will do for those who wait for you" (Isaiah 64:3).[160]

Second, this affirmation gives a theological reason, and not just a historical one, why Jews have not proselytized for many centuries and why very few of us see any need to do so at this point in history, even when it is politically possible in just about every place where Jews are now found. The reason is that proselytizing is a supreme form of human pride, and something which more often than not in human history has gone in tandem with conquest and domination of others. In one way or another, it implies that we have the whole truth, that we have already been redeemed, and that we want nothing in the world to contradict that which we are so proud of. But to Israel God declared "you are my witnesses ... who know me and have faith in me, and who understand that I am he before whom nothing was created and after whom nothing will be" (Isaiah 43:10). That witness is first of all to ourselves.[161] The testimony

---

[159] Following Nahmanides, *Commentary on the Torah*: Gen. 15:6. For the sources that follow Nahmanides and the numerous sources that, conversely, interpret *tsedaqah* here as Abraham's merit (*zekhut*) for having faith in God's promise, see Novak, *The Theology of Nahmanides*, 42.

[160] Following B. Berakhot 34b.

[161] A good example of this is the law pertaining to the display of the Hanukkah lights. Under optimal conditions, they are to be displayed to the outside world in order to proclaim the miracle (*parsumei nisa*). Yet under less than optimal conditions, when the world is not only uninterested in our Jewish proclamation but hostile to it, it is sufficient to display them inside one's own home to the members of one's own household alone. See B. Shabbat 21b and Rashi, s.v. "mi-ba-huts," and Tos., s.v. "d'i"; R. Joel Sirkes, *Bach* on *Tur*: Orah Hayyim, 671, s.v. "u-ve-sh'at ha-sakkanah."

of witnesses first of all has to be self-consistent.[162] It means that we must positively realize that if God's presence had not been with us we would have died as a people. Our only authentic life, collectively and individually, is when we witness our election to ourselves. As Moses said to God, "If your presence does not go with us, do not take us out of this wilderness" (Exodus 33:15). However, now our testimony to the nations of the world is not positive but negative. It is to remind them by our very vulnerable and incomplete life that God is not present in the world, that redemption is not to be expected by human criteria, that redemption will only come when God decides by his own mysterious criteria that the time is right for us and for them along with us. And so our testimony is to belie those who say that the world is redeemed and to insist that the world wait with Israel for her and its redeemer. "I know my redeemer lives, even if He be the last to rise on earth" (Job 19:25).[163]

With this basis in Scripture now in clearer view before us, we can proceed to examine how the Rabbis' imagination and reason elaborated the central Jewish doctrine of the election of Israel by God.

---

[162] See M. Sanhedrin 5.1ff.
[163] Following Robert Gordis, *The Book of God and Man* (Chicago, 1965), 264. See Novak, *Jewish–Christian Dialogue*, 155–156.

CHAPTER 5

The rabbinic development of the doctrine

WHO CHOSE WHOM?

In the biblical presentation of the doctrine of the election of Israel, the roles of God as the elector and of Israel as the elected are evident and consistent. It is God who initiates the relationship with Israel, and it is Israel who is to respond to that initiation. Even when Israel does not respond to God's election of her, when she turns away from the God who chose her, the election is not thereby annulled. It is simply reiterated by whatever means God so chooses at the time. Any attempt to see this relationship as some sort of contract, some sort of bilateral pact between two autonomous parties, is clearly at odds with biblical teaching. In the Bible, God alone is autonomous, and God alone can make initiatory choices with impunity. Israel's only choice seems to be to confirm what God has already done to her and for her. To choose to reject what God has done to her and for her is an unacceptable choice that cannot be allowed to persist. For Israel, there are no multiple options, as we understand that term today.

Nevertheless, as we have already seen in some of the rabbinic teachings brought in to explain Scriptural texts in the previous chapter, the relationship of God and Israel is more than one *from* God *to* Israel, one where God is the active initiator and Israel the passive recipient. If that were all there is to the relationship, it would be much less rich than the actual covenant (*berit*) that exists *in which* both God and Israel are joined.

Being that which is *between* God and Israel, the covenant requires more than acquiescent acceptance on Israel's part. It requires that the relationship in some real sense be one *from* Israel *to* God as well. Yet the relationship is not initiated by Israel, as Spinoza and the moderns he influenced assume. Nor is the relationship a reward for Israel's precovenantal merits.[1] Even the necessity of a prior adherence to natural law, as we saw in the previous chapter, is not the ground of the covenant, but only its human precondition.[2] Accordingly, the task in this chapter is to discover how the Rabbis saw a more active covenantal role for Israel than one would discern from the reading of Scripture alone without, however, concluding that the covenant itself is essentially contingent upon Israel's choice.

Occasionally Scripture itself does assert that Israel is to choose God. Thus at the end of his career, Joshua says to the assembled people of Israel, "for it is the Lord you yourselves have chosen (*behartem*) to serve him," and they respond by saying "so we do attest (*edim*)" (Joshua 24:22). And when Elijah on Mount Carmel insists that the people of Israel stop "hopping between two opinions, that if the Lord is God go after him, but if it is Baal go after him" (I Kings 18:21), the people soon respond with an enthusiastic affirmation that "the Lord he is God, the Lord he is God!" (18:39). Nevertheless, both these cases are ones where the people themselves have

---

[1] Even though a few rabbinic texts seem to suggest that Israel was chosen *because* of this or that virtue (see, e.g., *Vayiqra Rabbah* 32.5 and parallels), the emphasis being made there seems to be retroactive. That is, postcovenantal virtues (primarily response to the covenant in general – see, e.g., B. Shabbat 88a re Cant. 2:2) are retrojected into the precovenantal past. (For this type of reasoning, see pp. 205–207 below.) However, as Solomon Schechter pointed out about one such text that begins by asserting the merit of Israel's humility before God and concludes by asserting God's gracious election of her (*Tanhuma*: Eqev, no. 4, ed. Buber, 9a–b re Hos. 14:5 and Isa. 2:2), "this suggests that even those Rabbis who tried to establish Israel's special claim on their exceptional merits were not altogether unconscious of the insufficiency of the reason of works in this respect, and therefore had also recourse to the love of God, which is not given as a reward, but is offered freely ... The great majority of the Rabbis are silent about merits, and attribute the election to a mere act of grace (or love) on the part of God" (*Some Aspects of Rabbinic Theology* [New York, 1936], 6–61). See also H.-J. Schoeps, *Ausfrühchristlicher Zeit* [Tübingen, 1950], 196ff.).

[2] See pp. 145–146 above.

been overwhelmed by the power of the Lord. In the case of Joshua and the people, it was the power of the Lord to give Israel the land over the resistance of the Canaanites. In the case of Elijah and the people, it was the power of the Lord to send fire from heaven to accept the offering of Elijah, but not the offering of the priests of Baal.[3]

However, because of the basic duress one sees in both of these cases, the results are not positive at all. No sooner is Joshua dead than, as Scripture puts it, "the children of Israel did evil in the eyes of the Lord and they served the Baalim" (Judges 2:11). And no sooner has the Lord answered Elijah on Mount Carmel than Elijah wants to die, convinced that "I am no better than my fathers" (I Kings 19:4). So, if the covenant is to endure on earth, it must be freely taken up by the people of Israel. That requires that they do more than accept the covenant; they must actively implement it, even supplement it by their own reason and will. As Hillel the Elder used to say, "when one does not add, he subtracts."[4] Israel, at times, must act *as if* she herself chooses God.

Commenting on the verse, "for the Lord has chosen Jacob for himself *(bahar lo)*" (Psalms 135:4), an early *midrash* says "the matter is still inconclusive, for we do not know whether it is God who has chosen Israel or it is Israel who has chosen God."[5] In other words, it seems unclear whether the Lord is the subject of the verb "has chosen" and Israel its object, or whether Israel is the subject and the Lord the object. Finally,

---

[3] Elijah's offering a sacrifice on Mt. Carmel violates the Deuteronomic law that limits sacrifice to the central sanctuary (Deut. 12:5ff.), which finally became the Davidic sanctuary in Jerusalem (see *Sifre*: Devarim, no. 62; Zevahim 119a). The act is justified by the Rabbis as being an extraordinary ad hoc edict that a bona fide prophet may prescribe, presumably because of a grave threat to the covenantal fidelity of the people (see B. Yevamot 90b re Deut. 18:15). But since prophetic authority is validated by overwhelming supernatural phenomena rather than by exegesis or reason, prophetic edicts such as that of Elijah are *ipso facto* confined to the particular situations that elicited them (see Tos., s.v. "ve-li-gmar" thereon). Thus they are all sui generis. See B. Megillah 2b re Lev. 27:34; *Midrash Ha-Gadol*: Bemidbar, ed. Rabinowitz, chap. 32 re Deut. 19:16. Cf. B. Baba Batra 12a re Ps. 90:11; R. Judah Loewe (Maharal), *Gevurot Ha-Shem* (Cracow, 1582), intro.

[4] M. Avot 1.13.

[5] *Sifre*: Devarim, no. 312, ed. Finkelstein, 353–354. See *Testament of Naftali*, in *Batei Midrashot*, ed. Wertheimer, 196; also, 203.

though, this midrash concludes by quoting the verse, "it is you the Lord has chosen (*u-vekha bahar*) to be for him a treasure people (*l'am segulah*)" (Deuteronomy 14:2). Then it adds that "Jacob also (*she'af*) chose the Lord," the Scriptural prooftext being "not like these is Jacob's portion" (Jeremiah 10:16). The "also" here is significant because the rabbinic homilist does not want to make Israel's role absolutely initiatory but, rather, always relative to the first choice of God.

The use of this prooftext from Jeremiah is important because, as with many rabbinic homilies, one must know not only which part of a verse has been quoted, but also which part of it has not been quoted. The part of the verse not quoted states "for He is the creator (*yotser*) of all, and Israel is His very own tribe (*shevet nahalato*)." Thus the verse in its entirety seems to be asserting the consistent Scriptural doctrine that it is God who chooses Israel. If so, how do the Rabbis turn its meaning around? But, as the late Israeli rabbinics scholar Ephraim E. Urbach astutely comments, the Rabbis are reading this verse in the context of the preceding two verses of this chapter (14–15), which speak of the nations of the world choosing their own, unsubstantial, gods.[6] Just as they choose their gods, Israel chooses her God. The act itself is similar; it is the respective objects that are different in kind. The object of Israel's choice is true; the object of their choice is false.

The questions that now arise are: (1) When did Israel assume this more active role in the covenant, supplementing God's choice of her with her own choice of God? (2) What made this choice more effective than the choices we have seen were made in biblical times, such as in the days of Joshua and the days of Elijah? The Talmud itself answers both of these questions in a remarkable passage. Drawing out the implications of this passage will be most useful for our inquiry now.

Commenting on the Scriptural description of Israel at the time of the giving of the Torah to them at Mount Sinai, "and they stood at the base (*be-tahteet*) of the mountain" (Exodus 19:17), one sage interprets the words *be-tahteet* as meaning

---

[6] *Hazal* (Jerusalem, 1971), 470–471.

"under the mountain."[7] Thus he imagines that God held Mount Sinai over the heads of the people below, offering them the following choice: "If you accept the Torah, it is well and good; if not, there will your grave be." But, of course, this does not seem to be much of a "choice" at all, inasmuch as it is being offered under extreme duress. So, another sage points out that in an interhuman agreement, such duress would be sufficient grounds to have the agreement declared null and void. Indeed, he invokes the very legal term "protest" (*moda'a*) used to nullify such an interhuman agreement made under this kind of duress, showing that this is not just duress but extraordinary (*rabba*) duress.[8] If heteronomy in an agreement seems to be inappropriate, then extraordinary heteronomy seems to be extraordinarily inappropriate. Has not God come to Israel as a tyrant?[9]

Now it is important to remember that the easiest answer to this objection is not raised in the text before us. That answer would be that God the creator can do with any of his creatures whatever he pleases. His decrees need not consider the objections of their recipients. Nevertheless, this only answers the question of truth, namely, God is by definition authoritative (*elohim*), as we saw in the previous chapter.[10] It does not, though, answer the question of good, namely, why should the recipients of God's law actually desire to accept it and keep it? And without that desire, the covenant has no real meaning in the human world in which it is supposed to be normative. As such, the fourth-century Babylonian sage Rava states that the Torah was freely accepted during the time of King Ahasuerus. The medieval commentator Rashi explains that this was because of the love of God that was the people's response to what God had miraculously done for them by saving them from the plan of Haman to exterminate them all.[11]

The answer from love is of great philosophical significance,

---

[7] B. Shabbat 88a. For my earlier theological treatment of this text, see D. Novak, *Jewish Social Ethics* (New York, 1992), 28–29.

[8] See B. Baba Batra 39b–40a and Rashbam, s.v. "ve-khen moda'a" thereon.

[9] See B. Avodah Zarah 3a.

[10] See pp. 118–119 above.   [11] B. Shabbat 88a, s.v. "bi-ymei Ahasuerus."

because a phenomenology of love indicates that the strict divisions between freedom and coercion and between action and passion that can be maintained elsewhere are inadequate to describe the experience of love. For when I love someone I am both free and coerced, both active and passive. Thus in this type of relationship, these polar terms must be constituted dialectically.[12] That is, when I feel that freedom characterizes the relationship, I must be reminded that I have *fallen in* love; and when I feel that coercion characterizes the relationship, I must be reminded that it is what I *myself* have always *desired*. So also, when I feel that I am active, I must be reminded that I desire *to be* pleased; and when I feel that I am passive, I must be reminded that I desire *to* please the other one.[13] Therefore, in the case of the covenantal relationship of God and Israel, Israel is both elected and electing.

It is important to ascertain when Israel discovered her renewed love for God because it helps us understand the significance of what came to be Rabbinic Judaism, something biblically based but not totally reducible to the Judaism of Scripture itself. Thus Nahmanides, the great thirteenth-century Spanish exegete and theologian, in commenting on this Talmudic text, notes that if the Torah is the "decree of their king" (*gezerat malkam*), then the people had no grounds for protesting the severity of its imposition.[14] Furthermore, they had accepted the Torah willingly at Sinai when they declared "everything the Lord has spoken we will do and we will hear" (Exodus 24:7), which is a point the Rabbis made much of.[15] But Nahmanides emphasizes that the covenantal character of the normative relationship between God and

---

[12] See Martin Buber, *I and Thou*, trans. W. Kaufmann (New York, 1970), 143–144.

[13] Cf. R. Obadiah Bertinoro, *Commentary on the Mishnah*: Avot 1.3, which seems to be based on Y. Berakhot 9.5/14b. Also, note B. Nedarim 7b–8a re Ps. 119:106 (and *Midrash Ha-Gadol*: Bere'sheet, ed. Margulies, 662), which teaches that an individual Jew may "motivate himself or herself" by taking a personal oath (*shevu'ah*) to observe a commandment, i.e., act *as if* he himself or she herself initiated the commandment to himself or herself, even though in truth all Jews are already sworn to observe all the commandments at Sinai (see *Tanhuma*: Nitsavim, printed ed. and ed. Buber, 25b re Deut. 29:14).

[14] *Hiddushei Ha-Ramban*: B. Shabbat 88a, ed. Hirschler, 303.

[15] See B. Shabbat 88a re Cant. 2:3.

Israel requires the factor of free acceptance (*qabbalah u-vrit*). And this factor was even more pronounced during the Exile, with its miracle of the survival of the Jewish people as a people, and the return to the land of Israel led by Ezra, when the people themselves restored the covenant by their own will (*ve-qibbluha be-ratson*). The point to be remembered here is that unlike the Exodus, when Israel was forced out of Egypt by God, in the return to the land of Israel from Babylonian (and then Persian) exile, the people did have a real choice. They could assimilate into Babylonian society and culture, as was the case with other captive peoples.[16] Furthermore, even after Cyrus the Great permitted the Jews to return to their land, those who chose to remain in Babylonia did not seem to be punished by divine power. Accordingly, when the Jewish people were reconstituted as what historians call the Second Jewish Commonwealth, their reconstitution was based on more freedom than had been the case in the First Jewish Commonwealth when the power of their state was intact.

This new freedom is what is being emphasized by Rava in the prooftext he brings to show how the Torah was finally accepted in love with the greater freedom that entails. The verse reads, "the Jews upheld and accepted (*qiyyamu ve-qibblu*)" (Esther 9:27). Now, in the biblical context of this verse, what the Jews "upheld and accepted" was the new holiday of Purim that Mordecai had decreed be observed annually to commemorate the saving of the Jews from the extermination plot of Haman.[17] However, in the use of this verse by Rava, the verse now refers to the reacceptance of the Torah itself by the Jews in exile. As he puts it, "they upheld what they had already (*kevar*) accepted." Indeed, in a parallel passage in the Talmud, this verse is used to make the point that even during the last days of Moses the people not only reaffirmed their commitment to the Torah given to them at Sinai forty years earlier, but also accepted those commandments that would be innovated (*le-hithadesh*) in the future, such as the reading of the Megillah on

---

[16] See Ezek. 20:32.

[17] For attempts to tone down the innovative character of the new holy day, see Y. Megillah 1.5/70d re Exod. 17:14.

Purim.[18] And, finally, Rava himself interprets the original object of the verse, which refers to the legal institution of Purim, along the lines of the earlier Babylonian sage Samuel of Nehardea to mean: "they upheld above what they had accepted below."[19] That is, God confirmed what the Jewish authorities on earth had themselves decreed for the people.[20] And, of course, Purim is just one example of the new decrees initiated on earth for the sake of God (*le-shem shamayim*), decrees that supplement the Torah's own commandments decreed by God from heaven (*min ha-shamayim*) for the sake of Israel on earth.[21] In other words, God's active love for Israel shown in his election of her and the giving of the Torah to her is eventually reciprocated by Israel's election of God and the giving of her supplemental Torah to him.

THE HUMAN SIDE OF THE COVENANT

The more active role of the Jewish people in the covenant is the very hallmark of Rabbinic Judaism. This more active role can be seen in two factors: (1), the institution of human legislation; and (2), the institution of popular consent.

The Torah itself only seems to provide for the institution of human adjudication of the law of God. Thus in Exodus, Moses is advised by his father-in-law Jethro not to judge each case by himself on an ad hoc basis but, rather, to set up a system of judges "whom you will instruct (*ve-hizharta*) in the laws and teachings" (Exodus 18:20). In accepting this advice, Moses not only realizes that a division of judicial labor is a political necessity, but also realizes that cases must be decided according to preestablished rules and principles and that they cannot be directly referred to God any more for individual judgment. Indeed, after accepting this advice, Moses only refers two unusual cases to God: the first, a difficult case of Sabbath desecration (Numbers 15:32–36); the second, the difficult case

---

[18] B. Shevu'ot 39a.   [19] B. Megillah 7a.
[20] See B. Shabbat 87a; B. Baba Metsia 59b.
[21] See Maimonides, *Mishneh Torah*: Sanhedrin, 24.10.

of the inheritance of the estate of a man who had daughters but no sons (Numbers 27:1–11).[22]

By the time of Deuteronomy, the institution of adjudication by more general prior rules and principles is firmly established. Thus Moses, providing for the system of law that is to survive him, states: "According to the teaching (*al-pi ha-torah*) they [the contemporary judges] shall instruct you and by the judgment (*v'al-ha-mishpat*) they shall declare unto you what shall do; you shall not deviate (*lo tasur*) from the matter they shall tell you, neither to the right nor the left" (Deuteronomy 17:11). Clearly, here "the matter" (*ha-davar*) is the law of God already revealed to the people through Moses. And about this law, earlier in this book of the Torah it states: "The whole matter (*et kol-ha-davar*) which I command you shall be careful to do it; you shall not add anything (*lo tosef*) onto it, and you shall not detract (*lo tigr'a*) from it" (Deuteronomy 13:1).

At this level, it would seem that just as adjudication is mandated, supplemental legislation is proscribed. However, this is not the way the Rabbis read either verse from Deuteronomy. The key to understanding the rabbinic reading is to grasp how the Rabbis interpreted the word *davar* ("matter" or "thing" or "word") in Deuteronomy 13:1 and 17:11. By grasping this, we can begin to understand not just how they read these two verses, important as they are, but how they understood the Scriptural warrant for their whole project of actively contributing to Israel's covenant *with* God.

The word *davar* can either be read as a specific term or as a general term. In Deuteronomy 13:1, it seems to be meant as a general term, that is, one is not to add to or detract from the entire corpus of the law.[23] A similar use of the word can be seen in Isaiah 40:8, namely, "and the word (*u-dvar*) of our God shall endure forever." In Deuteronomy 17:11, conversely, *davar* seems to be meant as a specific term, that is, one is to follow the decision of the court in his or her particular case before the judges.[24] A similar use of the word can be seen in Exodus 18:16,

---

[22] For the relation between these two extraordinary cases, see B. Shabbat 96b.
[23] See Prov. 30:5–6; Malbim, *Commentary on the Torah*: Deut. 4:2.
[24] See LXX and Targumim on Deut. 17:11.

namely, when Moses tells Jethro about the individual cases brought to him, "whoever has a [legal] matter (*davar*), he comes to me."

The force of the rabbinic interpretation, however, is that it reverses these two meanings. That is, Deuteronomy 13:1 is now understood by the Rabbis to mean that one is prohibited from adding onto or detracting from any of the specifics of *a* commandment. Thus "the *whole* matter" (*kol-ha-davar*) is now understood as "*any* matter." An example given is that one is not to add to the number (four) of plants to taken in hand on the holiday of Sukkot or subtract from it.[25] What this accomplishes is to eliminate any Scriptural obstruction to the idea of general rabbinic legislation. One may, in effect, add onto the whole, only being careful not to distort any of the previously determined parts. And by reading *davar* in Deuteronomy 17:11 as a general term rather than as a specific term, one is mandated by the Torah not only to heed rabbinic adjudication of individual cases, but to heed rabbinic legislation in general.[26] That is, the Rabbis themselves are not only empowered to apply the law already given, but are also empowered to make supplemental law for the present and the future. Legislation being more active and adjudication being more reactive, legislation is more general than adjudication because the former is concerned with the open future whereas the latter is concerned with the closed past. The only proviso is that the formal distinction between Scriptural law (*d'oraita*) and rabbinic law (*de-rabbanan*) be kept in view, and that the normative priority of Scriptural law over rabbinic law be consistently maintained.[27]

The use of Deuteronomy 17:11 as the Scriptural warrant for rabbinic legislation is centered around the discussion in the Talmud concerning the formula for the blessing to be recited over the Hanukkah lights. After the formula of "[blessed are You Lord our God king of the universe] who has sanctified us with his commandments and commanded us to kindle the

---

[25] *Sifre*: Devarim, no. 82. See R. Joseph Albo, *Iqqarim*, 3.14.   [26] B. Berakhot 19b.
[27] See B. Betsah 3b; Maimonides, *Mishneh Torah*: Mamrim, 2.9.

Hanukkah lights (*ner*)" is accepted, the fundamental theological question is raised: "Where were we so commanded (*ve-heikhan tsivanu*)?"[28] In other words, what justifies calling the clearly nonbiblical institution of Hanukkah a divinely mandated commandment? The answer is that Deuteronomy 17:11 (abbreviated to the two words *lo tasur*) justifies calling rabbinic law divine law by its general warrant. The Torah itself gave the Rabbis this power to connect their law with its law.

Of course, this power given to the Rabbis is not unqualified. First and foremost, it must function for the sake of the covenant. Their law stems from a covenant made between the people and their leaders before God.[29] This means that rabbinic law is designed either to protect specific Scriptural laws that comprise the basic substance of the covenant or to enhance the covenant by the inclusion of new celebrations in it.[30]

In the case of the protective rabbinic measures (*gezerot*), what was early on called "fences for the Torah (*siyyag la-torah*)," it meant the addition of practices that would make the violation of Scriptural commandments less likely.[31] The classic example of this is in the area of Sabbath law (*shevut*), where, among other things, it is prohibited even to discuss business matters on the Sabbath.[32] That, of course, makes the actual conduct of business, which is prohibited by Scriptural law, much less likely. It also enhances the whole spiritual atmosphere that is one of the purposes of the Sabbath itself as the archetypal celebration of the creation of the world by God and the covenant between God and Israel. Making the law even stricter is seen as being a sign of Israel's active love for God, that is, doing even more than God himself expected of her.[33]

In the case of the enhancing rabbinic measures (*taqqanot*), practices like Purim and Hanukkah, one can see how the

[28] B. Shabbat 23a. Cf. Y. Sukkah 3.4/53d.
[29] See Ezra 10:3 and Neh. 10:1; B. Yevamot 89b; also, pp. 31–32 above.
[30] See Maimonides, *Mishneh Torah*: Mamrim, 1.1–2.
[31] See M. Avot 1.1; also, B. Eruvin 21b.
[32] B. Shabbat 113b re Isa. 58:13 and Rashi, s.v. "she-lo" thereon. See Novak, *Jewish Social Ethics*, 145.
[33] See B. Berakhot 20b re Deut. 8:10.

Rabbis did not want to limit celebrations of the covenant to the commemoration of a finite number of what were even by their time ancient events. They were convinced that the Jewish people were still capable of experiencing the saving presence of God in their communal life. Furthermore, it seems as though they were also convinced that if postbiblical, memorable events were not incorporated into the covenant, their popular commemoration could develop into counter-covenantal celebrations.[34] For that reason, the rabbinic institution of reciting Hallel (specific chapters of praise from Psalms 113–118) as part of the official liturgy was not limited to Scripturally mandated occasions like Passover, but was extended to Hanukkah as well.[35] (And one can see the same dynamic at work at the present time in the efforts of many religious Zionists to give a religious character to Israel's Independence Day – *Yom Ha'Atsma'ut* – by such practices as the full recitation of Hallel.[36]) Furthermore, there were numerous rabbinic enactments (*taqqanot*) in the areas of civil and criminal legal procedures that were designed to enhance the common good (*tiqqun ha'olam*) of the Jewish people.[37] The assumption here is that that which pertains to interhuman relationships (*bein adam le-havero*) is of ultimate significance in the relationship between God and man (*bein adam le-maqom*).[38] Ultimately, everything that is being done by and for the Jewish people themselves is for the sake of the covenant. It is all part of Israel's electing the God who elects her.

Finally, there is the factor of popular consent. In the area of Scriptural law, this factor does not seem to be at work. Although it is assumed that the law of God is for the good of man, nevertheless, its authority is assumed whether one sees the good the law is intending or not. Popular consent is something always *post factum*; *ab initio* it is irrelevant. At the

---

[34] See D. Novak, *Law and Theology in Judaism* (2 vols., New York, 1974, 1976), 2:129ff.

[35] *Arakhin* 10a.

[36] For a halakhic endorsement of liturgical innovation for *Yom Ha'Atsma'ut*, see Shlomo Goren, *Torat Ha-Mo'adim* (Tel Aviv, 1964), 576ff. Cf. Ovadia Yosef, *Teshuvot Yabi'a Omer*: *Orah Hayyim*, 6, no. 42.

[37] See M. *Gittin* 4.2ff. and Talmudim thereon.   [38] See pp. 143–148 above.

most elementary level, the laws of God are divine decrees (*gezerot*).[39] In fact, in one famous rabbinic passage, the first-century CE sage R. Eleazar ben Azaryah openly admits that he would love to do many of the things the Torah prohibits, but it is only that "my Father in heaven has decreed so for me (*gazar alay*)" that prevents him from exercising his own will.[40]

With rabbinic law, on the other hand, popular consent is indeed a major factor *ab initio*. Thus the Talmud assumes that "a decree (*gezerah*) cannot be decreed unless it is obvious that the majority of the community will abide by it."[41] In other words, not only the Rabbis but the ordinary people too have more power in the area of man-made law than they do in the area of God-made law. Nevertheless, the fact that this power is not construed to be for the sake of autonomy *from* the covenant but to be more like autonomy *for* the covenant enables one to look to the Jewish people themselves as a source of revelation. "If they themselves are not prophets, then they are the children of prophets."[42] In cases of doubt about what the actual law is, where there are good theoretical arguments by Rabbis on both sides of the issue, one is to "go out and look at what the people are doing."[43]

The human contribution to the covenant is most intensely seen in the whole institution of worship. For even in Scripture itself, it is recognized that worship is essentially a human reaching out to God. Thus the institution of sacrifice, the most original and pervasive form of human worship of God, is initiated by Cain and Abel (Genesis 4:3–5).[44] Along these lines, Jeremiah reminds the people in his time that sacrifice, being the basically human institution that it is, must be subordinate to the covenant and its law that are initiated by God. "For I spoke not with your ancestors nor did I command them

---

[39] See B. Berakhot 33b; *Bemidbar Rabbah*, 19.1.

[40] *Sifra*: Qedoshim re Lev. 20:26, ed. Weiss, 93d.

[41] B. Avodah Zarah 36a and parallels; Maimonides, *Mishneh Torah*: Mamrim, 2.7 (cf. R. Joseph Karo, *Kesef Mishneh* thereon).

[42] B. Pesahim 66a. See T. Yadayim 2.16 re Ps. 25:14 and Amos 3:7.

[43] See B. Berakhot 45a and parallels; Y. Pe'ah 7.6/20c; *Otsar Ha-Ge'onim*: Rosh Hashanah, ed. B. M. Lewin (Haifa and Jerusalem, 1932), 62 (responsum of R. Hai Gaon).

[44] Cf. B. Avodah Zarah 8a; B. Berakhot 28b.

in the day that I took them out of the land of Egypt for the sake of (*al*) burnt offerings and sacrifices. But this thing did I command them, namely, hearken to My voice" (Jeremiah 7:22–23).[45] Furthermore, although there is a medieval debate about whether the institution of prayer worship is actually mandated by the Torah or not, even Maimonides, who holds the view that it is, also reiterates the consistent rabbinic view that the content and structure of prayer worship is humanly ordained, beginning with the Men of the Great Assembly, who lived after the return of the Jewish people from Babylonian Exile in the fifth century BCE.[46] And it is quite clear that the whole development of Jewish liturgy has been as much contingent on popular will and custom as it has been on official rabbinic enactments. Indeed, the late American Jewish theologian Joseph B. Soloveitchik made the profound point that prayer worship was not officially instituted among the Jewish people until the time that prophecy was already on the wane. This implies that the people were so devoted to the covenant that they were prepared to talk more to God at the very time when God was talking less to them.[47]

Moreover, this is consistent with the overall tendency in Talmudic times for the Rabbis to reenact by their own authority (*de-rabbanan*) certain Scriptural commandments that by Scriptural criteria could no longer be seen as operative in their original form (*d'oraita*). The reason for this seems to have been that the Rabbis were convinced that these commandments still had covenantal significance even though in strictly legal terms the preconditions for their observance were no longer at hand. Here too it would seem that the Rabbis were as much influenced by popular practice as they were influencing it. A prime example of this tendency is the rabbinic reenactment of the commandment to eat bitter herbs (*maror*) at the Passover

---

[45] Here I follow the translation of L. E. Binns quoted by H. Freedman in his commentary on Jeremiah in Soncino Books of the Bible (London, 1949), 56.

[46] *Mishneh Torah*: Tefillah, 1.1 re Exod. 23:25 à la B. Ta'anit 2a re Deut. 11:13. Cf. Nahmanides, *Notes on Maimonides' Sefer Ha-Mitsvot*, pos. no. 5; also, B. Berakhot 20b, Rashi, s.v. "hakhi garsinan."

[47] *The Lonely Man of Faith* (New York, 1992), 58.

Seder. In strictly legal terms, that is only a requirement when it can be done in conjunction with the eating of the Paschal Lamb. Thus if there is no Paschal Lamb, which became the case after the destruction of the Second Temple in 70 CE, then there is no further requirement to eat the bitter herbs. Nevertheless, because the remembrance of the bitter suffering of Egyptian slavery is such an integral part of the experience of Passover, it was seen as a covenantal imperative, one which found a new humanly initiated legal form.[48] Here again, Israel elected to be elected.

THE ELECTION OF THE CONVERTS

The whole matter of electing to be elected lies at the core of the institution of conversion to Judaism (*gerut*). A careful look at the classical sources indicates that the development of this institution as an integral part of Normative Judaism itself presupposes the new postexilic sense of the greater role for the human contribution to the covenant between God and Israel.[49] The theological question is what sort of election is taking place here. How exactly is conversion to Judaism part of the larger covenant between God and Israel? The philosophical question concerns what is the volition of God and what is the volition of humans in this relationship. For although the factor of human volition is obvious in the case of a convert, it is not so obvious just what God's volition is here. The answers to these questions require both halakhic and historical inquiry.

In the biblical period, especially in pre-exilic times, conversion of a gentile into a Jew (or, more accurately, into an Israelite) appears to have been much more of a process than a single, all-encompassing event.[50] In fact, to call such persons "converts" as we use that term today is actually misleading, as

---

[48] B. Pesahim 115a. See *ibid.*, 116b and R. Yom Tov ben Abraham Ishbili, *Teshuvot Ha-Ritva*, no. 97, ed. Kafih, 115.

[49] Much of this section is adapted from my article, "The Legal Question of the Investigation of Converts," *Jewish Law Association Studies* (1987), 3:153ff.

[50] In classical halakhic parlance, it is more a matter of presumption (*hazaqah*) than one of demonstration (*ray'ah*). See, e.g., M. Kiddushin 4.10 and B. Kiddushin 79b–80a.

we shall see. Moreover, during this period, there seem to have been several levels of *gerim* – most accurately termed "sojourners" – having different degrees of privileges and obligations.[51]

In the area of civil and criminal law, including such acts as damage to the property of others, injury to other persons, and blasphemy, the Torah prescribes equality of both privilege and obligation for the native-born Israelite (*ezrah*) and for one permitted to live (*gur*) in Israelite society. "There shall be one judgment (*mishpat*) for you: the sojourner is like the native born" (Leviticus 24:22). There are many parallels to such legislation in the ancient world.[52]

In the area of cultic law, one can note several gradations as regards the privileges and obligations of converts. Thus in the case of Passover, which as we have already seen is the archetypal covenantal experience and celebration, when the *ger* wishes to have his dwelling with "the assembly of Israel (*adat yisra'el*)," then "no leaven is to be found" (Exodus 12:19) in his house as in an Israelite house. But only when the *ger* desires the full participation in the Passover ritual of eating the Paschal Lamb is circumcision finally required.

If a sojourner who dwells along with you (*itekha*) would offer the Passover offering to the Lord, all his males must be circumcised; then he shall be admitted (*ve'az yiqrav*) to offer it; he then shall become like a citizen of the country (*ve-hayah k'ezrah ha'arets*) ... There shall be one law for the native born citizen and for the sojourner who dwells in your midst (*be-tokhekhem*). (Exodus 12:48–49)

Here it should be noted that only at this point is the sojourner living "in your midst" rather than merely living "along with you."[53] The process might well extend over several generations.[54]

Nevertheless, despite all this legislation, nowhere in Scripture are we told *how* one becomes a *ger* in the first place *de jure*.

[51] See T. Meek, "The Translation of Gêr in the Hexateuch," *Journal of Biblical Literature* (1930), 49:177; D. Novak, *The Image of the Non-Jew in Judaism* (New York and Toronto, 1983), 14ff.

[52] See Novak, *The Image of the Non-Jew in Judaism*, 18–19.

[53] See M. M. Kasher, *Torah Shlemah* (Jerusalem, 1992), 3:86, n. 716.

[54] See Lev. 25:47 and R. Samuel David Luzzatto, *Commentary on the Torah* thereon.

All that we see is a process, initially entailing participation in the civil life of Israel and ultimately, at least in some cases, greater involvement in her cultic life as well. Initially, the simple fact of extended domicile seems to start the whole process *de facto*. Even in the clearly postexilic text of Deutero-Isaiah, where we do see mention of what could be strictly defined as religious conversion, namely, "the aliens who are joined (*u-venai nekhar ha-nilvim*) to the Lord, to serve him and to love the name of the Lord to be his servants" (Isaiah 56:6), even here the precise procedures for this "joining" and its precise demarcation in time are not explicated.[55]

It is only in early rabbinic times that we see conversion defined as an event with the stipulation of precise procedures and the precise demarcation of exactly when this event begins and ends. By this time, the Rabbis only recognized two kinds of *gerim*. The first is in essence a resident-alien (*ger toshav*), having definite privileges and obligations in Jewish civil and criminal law.[56] The second is one who is a full convert to Judaism (*ger tsedeq*), having complete privileges and obligations in virtually all areas of Jewish law. Furthermore, the Talmud indicates that the operation of the institution of the resident-alien is contingent on full Jewish sovereignty throughout the historic land of Israel. As such, it ceased to operate after the destruction of the First Temple in 586 BCE.[57] Thus for all intents and purposes, there is only fully religious conversion since that time.[58]

By the time of Rabban Yohanan ben Zakkai, probably shortly before the destruction of the Second Temple in 70 CE, the requirements for the event of conversion were codified. The requirements are: (1) circumcision, (2) immersion (*tevillah*), and (3) bringing a sacrifice. The event of conversion is compared to the event of the covenantal commitment made by the people of Israel when they accepted the Torah at Mount Sinai.

---

[55] See Ezra 6:21 and Yehezkel Kaufmann, *Toldot Ha'Emunah Ha-Yisra'elit* (4 vols., Jerusalem and Tel Aviv, 1966), 5:459, n. 5; also *ibid.*, 3:636.
[56] See B. Avodah Zarah 64b; Maimonides, *Mishneh Torah*: Melakhim, 8.10.
[57] Arakhin 29a.
[58] See Meiri, *Bet Ha-Behirah*: Yevamot 48b, ed. Dickman, 192.

Thus the presupposition for these ritual requirements is existential: the unconditional acceptance of the Written Torah and the Oral Tradition.[59] Conversion had now become one multifaceted cultic event.

Rabbi [Judah the Prince] says that "like you" (*kakhem* – Numbers 15:15) means like your ancestors. Just as your ancestors did not enter the covenant (*nikhnesu la-berit*) except through circumcision, immersion, and being sprinkled with sacrificial blood, so they may not enter the covenant except through circumcision, immersion, and being sprinkled with sacrificial blood.[60]

The requirements of circumcision and being sprinkled with sacrificial blood are explicitly Scriptural; as for the requirement of immersion, it is seen as the prerequisite for being sprinkled with sacrificial blood. Indeed, immersion is seen as the necessary transition for the assumption of any new sacred state.[61]

It is also important to note that the gentile's decision to become a Jew is not only a decision to accept the authority of the Torah and the practices it prescribes. It is also, indeed equally, a decision to be part of the Jewish people. For much of its history, being part of this people is to expose onself to persecution and contempt. Thus another rabbinic text, probably composed sometime around the Hadrianic persecution of the Jewish people in the land of Israel early in the second century CE, states:

When one comes to convert to Judaism in this time, they [the Jewish authorities] are to say to him: "what benefit do you see in coming to convert? Do you not know that Israel in this time is beset, downtrodden, lowly, distraught, and persecuted?" If he says, "I know and I am not worthy to be part of them," they are to accept him immediately.[62]

---

[59] T. Demai 2.5; Bekhorot 30b. Cf. B. Shabbat 31a and B. Yevamot 24b, Tos., s.v. "lo" re Menahot 44a.

[60] Keritot 9a. See J. Neusner, *A Life of Yohanan ben Zakkai* (Leiden, 1962), 162ff.

[61] See M. Yoma 3.6; B. Yoma 30a; Y. Yoma 3.3/40b; M. Pesahim 8.8; Jubilees 21:16; Testament of Levi in *Apocrypha and Pseudepigrapha of the Old Testament*, ed. and trans. R. H. Charles (Oxford, 1913), 2:248. See also Louis Finkelstein, "The Institution of Baptism for Proselytes," *Journal of Biblical Literature* (1933), 52:206ff.

[62] B. Yevamot 47a. See *Shemot Rabbah* 30.9.

The rest of the text prescribes a selective course of study in the commandments. If the convert accepts their full authority, then the actual rites of conversion are to be performed forthwith. The event is irreversible. Any transgression committed by the convert after a bona fide conversion, even a return back to his or her former religion, makes the convert a "Jewish apostate" (*mumar yisra'el*), but never again a gentile.[63]

What emerges from this text is that conversion not only imitates the receiving of the Torah by Israel, but also imitates the election of the Jewish people and their precarious position within the course of human history. As I shall argue in the conclusion, although these two realities are interrelated, neither is merely reducible to the other. They function together with a certain amount of dialectical tension.

By making conversion into an event, Jewish tradition emphasizes the role of human volition in the covenant. One cannot become a convert without his or her explicit consent. Being given at a particular time, that explicit consent becomes a condition of an event. One no longer becomes part of Israel through a gradual process whose moments are often imperceptible. In fact, although the Halakhah permits the conversion of children, even infants, those so converted have the option of repudiating what was, in effect, done by others on their behalf without their consent, when they reach the age of consent themselves.[64] It might well be that the memory of the forced conversion of the Idumeans during the reign of the Hasmonean king John Hyrcanus late in the second century BCE had some influence on the rabbinic emphasis of the condition of volition for the conversion of gentiles to Judaism and the Jewish people. For this political policy did not lead to the integration of the Idumeans into Judaism and the Jewish people. On the contrary, it led to great animosity against both Judaism and the Jewish people.[65]

---

[63] B. Yevamot 47b. Cf. B. Kiddushin 17b and B. Avodah Zarah 64a.

[64] B. Ketubot 11a. Cf. M. Nazir 4.6; Y. Nazir 4.6/53c and T. Eduyot 2.2. For further discussion of this whole issue, see Novak, "The Legal Question of the Investigation of Converts," 167ff.

[65] See Josephus, *Antiquities*, 13.257; also, Jubilees 15:26–27 and LXX on Est. 8:17; Novak, *The Image of the Non-Jew in Judaism*, 13.

The role of human volition as a *sine qua non* of the event of conversion does, however, raise serious problems both theological and philosophical. Theologically we might ask: How is this event an *imitation* of the covenantal event of God and Israel at Sinai? Is not the Sinai event one which is initiated by God? Philosophically we might ask: Is not the initiation of the covenant a matter of God's volition, but not Israel's? Have we not seen previously that Israel is only free to confirm that which God has *already* done to her and for her? And have we not seen previously that Israel is not free to reject the covenant with any impunity at all? Does not all of this suggest that the event of conversion is an exception to the normal course of the covenant rather than an extension of it? In other words, converts seem to become "Jews by choice," to use a currently popular term; native-born Jews seem to become Jews "by force" (*b'al korham*), to use a rabbinic term.[66] And as far as the Halakhah is concerned, a gentile who decides not to convert to Judaism has not committed any sin at all because there is no legal obligation to do so.[67] The answer to these serious questions lies, it seems to me, in the discovery that Jews have more freedom when entering the covenant than is usually assumed, and that gentiles have less freedom than is usually assumed.

This can best be seen when examining a famous rabbinic legend concerning the giving of the Torah. "When the Holy-One-blessed-be-he appeared to give the Torah to Israel, he did not appear to Israel alone but to all the nations."[68] The text continues and states that the Edomites refused the Torah

---

[66] See M. Avot 4.22.

[67] Thus in an interesting responsum written in 1926, the Lithuanian-German halakhist R. Jehiel J. Weinberg (d. 1966) dealt with the question of a Hungarian Rabbi who inquired whether a hemophiliac could be converted to Judaism without circumcision since circumcision would certainly endanger his life. R. Weinberg concluded that this was not permitted because "no one is obligated (*mehuyyav*) to convert to Judaism" and, moreover, the would-be convert must not be allowed by a rabbinical tribunal to do so even if he himself was willing to undergo the risk because such permission would be a "profanation of God's name" (*hillul ha-shem*), i.e., it would lead non-Jews to morally condemn Judaism. This responsum was published in *The Leo Jung Jubilee Volume*, ed. M. M. Kasher *et al.* (New York, 1962), Heb. sec., 27.

[68] *Sifre*: Devarim, no. 343, ed. Finkelstein, 396–397. See Novak, *The Image of the Non-Jew in Judaism*, 257ff.

because they could not accept the prohibition of murder; the Ammonites and Moabites because of the prohibition of incest; the Ishmaelites because of the prohibition of robbery. The text then continues "Not only did they not hearken to it [the Mosaic Torah], but even the seven commandments which the Noahides accepted upon themselves they were unable to persevere in them, finally casting them off." In another version of this legend, one of the Rabbis says that "if the seven commandments the Noahides were commanded and accepted upon themselves, they were unable to persevere in them, then all the more so could they not persevere in the commandments of the Torah."[69]

What we see here is that the free acceptance of the Noahide laws, which the Rabbis assumed are the basis of universal morality, is the prerequisite for the acceptance of the full Torah, the constitution of the Jewish people. That notion goes back as far as the famous retort of Hillel the Elder (who lived around the beginning of the Common Era) to the would-be convert: "What is hateful to yourself, do not do to someone else. That is the whole Torah, the rest is commentary; now go and learn."[70] Of course, that most general moral maxim is not the whole Torah. It is found in many other "Torahs" as well as Israel's, and there is much in the Torah that is more than mere "commentary" on it.[71] It is the bare minimum of the Torah, however. That is, following the full intent of morality leads one to seek the direct revelation of God and his law. It is not that the law is the creation of human freedom, as is the case with the autonomous moral law advocated by Kant and all his modern disciples. Instead, it means that God's law can only be approached when one proceeds out of a human awareness of his or her own freedom of choice to respond to the claims made by what truly transcends it. Nevertheless, that freedom is only a condition of revelation, not its cause. God is totally free to "be wherever and whenever he will be" (Exodus

---

[69] *Mekhilta*: Yitro, ed. Horovitz–Rabin, 221–222. See B. Yevamot 48b.
[70] B. Shabbat 31a.
[71] For further sources, both Jewish and non-Jewish, regarding this maxim, see Novak, *Jewish Social Ethics*, 182, nn. 29–30.

3:14).[72] There is no guarantee of revelation, only preparation for it. The preparation only deals with the possibility of revelation; it is not a potential that has its own actualization already within itself.[73]

If this is understood, then the freedom of the convert to accept the Torah is also a condition of his or her acceptance into the covenant, but not its cause. The convert does not "convert himself or herself" (*mitgayyer*); rather the convert "is converted" (*nitgayyer*) to Judaism by a Jewish tribunal acting in God's stead as it were.[74] That is, they have the power to accept or reject a candidate for conversion not only because of qualities the candidate has or does not have, but also because of reasons having nothing to do with the particular candidate. This has been the case, especially, when conversion would adversely affect the welfare of the Jewish community as a whole. This is like God's election of Israel, which is more because of God's own reasons than Israel's inherent qualities. Thus the Talmud presents the view that converts were not accepted during the days of King David and King Solomon because it could not be ascertained whether or not they were converting only because they desired a share in Jewish wealth or Jewish power.[75] Also, during the Middle Ages, in many times and places, converts were not accepted because such Jewish acceptance of them would expose the Jewish community to the wrath of their Christian or Muslim host societies.[76] For, after all, who would these converts be if not apostates from Christianity or Islam?

Nevertheless, the converts are able to prepare themselves for the possibility that the Jewish tribunal will accept them into the community of Israel. And, surely, the moral character of

---

[72] See the translation of Martin Buber and Franz Rosenzweig, *Die Fünf Bücher der Weisung* (Olten, 1954), 158.

[73] See D. Novak, *Jewish–Christian Dialogue* (New York, 1989), 129ff.

[74] See B. Yevamot 22a and 47a re Deut. 1:16. Cf. B. Kiddushin 70b, Rashi, s.v. "be-yisra'el ketiv."

[75] B. Yevamot 24d.

[76] See Salo W. Baron, *The Jewish Community* (3 vols., Philadelphia, 1942), 1:222; *Jewish Encyclopedia* (12 vols., New York, 1916), 4:236; *Encyclopedia Judaica* (16 vols., Jerusalem, 1972), 13:1190.

the convert is a factor therein. According to the Talmud, converts must regard themselves as going from a lighter type of holiness to a heavier one.[77] In other words, converts prepare themselves for conversion to the Jewish people and Judaism in much the same way as Israel prepared herself for God's election and revelation of the full Torah to her. With this analogy as a model, we can now see how it teaches us that the freedom of Israel in the covenantal relationship with God is more than passive acceptance but less than autonomy.

Because the analogy between Israel and the converts is so theologically significant, it explains why twice in Jewish history, when there seemed to be insuperable halakhic impediments to the continuance of the whole institution of conversion (*gerut*), the Rabbis found the legal means to let it continue.

The first such impediment itself arose after the destruction of the Second Temple in 70 CE. As we saw before, in addition to circumcision and immersion, the third ritual requirement of conversion is that the convert bring a sacrifice and be sprinkled with its blood. But how could this be fulfilled when there is no longer any Temple? The Talmud notes, "R. Aha bar Jacob said, [Scripture says] 'when a sojourner dwells with you ... who is in your midst throughout the generations (*le-doroteikhem* – Numbers 15:14).'" This is in answer to the question, "since there is no sacrifice today, are we not to accept converts any more?"[78] One solution reported is that the minimal sum for a sacrifice be put in escrow by the convert, the assumption being that the Temple will soon be rebuilt. But Rabban Yohanan ben Zakkai eliminated even this conditional act because it entails more problems than it would solve. Thus conversion as an integral part of the covenant determines the legal adjustments needed to insure its normative character. The verse from Numbers 15:14 is quoted to indicate that in every generation of Jews there will inevitably be converts or would-be converts dwelling in their midst or along with them and that the law must find a *modus operandi* to justify *de jure* what is already *de*

---

[77] B. Yevamot 22a. See B. Horayot 13a; R. Judah Halevi, *Kuzari*, 2.48; *Sefer Hasidim*, ed. Bologna, no. 511.
[78] Keritot 9a.

facto a *modus vivendi*. This same sort of logic is used elsewhere in the Talmud to justify, *ex post facto* to be sure, conversions initially motivated by social ends rather than the purely religious end of accepting the Torah and its commandments per se.[79]

A similar problem arose in connection with the possibility of disqualifying all rabbinical judges who are needed for supervising and approving the event of conversion. For with the cessation of the rabbinical ordination that was seen as being in unbroken succession from Moses on (*semikhah*) in the third century CE, no subsequent judge could qualify for this role in the precise sense stipulated by R. Yohanan bar Nappaha, who said, "a convert requires a court of three since the term 'judgment' (*mishpat*) is written in connection with him."[80] Several commentators see the reference here as being to Numbers 15:15, "one judgment (*mishpat ehad*) there shall be for you and for the sojourner (*la-ger*) who dwells with you."[81] Such a "judgment" requires a court of three judges ordained in what the Rabbis considered to be direct succession from Moses himself (*mumhin*).[82] And already, in later Talmudic times, outside the land of Israel, Rabbis with this type of ordination were no longer to be found. However, some commentators solve this problem by citing another Talmudic source which rules that even Rabbis who do not have "Mosaic" ordination are still allowed "to function as the agents" of earlier Rabbis who did have it. Now, this extension of authority through the legal fiction of agency stipulated by the agent (*shaliah*) rather than the party on whose behalf he acts (*ha-meshaleah*) is limited to those areas of law whose application is regularly required.[83] These commentators consider conversion to be such an area of law. Furthermore, they indicate that just as the right of adjudication was extended to the area of loans (where fully ordained

[79] B. Yevamot 24b. Cf. Gerim 1.7. Also, see R. Ben Zion Uziel, *Teshuvot Mishpatei Uziel*: Even Ha'Ezer (Jerusalem, 1964), sec. 18 .

[80] B. Yevamot 46b.

[81] See Rashi and Tosafot on B. Yevamot 46b, s.v. "mishpat."

[82] See B. Sanhedrin 2b–3a.

[83] See B. Gittin 88b. Cf. B. Kiddushin 32b, Tos., s.v. "v'ayn."

Rabbis are in principle required for adjudication) "because they [the Rabbis] were concerned that lending might stop [if lenders did not have the protection of the due process of law in the event of nonpayment by debtors]," so were they concerned lest conversion stop.[84] Elsewhere it is noted that conversion was a legal institution in Babylonia even though the Rabbis there did not have Mosaic ordination.[85] And, finally, the thirteenth-century Spanish halakhist and theologian Nahmanides connects this legal fiction with the earlier legal fiction that we have seen before, namely, the decision after the destruction of the Second Temple that made the ability to bring a sacrifice no longer a *sine qua non* of conversion.[86]

The last point to be made in connection with the covenantal significance of conversion concerns the analogy between Israel entering the covenant at Sinai and converts entering the Jewish people and Judaism at the time of their conversion. Who is being compared to whom? Is Israel to be compared to a convert, or are converts to be compared to Israel? Is the analogy between true equals, or is the analogy one between a major and a minor party?

There is some evidence that would suggest that Israel is to be compared to a convert. The best example of this can be seen in the old custom of reading the book of Ruth in the synagogue before the reading of the Torah on the festival of Shavuot.[87] Now, Shavuot in Rabbinic Judaism is "the time of the giving of our Torah" (*zeman mattan torateinu*).[88] The Torah reading for that day is the selection from Exodus (19–20) describing the

---

[84] B. Yevamot 46b, Tos., s.v. "mishpat."

[85] B. Gittin 88b, Tos., s.v. "be-milta." Cf. T. Rosh Hashanah 1.18 and B. Rosh Hashanah 25a–b.

[86] *Hiddushei Ha-Ramban*: B. Yevamot 46b, ed. Meltzer. See also Nahmanides' most influential disciple, R. Solomon ibn Adret, *Hiddushei Ha-Rashba* thereon; and R. Simon ben Zemah Duran, *Teshuvot Tashbats*, 2, no. 290.

[87] Although the conceptual connection between the book of Ruth and Shavu'ot is obvious, the actual source of the practice of reading it at this time for this reason is obscure. See *Yalqut Shim'oni*: Ruth, no. 596; R. Abraham Gumbiner, *Magen Avraham* on *Shulhan Arukh*: Orah Hayyim, 490, n. 8. Also, see R. Abraham Isaac Sperling, *Sefer Ha-Minhagim U-Meqorei Ha-Dinim* (Jerusalem, 1972), Inyanei Pesah, no. 585 re B. Yevamot 48b à la Ruth 1:16–18. Re the superiority of converts, see *Tanhuma*: Lekh Lekha, no. 6, ed. Buber, 32a.

[88] See B. Pesahim 68b.

covenant between God and Israel consummated at Mount Sinai and the prescription of its legal foundation: the Ten Commandments.[89] Hence reading the story of Ruth, the paradigmatic convert to Judaism, seems to suggest that she is the model for all Israel. Nevertheless, if one looks at the book of Ruth itself, one will notice that Ruth herself says [to her mother-in-law Naomi], "your people will be my people, and your God my God" (Ruth 1:17). In other words, Ruth's acceptance of Judaism is contingent on the people of Israel already being in relationship with *their* God. Thus a favorite rabbinic phrase used to denote irony is: "Is the native born (*yatsiva*) on earth and the convert (*ve-giyora*) in heaven?"[90] Ultimately, to compare Israel to converts is to make the covenant too contingent on human volition. In truth, the converts could not decide to come to Israel if Israel had not already been first chosen by God. Israel's election, to use a rabbinic term, is "the root" (*iqqar*); the converts' conversion is "grafted" (*tafel*) onto it.[91]

Therefore, it is not so much that Israel "converts" to the covenant but that the convert is "born again" (*ke-qatan she-nolad dami*), that is, the convert becomes a Jew analogously to the way Jews become Jews: by birth.[92] This is a consistent principle in the treatment of converts in the Halakhah. The only exceptions seem to be based on a kind of nature–grace dialectic. That is, there are certain natural facts, such as the relationship with one's biological parents, that even revelation must respect and cannot simply obliterate.[93] And this too is similar to the fact that the covenant between God and Israel does not obliterate certain universal factors of the human condition – even for the Jews who have been elected by God.[94]

---

[89] B. Megillah 31a.   [90] B. Baba Kama 42a and parallels.
[91] See Menahot 91b and parallels.
[92] B. Yevamot 22a and parallels.
[93] See, e.g., T. Demai 6.12–13; B. Kiddushin 17b; also, Novak, *Law and Theology in Judaism*, 1:72ff.
[94] See B. Sanhedrin 59a; *Mekhilta*: Mishpatim, ed. Horovitz–Rabin, 263 re Exod. 21:14.

THE PROBLEM OF APOSTASY

The factor of human freedom in the covenant between God and Israel, which as we have seen was considerably developed in Rabbinic Judaism, does not extend, however, to the freedom to leave the covenant. Just as converts who revert to their former non-Jewish religious practices and beliefs are still considered Jews, albeit apostates (*mumarim*), it is all the more so with native-born Jews.[95] The covenant has two entrances, birth and conversion, but no exit. Even death only relieves Jews of their legal obligations, all of which are this-worldly; it does not, however, relieve them of being part of the covenant which extends to the world-to-come.[96] And even those Jews who have forfeited their portion in the world-to-come are still under the legal obligations of the covenant in this world until the moment of their death.[97] All of this is, of course, fully understandable *de jure*. That which God has established to be perpetual may not, cannot, be eliminated by human creatures. Nevertheless, Jews do leave the covenant *de facto*. They can and do assume gentile identities in the human world all the time. That is a well-demonstrated historical fact. How, then, does the tradition deal with this often great disparity between law and life, between theology and history? What are the approaches to dealing with the situation of Jews who have elected not to be elected?

In the course of the development of the Halakhah, the *locus classicus* for dealing with this whole issue is the following passage from the Talmud:

R. Nehemiah said to him [to R. Judah] ... just as Israel was not punished for sins committed [by individuals] in secret (*al ha-nistarot*), so they were not punished for sins committed in public (*she-ba- galui*) until they had crossed over the Jordan [into the Promised Land]. So why, then, was Israel punished on account of Achan? That was because his wife and children knew about it. "Israel sinned" (*hata yisra'el* – Joshua 7:11): even though they have sinned, they are still Israel (*af-al-pi she-hata yisra'el hu*).[98]

---

[95] See B. Yevamot 47b. [96] See Niddah 61b re Ps. 88:6 and M. Sanhedrin 10.1.

[97] See M. Avot 2.10 and B. Shabbat 153a re Eccl. 9:8; also, Maimonides, *Mishneh Torah*: Teshuvah, 3.13 and R. Joseph Karo, *Kesef Mishneh* thereon.

[98] B. Sanhedrin 43b–44a.

Since this passage is written in the type of shorthand typical of rabbinic discourse, its meaning and implications must be unpacked before we can see its subsequent application within the history of the Halakhah.

The verse that stimulated the above discussion is from Deuteronomy 29:28 – "The secret things (*ha-nistarot*) are for the Lord our God, but the public things (*ve-ha-niglot*) are for us and for our children forever (*ad olam*) to do: all the words of this Torah." Since in the received text of the Pentateuch (*masorah*), dots appear over the words "for us and for our children" and the first letter of "forever" (*ayin*), there seems to be particular urgency to explain the verse.[99] Thus for R. Nehemiah, the emphasis of the verse is to indicate that there is only collective punishment for individual sins when these sins are committed with public knowledge of them. Achan son of Zerah is a man who violated the ban on appropriating the condemned property (*herem*) of vanquished Canaanites during the conquest of the land of Israel led by Joshua. For all intents and purposes, his wife and children constituted such a knowing public. Apparently they, *in loco populorum*, should have restrained him or reported him to the community authorities, but they did not.[100] And the purpose of the quotation from Joshua 7:11 is to show that *the people of Israel* do not lose *their* elected status because of this sin and, presumably, because of any other sin as well. Perhaps this homily is a Jewish attempt to answer the charges of Christian supercessionists that the Jewish people are no longer the elect people of Israel because of their sins.[101] "Israel" here is understood collectively.[102]

---

[99] See *Sifre*: Bemidbar, ed. Horovitz–Rabin, no. 69.

[100] Cf. B. Sanhedrin 27b re Lev. 26:37; *ibid.*, 82a re Prov. 21:30.

[101] See *Sifre*: Devarim, nos. 96, 308; B. Kiddushin 36a; *Ruth Rabbah*, petihah, 1. For some of the main Christian supercessionist sources, see Rosemary Ruether, *Faith and Fratricide* (New York, 1974), 124ff., and more fully, Marcel Simon, *Verus Israel*, trans. H. McKeating (New York, 1986). Nevertheless, not all Christian theology has been supercessionist in the sense of seeing God's covenant with the Jewish people ("the old Israel") as annulled. See, e.g., Rom. 3:1–3 and 11:1–2, 17–24; also, the statement on the Jews ("Nostre Aetate") in *The Documents of Vatican II*, ed. W. M. Abbott and trans. J. Gallagher *et al.* (London and Dublin, 1966), 66off.; and pp. 116–117, n. 23 above.

[102] See comment of Rabbenu Hananael on B. Sanhedrin 44a.

By the early Middle Ages, however, the phrase from the Talmud was used in the sense of "even though he sinned, *he* is still a Jew."[103] It is as if "Israel" referred to Achan as an individual rather than to the people of Israel collectively. And, furthermore, the phrase now assumed a more explicit connection to relations between Jews and Christians. Even those Jews who had converted to Christianity, and who presumably did so to alleviate themselves of their Jewish identity, even these persons are still considered to be part of the covenant between God and Israel because that covenant is established by God forever. And the perpetuity of the covenant applies to the Jewish people collectively as well as to every Jew, native born or convert, individually.

This halakhic use of the theretofore aggadic passage above has ample basis in the Talmudic sources themselves. But as the Israeli social historian Jacob Katz has shown in the most comprehensive study of this principle, this succinct new formulation into one slogan – *af-al-pi she-hata yisra'el hu* – was occasioned during the time of the First Crusade in the eleventh century, when many Jews in northern France and the Rhineland were being given the option of conversion to Christianity or death by the crusaders. The new slogan reminded them, and perhaps their persecutors as well, that no matter what these Jews did, they were still part of Israel, that God's election of them into the covenant is more powerful than either the threats of the crusaders or their own temptations to seek a more secure life in this world. Katz rightly shows that it was the new use of this slogan by the great eleventh-century French commentator and jurist Rashi that gave these six words, with their full implications, great halakhic authority from that time on.[104]

This new use of the Talmudic phrase stems from a time when apostasy on a large scale became a particularly acute problem

---

[103] The earliest use of the phrase in this sense I could find is in *Midrash Aggadah*: Mattot, ed. S. Buber (Vienna, 1894), 162. See also David Weiss Halivni, *Meqorot U-Mesorot*: Nashim (Tel Aviv, 1968), 67, n. 3. Cf. *Sifre*: Devarim, no. 96 re Deut. 14:1 (the view of R. Meir), ed. Finkelstein, 157 and n. 14 thereon.

[104] "Af-al-pi She-Hata Yisra'el Hu," *Tarbiz* (1958), 27:203ff. The *locus classicus* in Rashi is *Teshuvot Rashi*, ed. I. Elfenbein (New York, 1943), no. 171.

for European Jewish communities. Before that time, however, especially during the relatively peaceful time for Babylonian Jewry during the period of the Geonim (roughly from the seventh to the eleventh century), the problem of apostates was much more a question of the effect of their apostasy on the rest of the Jews they left behind in their departure from the Jewish community than a question of their own status per se. Thus, for example, there were halakhic attempts at this time to remove the apostate from the levirate obligation. That is, if a man had died and had left his wife childless, according to Torah law (Deuteronomy 25:5–10) his brother is required either to marry the childless widow (*yibum*) or release her in a special ceremony (*halitsah*). But what if the brother were an apostate? According to some authorities, his apostasy removed him from the legal category of being the "brother" of the deceased.[105] Another example concerns the prohibition of paying interest to or accepting interest from a fellow Jew (Leviticus 25:35–37). But what if one had lent money to an apostate? Is the apostate to be accorded the covenantal privilege of an interest-free loan? Here again, according to some authorities, apostasy removed him from being the "brother" [Jew] of the lender.[106] Nevertheless, these interpretations were all of a highly specific character. Their general implications are not drawn out. As far as I know, no one at this time inferred from all of this that these apostates had removed themselves from the covenant *entirely*. So, when that issue did become the question, the authorities' answer had to be general. The answer, then, became a comprehensive slogan rather than specific exegesis. And I think it is evident that the theology of election and covenant very much informed this

---

105 See *Otsar Ha-Ge'onim*: Yevamot, ed. B. M. Lewin (Jerusalem, 1936), 34ff., 196ff. Building on these sources, the eighteenth-century German halakhist R. Jacob Emden argued that apostates had literally forfeited *any* claim to be considered Jews. However, since the principle *af-al-pi she-hata yisra'el hu* was so well established by his time, he argued that it only applied to sins less than apostasy. See *Sh'elat Ya'vets*, 1, no. 28.

106 See Rabbenu Asher (Rosh), *Baba Metsia*, 5.52; also, *Hiddushei Ha-Ramban* on Baba Metsia 71b, ed. Meltzer. Re the covenantal character of the prohibition of interest, see Novak, *Jewish Social Ethics*, 223–224.

whole response.[107] Finally, in more recent times, beginning in the early nineteenth century with the rise of Reform Judaism, when certain traditionalist authorities seemed to be prepared to read more religiously liberal Jews out of Judaism, the slogan was again invoked to remind these traditionalists – who soon began to call themselves "Orthodox" – that they had no such power in the covenant.[108]

Understanding the full implications, both theological and halakhic, of this slogan helps refute a Jewish folk practice that was justified by a faulty halakhic text. The text concerns, no less, Rabbenu Gershom of Mainz, who died around the middle of the eleventh century and who was the acknowledged leader of the Ashkenazic Jewry of northern France and the Rhineland a generation or so before the time of Rashi, and an authority whose edicts (such as the ban on polygamy) had a tremendous influence on the development of the Halakhah. According to the faulty text, Rabbenu Gershom "mourned as dead (*nit'abel*)" a son of his because this son "had become an apostate (*ke-she-nishtamer*)."[109] This text has been used to justify a practice among some Jews to mourn formally as dead a family member who has converted to another religion, even one who has married a gentile.[110]

However, as we can surely see by now, this text raises severe halakhic and theological problems. The halakhic problem is how one can engage in the formal act of mourning (as opposed to simply experiencing great sorrow over the apostasy of a family member), which relieves one of many normal legal obligations, for someone who is not really dead.[111] The theological problem is how one can acknowledge the power of the apostate to really and finally remove himself or herself from the

---

[107] See B. Shabbat 87a, Tos., s.v. "u-mah" (no. 2); B. Pesahim 120a, Tos., s.v. "kol benei nekhar"; Katz, "Af-al-pi," 212.

[108] See Katz, "Af-al-pi," 216–217. Cf. R. Moses Schreiber, *Teshuvot Hatam Sofer* (3 vols., New York, 1958), 6, no. 89.

[109] R. Isaac of Vienna, *Or Zaru'a*: Avelut, no. 428; Rabbenu Asher (Rosh), *Mo'ed Qatan*, 3.59.

[110] For the Karaite practice of literally regarding an apostate as dead, see R. Isaac Abrabanel, *Commentary on the Torah*: Ki Tetse, no. 14.

[111] See R. Joseph Karo, *Shulhan Arukh*: Yoreh De'ah, 380ff.

covenant initiated by God between himself and *all* his people Israel. These problems help us appreciate that the correct version of this famous incident is actually the earlier version of it. In this version, the text reads, "Rabbenu Gershom mourned for his [deceased] son who had become an apostate (*she-hemeer*)."[112] And then the text continues that the sage who reported this concluded, "but this is not to be taken as any precedent (*she'ayn li-lmod mimenu*) because he [Rabbenu Gershom] did this out of his great anguish that his son [before he died] was not privileged to repent (*she-lo zakhah la-shuv bi-teshuvah*)."

Now, what is *not* to be derived from this version of the incidence of apostasy of Rabbenu Gershom's son and Rabbenu Gershom's mourning for him *after his death* is that even an apostate deserves the honor of being mourned after his death. For the apostate is considered to be "wicked" (*rasha*), and such wicked people are specifically removed from the category of those for whom family members are required to mourn.[113] Nevertheless, even these apostates are not considered to be removed from the covenant while they are alive. Undoubtedly, then, Rabbenu Gershom hoped and prayed that his son would return to Judaism while there was still time for him to do so in this world. Thus his mourning is understandable on emotional grounds, but it is not justifiable on halakhic grounds.

On theological grounds, this perpetuity of the covenant is emphasized as far back as the time of the prophets. Thus Jeremiah, speaking about "the lost tribes of Israel," says, "Is not Ephraim my precious son, my darling child? Even when I rebuke him, I remember him with affection, my heart yearns for him; I will surely be compassionate towards him, says the Lord" (Jeremiah 31:20). This verse plays a key role in the New Year's rite of Rosh Hashanah in the part of the synagogue liturgy where God's faithfulness to the covenant (*zikhro-*

---

112 See Mordecai, *Mo'ed Qatan*, no. 886; R. Moses Schreiber, *Teshuvot Hatam Sofer*: Yoreh De'ah, no. 326; R. Yekutiel Y. Greenwald, *Kol Bo Al Avelut* (New York, 1965), 317.

113 See B. Sanhedrin 47a–b; Semahot 2.7ff.; Maimonides, *Mishneh Torah*: Evel, 1.10.

not) is emphasized.[114] And Ezekiel says, "I have no pleasure in the death of any man, says the Lord, repent then and you will live" (Ezekiel 18:32). This verse plays a key role in the all-day atonement rites of Yom Kippur in the part of the synagogue liturgy just before the end of the service which is called "the closing of the gate" (*ne'ilah*).[115] It is seen as teaching that this might very well be the last chance for any sinner, even the apostate, to return to the covenant with God.

During the course of Jewish history, there were many occasions when apostates did return to the fold. These apostates were generally of two kinds: (1), those who had sincerely converted to Christianity or to Islam, but who later realized that they had been religiously mistaken; (2), those who had converted to Christianity or to Islam because they had been forced to do so by Christians or by Muslims, who had given them the choice of conversion or death. Now the Talmudic rule, formulated at the time of the Roman persecution of the Jews under the pagan Emperor Hadrian early in the second century of the Common Era, is that one is to die as a martyr when such a choice is presented.[116] Later authorities considered Christianity and Islam to be no different from any pagan religion in this specific situation.[117] Yet there were many Jews who decided to feign conversion in order to escape death, but who secretly considered themselves still to be Jews and still practiced as much Judaism as they could without being detected. Many of these secret Jews (eventually called Marranos in late medieval Iberia) did return to the Jewish community to practice Judaism openly when the opportunity presented itself to them.[118] (The quintessential modern apostate from Judaism, Baruch Spinoza, was the son of two such returners to

[114] See *High Holyday Prayerbook*: Rosh Hashanah, ed. and trans. P. Birnbaum (2 vols., New York, 1960), 307.

[115] See *ibid.*: Yom Kippur, 698.

[116] B. Sanhedrin 74a; Y. Sanhedrin 3.6/21b. See Maimonides, *Mishneh Torah*: Yesodei Ha-Torah, 5.1ff.

[117] See, e.g., R. Abraham Gumbiner, *Magen Avraham* on *Shulhan Arukh*: Orah Hayyim, 128.37.

[118] For a moving account of such a return by a Marrano, see Yitshak Baer, *A History of the Jews in Christian Spain*, trans. L. Schoffman (2 vols., Philadelphia, 1961), 2:296ff.

the Jewish community, although, as we have seen, his apostasy was novel inasmuch as he did not become an apostate from Judaism *to* any other historical religion.)

Despite the fact that these former "apostates" (at least in the legal sense) should have chosen martyrdom, Jewish communities were on the whole quite tolerant of them, realizing that one should not be punished for acts commited *in extremis*.[119] The general tendency was for Jewish communities to welcome them back to the fold with few if any questions asked. The general Talmudic principle of removing obstacles from the path of the penitent (*mi-shum taqqanat ha-shavim*) seems to be at work here.[120] After all, if these returners thought that they would be stigmatized by the communities to which they desired to return, they might very well not return at all.[121] The theology behind all of this is quite clear.

However, there arose a halakhic problem in connection with these returners. What sort of ceremony should be conducted when they do return to the Jewish fold? Surely such a transforming occasion calls for a *rite de passage*. Now, as we have seen in connection with conversion to Judaism (*gerut*), such transformations are conducted by means of immersion in a specially designated body of water (*miqveh*).[122] But would that be appropriate in this type of case? The greatest halakhic authority in the Jewish community of early fourteenth-century Christian Spain, R. Solomon ibn Adret of Barcelona, said no in these words:

He [the former apostate who has returned] does not require immersion because he is not a convert (*de-l'av ger hu*) who would require this to elevate him from his [former] gentile status (*me-goyyuto*) because he was both conceived and born outside of the sanctity of Jewish identity. But this Jew who became an apostate to a non-Jewish

---

[119] The basis for halakhic leniency for returning Marranos is Maimonides, *Mishneh Torah*: Yesodei Ha-Torah, 5.4. Cf. *Encyclopedia Talmudit* (22 vols., Jerusalem, 1946–1993), 2:65a, n. 48. For the general principle advocating leniency regarding acts committed under duress (*ones*), see B. Baba Kama 28b re Deut. 22:26.

[120] See B. Baba Kama 94b; also, B. Eruvin 69b.

[121] Cf. R. Israel Isserlein, *Teshuvot Terumat Ha-Deshen*, 1, no. 241. R. Moses Isserles, *Darkhei Mosheh* on *Tur*: Even Ha'Ezer, 7.

[122] See n. 58 above.

religion, his conception and birth were inside the sanctity of Jewish identity; therefore, he does not require immersion. For even a convert to Judaism (*ger*) who was circumcised and immersed, if he reverted to his gentile ways (*le-goyyuto*) and then took on Judaism again (*ve-hazar ne-nityyahed*), even he does not require immersion [again].[123]

It is important to note how R. Solomon uses identical terms in the same passage both *de jure* and *de facto*. On the *de jure* level, neither the native-born Jew nor the convert is able either to become a gentile *de novo* or to become a gentile once again. But on the *de facto* level, both transformations are certainly possible.[124] Therefore, for his purposes here, R. Solomon uses the terms literally when speaking *de jure*, but figuratively when speaking *de facto*. And in another responsum on the same subject, R. Solomon orders a ceremony where the returner makes a public commitment to keep the commandments (*divrei haverut*).[125] The point here is that immersion implies that the former apostate *really* left the covenant, which is not true *de jure* (which is the Jewish religious reality), whereas a public ceremony of commitment (for which there is a rabbinic source) implies that the returner only left Jewish practice but not the covenant per se.[126] As in the case of conversion, covenantal theology largely determines the law here too.

The last matter that we need to examine in analyzing the significance of apostasy for the indelible election of Israel by God and her perpetual covenant with God is the contemporary phenomenon of Jewish converts to Christianity who still consider themselves part of the Jewish people. Some of them even

---

[123] *Teshuvot Ha-Rashba*, 5, no. 66. Cf. *Otsar Ha-Ge'onim*: Yevamot, 111–112; R. Joseph ibn Habib, *Nimuqei Yosef* on *Alfasi*: Yevamot, ed. Vilna, 16b; Isserlein, *Teshuvot Terumat Ha-Deshen*, 1, no. 86; R. David ibn Abi Zimra, *Teshuvot Ha-Radbaz*, 3, no. 858; R. Moses Isserles (Rema) on *Shulhan Arukh*: Yoreh De'ah, 268.12.

[124] Re the propensity of converts to return to their gentile ways, see B. Kiddushin 17b; B. Avodah Zarah 64a.

[125] *Teshuvot Ha-Rashba*, 7, no. 411. For another "reentry" procedure, namely, shaving the entire body of the returned apostate and the halakhic problems it entails, see R. Jacob Reischer, *Teshuvot Shevut Ya'aqov* (Jerusalem, 1971), 3, no. 90 re R. Shabbtai Ha-Kohen, *Siftei Kohen (Shakh)* on *Shulhan Arukh*: Yoreh De'ah, 268.7, and R. David Ha-Levi, *Magen David (Taz)* on *Shulhan Arukh*: Orah Hayyim, 531.7. The earliest source I have been able to find for this procedure is Hizquni, *Commentary on the Torah*: Num. 8:7 (cf. Rashi thereon).

[126] See T. Demai 2.5 and Bekhorot 30b.

consider the religion they are now practicing to be Judaism.[127] This is very much a *novum* in Jewish history, at least since the early Christians separated themselves or were themselves separated from the rest of the Jewish people. At least for the past seventeen hundred years or so, when Jews converted to Christianity, they no longer considered themselves to be part of the Jewish people any more. As such, their conversion was as much a social and political act as it was a religious act.

The claims of these new Jewish-Christians (who sometimes call themselves "Messianic Jews" or some similar name) have caused a good deal of consternation in the contemporary Jewish community. For in the past, both Jews and Jewish apostates agreed that the apostates were no longer functioning members of the Jewish community. And it was the Jews who made a claim on them that the apostates denied, namely, that the apostates were still part of Israel despite their apostasy; they were still Jews, albeit very bad ones. Now, however, it is the Jewish converts (or at least some of them) who are making a claim on the Jewish community to include them still. Many in the Jewish community have been unprepared for claims such as this, because past experience with apostates has been the exact opposite. The earlier claim was to be let go, not to be allowed to remain. In fact, more often than not, most Jews have assumed that the stated religious motives of Jewish converts to Christianity have been a rationalization of an essentially social and political act, one motivated by the advantages of being part of the larger powerful majority rather than being part of the much smaller and much weaker minority.

The claims of the new Jewish-Christians have become a uniquely legal problem in the State of Israel. For there, one's citizenship is both a relation to the secular state and also a relation to a "national" community (*le'umiyut*). That is, the majority of Israelis are both Israelis *and* Jews, and members of other communities are Israelis *and* Christians or Israelis *and* Muslims, etc. Several important cases have been brought

---

[127] See D. Novak, "When Jews Become Christians," *First Things* (November, 1991), 17:42ff.

before the Israeli Supreme Court (*bet ha-mishpat ha'elyon*) in which Jewish converts to Christianity have claimed Israeli citizenship and the recognition that they are still functioning members of the Jewish nation.[128]

In a recent case of this type, the court ruled against such a claim. However, even though the legal conclusion was unanimous, there were both a majority and a minority decision. That is, the reasoning of all the justices was not the same. The minority opinion based itself on sociological considerations. It argued that for all intents and purposes, common opinion is that a Jew is a Jew and a Christian is a Christian. One cannot claim to be a member of both communities.[129] To use a Talmudic term, these justices "followed after ordinary human language" (*ahar lashon benei adam*). But the majority of the justices, to use the converse of this Talmudic term, "followed after the language of Jewish tradition" (*ahar lashon torah*).[130] In their opinion, even though the Jewish-Christian is still to be considered part of Israel in the ontological sense, there is more than ample basis in the halakhic tradition of denying communal rights and privileges (*zekhuyot*) to those Jews who have adopted a religion separate and distinct from Judaism.[131] In other words, in a case involving the most important inter-Jewish question today, that is, Who is a Jew? (*mi hu yehudi*), the Supreme Court of an officially secular state had to adopt the legal reasoning of the Jewish *religious* tradition, reasoning that what we have already seen is heavily influenced by covenantal theology. Even in a secular Jewish context, the question of the election of Israel can never be permanently precluded. At most, it can be merely bracketed for a time.

After this analysis of some of the theological developments of the doctrine of election by the Rabbis as theologians, and the legal developments of it by the Rabbis as jurists, we can proceed to examine the two major philosophically influenced constitutions of the doctrine by medieval Jewish theologians.

---

[128] See Moshe Silberg, *Ba'in K'Ehad* (Jerusalem, 1981), 381ff.
[129] *Jerry Lee and Shirley Beresford* vs. *Interior Ministry* (1988), p. 36 (typescript).
[130] See B. Nedarim 49a.   [131] *Beresford*, pp. 46–47 (typescript).

CHAPTER 6

Two medieval views of election

TIME AND ETERNITY

The doctrine of the election of Israel, both as originally presented in Scripture and then developed by the Rabbis, is only philosophically cogent if one assumes that it designates a temporal relation. Real choice involves two or more objects being present to the elector and that one of them is elected at a certain time as distinct from any other time. The freedom that choice presupposes ("unfree" choice being a contradiction in terms) makes choice a practical rather than a theoretical issue. It is the concern of the realm of politics, taken in the broad classical sense that denotes the locus of free and purposeful public action between persons. It is not the concern of the realm of science per se, which describes the necessary behavior of entities.[1]

Accordingly, election is historical, that is, it is a humanly remembered temporal event, characterized by freedom rather than by necessity. And, even though I have argued elsewhere that there are natural limits that must be recognized *a priori* in order for there to be communities in which covenantal history

---

[1] Some of the views on temporality expressed here, especially the assertion of the temporality of God, would seem to suggest an affinity to those followers of the philosophy of A. N. Whitehead known as the "process theologians." However, there are two major differences between us. First, the relationship of consciously effecting and being effected is confined to to the historical relationship between God and man. Second, God is not part of the creative order of nature; he is *creator ex nihilo*. Cf. Whitehead, *Process and Reality* (New York, 1929), 219ff.; 263.

may occur and be sustained, these limits only make that history possible; it itself cannot be reduced to these limits as mere instantations of perpetual natural law. These natural limits are the *conditio sine qua non* of covenantal history, not its *conditio per quam*.[2] History as the arena of free personal action involves novelty in a way that nature does not. For in our constitution of nature, we see time as one continuum extending from past to present to future: the realm of causality. But in our constitution of history, we see radical gaps between present, future, and past: the realm of freedom. Freedom can only function in this latter temporal order.[3] It is only this sort of ontology, one that sees the primacy of divine historical activity for humans followed by their practical activity in response to it, and one that sees science (and even its furthest extension into meta-physics) as tertiary to them both that can enable one to retrieve philosophically the fundamental Jewish doctrine of election.[4]

In this ontology, both God and Israel are temporally related. The difference between them is that Israel, like any creature, is ultimately engulfed by death as the personal dissolution that time entails for her, whereas God is not engulfed by it. Thus the time of Israel as a creature is limited (finite); the time of God as creator is unlimited (infinite). God as infinite existence (which is not at all the same as Eternal Being) is coeval with time, whereas finite creatures are transcended by time. For this reason, a notion of human immortality (as opposed to the doctrine of the resurrection of the dead) destroys the essential difference between man and God and ultimately absorbs man into God.[5] Nevertheless, God only transcends the mortal, finite time of all creatures; he does not transcend time itself in the way he certainly transcends space.

---

[2] See D. Novak, *Jewish Social Ethics* (New York, 1992), 29ff.

[3] See pp. 25–26 above. Cf. Martin Heidegger, *Being and Time*, trans. J. Macquarrie and E. Robinson (New York and Evanston, 1962), 372ff. for the notion of time as ecstatic, i.e., discontinuous and, therefore, (at least) humanly experienced as the open realm of freedom, not a closed realm of causality. Cf. also Henri Bergson, *Time and Free Will*, trans. F. L. Pogson (New York, 1910), 222ff. for the notion of time as more than a coordinate of space.

[4] See Novak, *Jewish Social Ethics*, 16–17.

[5] See Appendix 3; also, Hizquni, *Commentary on the Torah*: Exod. 3:14.

For time in this sense is duration: that in which a sequence of events occurs. Thus all existence is temporal.[6] Even creation itself can be considered an event in the life of God – although obviously not in the life of man, because it is God's pre-historical experience.[7] Space, on the other hand, is external inasmuch as it can be constituted as something apart from the experiencing subject.[8] Thus all existence cannot be confined to space.[9] This is manifested by thought, which when it is creative is not *located* but *locating*.[10]

[6] I think Maimonides gets himself into a theological quandary when he asserts the doctrine of *creatio ex nihilo* while insisting simultaneously that time too is "a created thing" (*mi-khlal ha-nivra'im*) in *Guide of the Perplexed*, 2.13, trans. S. Pines (Chicago, 1963; Hebrew trans. of Samuel ibn Tibbon), 281. Here he follows Aristotle's scientific view that "time is consequent upon motion" (*ibid.*) without, however, following Aristotle's metaphysical conclusion of the eternity of celestial motion, namely, "that there exists a certain matter that is eternal (*qadmon*) as the deity is eternal; and that He does not exist without it, nor does it exist without Him" (*ibid.*, 283; cf. *Physics* 251b10ff.) He differs from Aristotle because Aristotle's view correlates God and matter in such a way as to compromise the absolute transcendence of God: "For the purpose of every follower of the Law of *Moses and Abraham our Father* or of those who go the way of these two is to believe that there is nothing eternal in any way at all existing simultaneously (*qadmon im Ha-Shem yitbarakh*)" (*ibid.*, 285). Nevertheless, if creation is not itself a temporal act/event because time is totally correlated with space and thus itself something created as is space, then how is God's transcendence of his creation anything more than logical priority (which itself cannot be taken as free) rather than real priority (see *Guide*, 2.30)? What else could it be, in Maimonides' view, not being either spatial or temporal? Cf. R. Isaac Abra-banel, *Rosh Amanah*, chap. 16, who senses the problem but who, nevertheless, refuses to criticize Maimonides directly.

[7] Note Kant, *Critique of Pure Reason*, B50, trans. N. Kemp Smith (New York, 1929): "Time is nothing but the form of inner sense, that is, of the intuition of ourselves and of our inner state" (p. 77).

[8] Note *ibid.*, A27: "we can indeed say that space comprehends all things that appear to us as external, but not all things in themselves, by whatever subject they are intuited, or whether they are intuited or not" (p.72).

[9] The rabbinic dictum: "He is the place of his world (*meqom olamo*), but the world is not his place (*meqomo*)" (*Bere'sheet Rabbah* 68.9 re Gen. 28:11, ed. Theodor–Albeck, 777–778 and see note thereon) is certainly using the spatial term "place" as a metaphor. It is essentially asserting the absolute priority of God to the world: the world needs to be related to God, but God need not be related to the world. Thus God *locates* his world whenever he so wills or chooses, but he is never *located* in that world. See I Kings 8:27–30; II Chron. 2:4–5.

[10] There is a perennial philosophical debate over whether thought is prior to language or language to thought. In the case of man, Scripture teaches that language is prior to thought. Humans do not attain the level of thought until they are addressed *in situ*: "And the Lord God took the man and placed him (*va-yannihehu*) in the Garden of Eden . . . and the Lord God commanded man saying (*l'emor*)" (Gen. 2:15–16 – see *Targumim* thereon; also, Gen. 3:9; 22:1; Exod. 3:4; I Sam. 3:4; Isa. 6:5). "Natural"

Moreover, as I have noted already, the unlimited time of God is not the same as "Eternal Being," as that idea has been constituted by philosophers since the time when philosophy arose in Greece.[11] In Biblical-Rabbinic Judaism, it makes no sense to speak of eternity. Even God is not eternal but, rather, *everlasting*. An *eternal* God, in the classical philosophic sense of unchanging and hence unresponsive Being, bears little or no resemblance to the creator God who associates himself with Abraham, Isaac, and Jacob and their progeny, who, in the unforgettable characterization of my late revered teacher Abraham Joshua Heschel, is a "God of pathos."[12]

However, there is one strand of rabbinic theology from which it seems one can infer otherwise, that is, it seems to suggest that the election of Israel does entail the idea of eternity. Although I shall first argue against this inference, in this chapter I shall show thereafter how the Greek idea of eternity did influence the theories of the election of Israel proposed by two of the most important Jewish philosophical theologians in the Middle Ages: Judah Halevi and Moses Maimonides. I shall finally argue that their respective views involve serious problems both theological and philosophical, especially for Jews attempting to retrieve the ancient doctrine at this juncture in our history.

The late Israeli rabbinics scholar Ephraim E. Urbach astutely located two different rabbinic views of the election of Israel. The first view he called "cosmic-eternal (*nitsheet*)," defining it as one that teaches that "the election of Israel was conceived together with the creation of the world," thus making it "something absolute (*le-muhletet*) and not contingent

---

languages emerge from particular locations and never wholly transcend them. "Artificial" languages are only abstractions from natural languages and are not in any way "transcendental" (see Ludwig Wittgenstein, *Philosophical Investigations*, 2nd ed., 1.18, trans. G. E. M. Anscombe [New York, 1958], 8). But in God's case, conversely, since Scripture teaches that he is prior to space (hence to any and all places), his thoughts do precede his creative utterances (see Isa. 55:8) "For He commanded and they were created. He made them [the heavenly bodies] stand for the duration of the world (*l'ad l'olam*); He put down an order (*hoq*) that will not change" (Ps. 148:4–5; cf. Ps. 33:9).

11 See appendix 3 below.
12 See *The Prophets* (Philadelphia, 1962), 221ff.

on any stipulations (*be-tena'im*) whatsoever." The second view he called "historical-relative (*yahaseet*)," defining it as one that teaches that election is "connected to stipulations and conditions (*u-ve-nesivot*), and in which the people fulfills an active role wherein it is also the elector (*ha-boher*)."[13] This second view, to be sure, forms a much stronger precedent for the understanding of the rabbinic view of election and its practical consequences, which was put forward in the previous chapter, than does the first. But what about the first view? Is it one that the theological argument of this book thus far must turn away from? Or, is it one that does not really imply an ontology of eternity as some scholars seem to think?

The cosmic-eternal view of the election of Israel is ascribed to the teaching of the second-century CE sage Rabbi Akibah by Urbach. He sees the *locus classicus* of this teaching in R. Akibah's famous dictum, "Beloved are Israel who are called God's children ... Beloved are Israel because the vessel through which the world was created was given to them."[14] This expresses the view, itself having precedents in earlier Hellenistic Jewish theology, that both Israel and the Torah are primordial entities.[15] From this type of assertion, it is an easy inference, for anyone who has studied classical philosophy, that is, to assume that Israel and the Torah are essentially eternal and not temporal in truth.

This inference, however, entails serious theological and philosophical problems. What does one do with the numerous passages in the Torah, both narrative and legal, that are clearly historical? And what does one do with the obvious contradiction between eternity and free choice?[16] Do not

---

[13] *Hazal* (Jerusalem, 1971), 468–469. See also Solomon Schechter, *Some Aspects of Rabbinic Theology* (New York, 1936), 59–60.

[14] M. Avot 3.14.

[15] See Urbach, *Hazal*, 469, citing IV Ezra 6:56–59. For the issue of preexistence in general and of the Torah specifically, see H. A. Wolfson, *Philo* (2 vols., Cambridge, Mass., 1947), 1:182ff.; also, Louis Ginzberg, *The Legends of the Jews* (7 vols., Philadelphia, 1909–1938), 6:30, n. 177.

[16] For the theological problem, see Maimonides, *Mishneh Torah*: Teshuvah, 5.5. Cf. R. Hayyim ibn Attar, *Or Ha-Hayyim* on Gen. 6:5; also, D. Novak, "Self-Contraction of the Godhead in Kabbalistic Theology," in *Neoplatonism and Jewish Thought*, ed. L. E. Goodman (Albany, 1992), 311ff.

virtually all the narrations and commandments of the Torah assume that there is human responsibility? But can there be human responsibility without free choice, which, as we have just seen, itself presupposes temporality?

Nevertheless, there is a possible solution to these problems, problems that are so central to the philosophical retrieval of the doctrine of election, and this solution can be derived from the rabbinic tradition itself without the addition of metaphysical assumptions that seem to be inconsistent with biblical–rabbinic doctrine.

The solution comes from an appreciation of the rabbinic notion of retroactivity (*bereira*). In this notion, something that is stipulated at a certain time after it has subsequently come to be is considered to have been so beforehand. In other words, it is retroactively projected back to the past *as if* it had *always* been the case.[17] The *locus classicus* of this notion is found in this passage in the Mishnah concerning the way one may stipulate the limited domicile one must establish before the Sabbath for the Sabbath about to come. "One may stipulate (*matneh*) his Sabbath domicile (*eruvo*) and state . . . if a sage has come to the east, let my Sabbath domicile be in the east; if from the west, let it be in the west."[18] Since one is only allowed to walk within the precincts of a town and a surrounding radius of two thousand cubits (*tehum*), and one can only have one real domicile, without this stipulation one might not be able to walk far enough to hear a particular sage preach on the coming Sabbath.[19] So, if one establishes his possible domicile both two thousand cubits east of the town and similarly west of the town, he can then choose which is his real domicile when he finds out on that Sabbath itself just where the sage he wants to hear preach is actually preaching. After he makes this discovery, it is as if he had originally made this desired stipulation alone, and it is as if he never made the undesired stipulation at all.

Furthermore, the same logic is applied more theologically in the case of marriage. On the one hand, it is a consistent

---

[17] See *Encyclopedia Talmudit* (22 vols., Jerusalem, 1946–1993), 4:217ff.
[18] M. Eruvin 3.5.
[19] See B. Eruvin 51a re Exod. 16:29.

rabbinic teaching that marriages are "made in heaven," that is, somehow or other they are preordained by God. But what about the free choice of the marriage partners themselves that is a legal prerequisite to a valid marriage covenant? And what about those marriages that do not endure but end in divorce? The usual explanation of this paradox is that when the marriage does endure for the right reasons, then it is *as if* it had been preordained all along (*le-mafre'a*), even before the married parties themselves came into the world.[20]

The point here is that once a significant decision has been made and has been sustained, it is almost impossible to conceive what the world would be like if the decision had not been so made.[21] When it comes to the election of Israel by God and the giving of the Torah to her, which are events of such cosmic significance (especially as we saw in chapter 4), it is understandable how R. Akibah and his school would be inclined to use language of this type. Indeed, in the continuation of his statement about the primordial character of Israel and the Torah, R. Akibah makes the enigmatic statement: "everything is foreseen (*tsafui*), but choice (*reshut*) is given."[22] The interpretation of this statement might well be that even though everything has been planned by God in advance in the sense that his purposes are before him, these purposes require the human choice of the covenantal partner Israel to cooperate in their realization. Only thereafter can one speak of what was *fore*seen. And along these lines, the fifteenth century Spanish exegete and theologian R. Jacob ibn Habib noted in discussing the notion of the Torah as primordial, which seems to contradict the doctrine of *creatio ex nihilo*, that this notion can be inter-

---

[20] See, e.g., B. Sotah 2a; *Bemidbar Rabbah* 3.4. For a full discussion of this issue, see D. Novak, *Law and Theology in Judaism* (2 vols., New York, 1974, 1976), 1:7ff. Also, one can see miracles in the same retroactive sense. See, e.g., M. Avot 5.6; B. Pesahim 54a.

[21] This logic has similarities to Aristotelian potency-act logic, i.e., what actually exists in the present retroactively indicates what its potentiality was in the past (see *Physics* 201a15). But viewing potentiality in the present is only viewing a possibility, and it does not predict with certainty even if it will be actualized in the future (see *Metaphysics* 1050b10). Cf. D. Novak, *Jewish–Christian Dialogue* (New York, 1989), 132ff.

[22] M. Avot 3.15.

preted to mean that the giving of the Torah (and the election of Israel as its correlate) reflects the purpose (*sibah takhliteet*) the full realization of which God already had in mind originally when he created the world.[23]

If this interpretation is correct (or, at least, plausible), then the two rabbinic views that Urbach delineated can be reconciled after all. The election of Israel is a historical event, contingent on temporal factors, as we have seen; however, without the emphasis of its primordial status, election could be seen as a merely local event, one having only parochial significance. Instead, though, its full significance must be correlated with God's relationship with his entire creation, with the world as a whole.[24] As such, it must be connected to the very inception of creation itself. And without this cosmic emphasis, the eschatological dimension of the covenant, the final redemption, becomes little more than a one-dimensional political event.

Nevertheless, it is also plausible that the teaching of R. Akibah and his school on election and the nature of the Torah is compatible with the philosophical idea of eternity, an idea that became very attractive to a variety of later Jewish theologians who had studied Platonic and Aristotelian philosophy. It is the assumption of this compatibility that lies behind the generic agreements between Halevi and Maimonides in the ontology they assumed in their respective theological constitutions of the traditional doctrines of election and Torah, despite the considerable differences in their specific interpretation of these correlated doctrines.

WILL AND CHOICE IN HALEVI

The early Zionist theorist Ahad Ha'Am (d. 1927) was typical of a number of modern Jewish scholars when he noted about Judah Halevi that "he recognized the character and value of the chosenness of Israel (*behirat yisra'el*) and made it the foundation of his system (*yesod le-sheetato*)."[25] And the leading Jewish

---

[23] *Ein Ya'aqov* (3 vols., New York, 1953), intro.   [24] See pp. 115–138 above.
[25] "Shinui He'Arakhin" (1898), in *Kol Kitvei Ahad Ha'Am*, 2nd ed. (Jerusalem, 1949), 157.

historian of recent times, Salo Baron, was just as typical when
he noted Halevi's "serene allegiance to history and the long-
range forces of destiny high above the ... forces of nature."[26] If
both of these characterizations were true, we could easily see
Halevi as a traditional rabbinic theologian, someone who gave
renewed expression to the ancient doctrine of the election of
Israel, and someone who anticipated modern historicism.
However, a closer examination of what Halevi himself actually
said on the subject of the election of Israel will lead us, I think,
to see him as a more independent thinker, one for whom
neither history (a word he himself never actually used) nor the
election of Israel – at least as we have come to understand these
ideas today – is foundational.[27] What was foundational for
Halevi was a realm above that of ordinary nature (that is, a
supernature), a realm in which the people of Israel in their
relationship with God are central.

The key to grasping Halevi's authentic view of the role of
Israel in the real cosmic order can be seen in two closely
connected ontological passages in his theological masterwork,
the *Kuzari*. There he writes,

God, may he be exalted, wills (*rotseh*). For everything that has
proceeded from him, it is possible (*efshar*) that it could be opposite, or
not have proceeded at all ... This agrees with the opinion of the
philosophers ... The will (*ratson*) of God is absolutely prior (*qadmon*)
and is consistent (*u-mat'im*) with his wisdom. As such, nothing happens
to it all of a sudden (*mithadesh*), nor is there any change in it.[28]

26 "Yehudah Halevi: An Answer to an Historic Challenge," *Jewish Social Studies*
   (1941), 3:272.
27 Although I cannot agree with his wholesale dismissal of philosophical method for
   the understanding of Judaism, I think that the late Max Kadushin was correct
   when he said about Halevi, "He has a conception of God, therefore, quite like that
   of the medieval Jewish philosophers" (*The Rabbinic Mind* [New York, 1952], 282).
   Indeed, in one of his poems, Halevi says, "The Servants of time (*zeman*) are the the
   servants of servants; the servant of the Lord, he alone is free" ("Helqi Adonai," in
   Selected Religious Poems of Jehudah Halevi, ed. H. Brody [Philadelphia, 1924], 121).
   God is thus contrasted with temporality. Almost any rationalist theologian of that
   period could have said the same thing.
28 *Kuzari*, 5.18. I translate from the Hebrew text of Y. Even-Shmuel (Tel Aviv, 1972),
   p. 220. I am most grateful to my friend Prof. Barry S. Kogan for his several
   suggestions for translation based on his own forthcoming translation of the Judeo-
   Arabic text of *Kuzari*. I am also grateful to him for his many suggestions regarding
   the argument of this section.

Soon afterwards, Halevi differentiates between will, in the primordial sense he has described just above, and choice (*behirah*). He places this definition in a full ontological context. "Actions are divine (*elohiyyim*) or natural (*tiv'iyyim*), accidental (*miqriyyim*) or chosen (*behiriyyim*)." Note that the two extremes are divine acts at one end and chosen acts at the other. Divine acts are those performed by no other cause (*sibah*) than "the will of God." Chosen acts, by clear contrast, are those whose cause is "the will of man at the time (*sha'ah*) it is found in the situation of choice (*be-matsav ha-behirah*)." And it is "within this domain (*be-tehum zeh*) that there is perpetual possibility (*tamid ha-efsharut*)."[29]

From these ontological passages, it seems quite clear that choice is temporal – historically situated – whereas the primary will, which is none other than the divine will, is not. To speak of God's will, then, is to speak of God's consistent transcendence of the world. God's will is primary in the sense that God himself is not subordinate or even coequal with anything else. But this very transcendence means that the ordinary world of creation is one that he does not really ever enter himself, but, as we shall soon see, it is a world that he does allow and enable some of his creatures to transcend at least partially too. Accordingly, the difference between the possibilities before God and the possibilities before man, for Halevi, is that the possibilities before God are merely logical, whereas the possibilities before man are realities. For this reason, human choice involves *a posteriori* responsiveness, something that cannot be posited of the will of God, which is always primordial: ever causing but never effected. The fact that temporal events are the result of this primordial divine will entails the philosophical problem that goes back to Plato's constitution of the primordial nature of eternity: How does mutable time emerge from immutable eternity?[30] Also, this constitution of will without real choice, and the absence of responsiveness that it entails, might well explain the virtual absence of a theory of covenant

---

[29] *Ibid.*, 5.20, p. 222. Re the uses of "will" in Halevi's thought, see A. Nuriel, "The Divine Will in the *Kuzari*," *Jerusalem Studies in Jewish Thought* (1990), 9:19ff.

[30] See *Timaeus* 37Eff.

in Halevi's theology in the *Kuzari*.[31] Thus one could say that for Halevi God *willed* Israel's existence *pre*historically, but not that God actually *chose* Israel *within* history.[32]

Choice, then, is something that is human, not divine. The question that must now be addressed is how this human choice is involved in the unique cosmic status Halevi assigns to the people of Israel.

It must be remembered that the *Kuzari* is written as an exposition of and argument for "the despised religion," which was the status of Judaism in the eleventh-century world of Judah Halevi. In this work, Halevi is defending Judaism against five different despisers: (1) pagans, (2) philosophers, (3) Christians, (4) Muslims, and (5) Jewish biblical literalists (Karaites), who rejected the Rabbinic Judaism of the majority of the Jews. By far the most important despisers not only to defend Judaism against but to argue with for its superiority are the philosophers.[33] Paganism, of which Halevi seems to think Hinduism is the most ancient (and thus the most formidable) variety, is dismissed as itself having no consensus regarding the written record of revelation and hence no coherent theology.[34] Christianity and Islam are quickly dismissed as being mere derivatives of Judaism inasmuch as they base the veracity of their respective revelations on the original revelations to the Jews.[35] As for the Karaites, they are trapped in the inconsistency of denying tradition but having to admit that Scripture itself is only intelligible when there is a tradition of interpreting it.[36]

The *Kuzari* is a dialogue between the pagan king of the nation known as the Khazars and a Rabbi. The effect of this dialogue is to persuade the king to convert to Judaism, and subsequently to bring the rest of his kingdom along with him.[37] That, of course, is a fundamental human choice. The great

[31] When Halevi speaks of *berit* in *Kuzari*, 1.34, p. 70, he does not develop its implications of real mutuality between God and man.

[32] See Y. Silman, "Ha-Ta'amim Ha-Shitatiyyim Le-Rayon Behirat Yisra'el Be-Sefer Ha-Kuzari," *Sinai* (1977), 80:260.

[33] See Leo Strauss, "The Law of Reason in the *Kuzari*," in *Persecution and the Art of Writing* (Glencoe, Ill., 1952), 103.

[34] *Kuzari*, 1.61.   [35] *Ibid.*, 1.4, 9.   [36] *Ibid.*, 3.35ff.   [37] *Ibid.*, 2.1.

bulk of the dialogue is to explain to the king the main tenets of the Judaism to which he has converted. This is usually done by answering the astute questions the king asks about those aspects of Judaism that seem puzzling or even irrational.

What brings the king to the quest that ends in his conversion to Judaism and integration into its teachings is a troubling dream that he keeps having in which he is told by an angel: "your intention is pleasing (*kavvanatekha retsuyah*) to God, but your action (*ma'asekha*) is not pleasing."[38] This is troubling to the king because he used to be "very zealous (*zaheer m'od*) in keeping the commandments (*mitsvot*) of the Khazar religion."[39] Therefore, his task is to correlate thought and action in a truly satisfying way. Since intention as directed thought is ultimately a philosophical matter, it stands to reason that the first person the king consults in his quest is a philosopher. For it would seem that a philosopher, who best understands intention's true finality, which is the knowledge of God as the absolute, should be best able to teach the king how to make his action consistent with thought. What is being addressed here is the classical philosophical question of the right relation between practical excellence and theoretical excellence, that is, the connection between the true and the good. This is especially important inasmuch as the inquirer is a king, a man who has political responsibility. Indeed, it would seem that Halevi had Plato's ideal of the philosopher-king in mind when developing this character in his dialogue.[40]

However, the philosopher's answer to the king is very disappointing. For he limits intelligent human choice to opting for the *vita contemplativa*, that is, "always to (*tamid*) choose (*li-vhor*) truth."[41] As for the *vita activa*, he merely says, "Do not be concerned (*al tahush*) by which means you worship God."[42] As for morality per se, he simply advocates that "you conduct yourself and your household and your land with good qualities (*be-middot tovot*)."[43] This being the case, the philosopher has not correlated thought and action; he has, rather, made action

---

[38] *Ibid.*, intro., p. 1.   [39] *Ibid.*
[40] See Strauss, *Persecution and the Art of Writing*, 114.
[41] *Kuzari*, 1.2, p. 4.   [42] *Ibid.*   [43] *Ibid.*

almost arbitrary. But if any reasonable course of action will do, then why is the king's present course of pagan action unacceptable? Is not his intention – his philosophical quest – something that should make his action acceptable already?

This inability to correlate practical and theoretical excellence is a particular failing of Aristotelian philosophy. Aristotle himself simply indicated that those who are truly involved in the *vita contemplativa* are so far removed from the concerns of ordinary human life in society as to be useless politically.[44] However, for Plato, there is the insistence that somehow or other the true philosophers can also be effective political leaders. In his more optimistic moments, Plato insists that the political effectiveness of the philosophers is not only in spite of their contemplative concern but because of it.[45] However, even though Plato emphasizes the rational character of philosophy, he has to admit that the realization of the vision of the philosophical polity will only take place through "some divine inspiration."[46] Only the divine factor, the *tertium quid*, as it were, can insure that there will be a human situation in which practical excellence and theoretical excellence will be fully correlated. But, alas, Plato was never able to see such a correlation brought into reality.[47]

With this in mind, we can now appreciate Halevi's rejection of the inadequacy of philosophy for the fullest human life with God and man. About this he says, "Considering the deeds of the philosophers and considering their knowledge, considering their quest for truth (*dorsham et ha'emet*) and considering their personal effort (*hishtadlutam*) in this matter, it should have been the case (*min hara'ui*) that prophecy became manifest and present among them owing to their attachment to spiritual things (*ha-deveqim be-ruhaniyyim*)."[48] Now, why is it a self-

---

[44] *Nicomachean Ethics* 1177a25–30.
[45] See, e.g., *Republic* 473D; also, D. Novak, *Suicide and Morality* (New York, 1975), 21ff.
[46] *Republic* 499B.
[47] For Maimonides' attempts to constitute a more cogent connection between theoretical and practical/political excellence, see *Guide of the Perplexed*, 3.54; also, D. Novak, "Maimonides' Concept of Practical Reason," in *Rashi 1040–1990: hommage à Ephraim E. Urbach*, ed. G. Sed-Rajna (Paris, 1993), 615ff.
[48] *Kuzari*, 1.4, p. 5.

contradiction of philosophers that they have never become prophets? Is it prophecy that their efforts intend? The answer is no if the intent of philosophers is to be philosophers in Aristotle's mold, that is, philosophers who are only really concerned with the *vita contemplativa*. But if the intent of philosophers is to be philosophers in Plato's mold, that is, those who strive to unify the theoretical and the practical, then the answer is yes. For as Maimonides emphasized less than a century later, largely following the Arab Platonist Alfarabi, the prophet is one who most thoroughly combines theoretical and practical excellence and is able to use this integral combination to rule best.[49]

THE SUPERNATURAL STATUS OF ISRAEL

Even though the true and good fulfillment of human life is the prophetic combination of theory and practice, this combination is more than the synthesis of these two human elements. Prophecy is a reality, not just a catalyst, and it is a reality that must come from a superhuman source and be operative in a supernatural realm.[50] In constituting this supernatural realm, Halevi traces a progression from the level of nature (understood as the bare minimum of life on earth) to the level of the ensouled (understood as those living beings possessing locomotion) to the level of the rational (*ha'inyan ha-sikhli*). Interestingly enough, what characterizes the rational realm is not theoretical but practical reason.[51] Finally, there is the level of the divine presence (*ha'inyan ha'elohi*). This level is the knowledge of the divine governance of the universe, and it is a matter that can only come from God himself.[52] It is something which is

---

[49] See *Guide of the Perplexed*, 2.36ff.; 3.27; also, Leo Strauss, "Quelques remarques sur la science politique de Maimonide et de Farabi," *Revue des Etudes Juives* (1936), 100:1–37.

[50] See *Kuzari*, 1.98; 2.50; 3.23; 4.3, 15.   [51] *Ibid.*, 1.31ff.

[52] For discussions of this key term in Halevi's theology (= *amr ilahi* in Arabic), see Julius Guttmann, *Philosophies of Judaism*, trans. D. W. Silverman (New York, 1964), 427, n. 151; I. Efros, *Studies in Medieval Jewish Philosophy* (New York and London, 1974), 14–145; H. A. Wolfson, *Studies in the History of Philosophy and Religion*, ed. I. Twersky and G. H. Williams (2 vols., Cambridge, Mass., 1977), 2:60; and, esp., Shlomo

given to the prophets qua prophets, but not something which the prophets as humans could ever have discovered for themselves or even inferred from the data of the ordinary world.

The level of the divine presence is something that is, therefore, apart from anything else in the world, even the world that can be apprehended by the highest levels of human reason. Indeed, this level was the original state of humans at the time of their creation. Thus in quoting the words of Genesis 1:28, "Let us make man in our image (*be-tsalmenu*) according to our likeness," Halevi addresses the obvious question of who the "us" are to which Scripture is referring in the creation of humans.[53] His answer that the "us" refers to God and the angels has rabbinic precedent, but his use of that precedent is more than just repetition of tradition.[54] It is recontextualized into the edifice of his own theology.

> This means: I am he who has made creation hierarchal (*she-higdarti et ha-yetsirah*) and have followed wisdom's arrangement from the primary elements ... to those beings that possess keen senses senses and marvelous instincts. Now there is no higher level than that except the level (*madregah*) which is close to the divine–angelic class (*ha-sug ha'elohi-ha-mal'akhi*). So did God create man in the form (*be-tsurat*) of his angels ... at their rank.[55]

Nevertheless, even though this was the beginning of human creation, when humans were privileged with direct connection to God and his will, the transmission of this connection with the divine was not the patrimony of all the children of Adam. Halevi points out that in each subsequent generation it was only a privileged few who received the divine wisdom.[56] However, when the children of Jacob became constituted as a people, the divine presence (*ha'inyan ha'elohi*) became the patrimony of an entire group, one which was constituted to preserve it as a spiritual and political reality, in the world but not of it.[57]

Pines, "Shi'ite Terms and Conceptions in Judah Halevi's *Kuzari*," *Jerusalem Studies in Arabic and Islam* (1980), 2:165ff.

[53] For further discussion of this point, see D. Novak, *Law and Theology in Judaism* 2:108ff.; *Halakhah in a Theological Dimension* (Chico, Calif., 1985), 96ff.

[54] See B. Sanhedrin 38b; Rashi, *Commentary on the Torah*: Gen. 1:26; also, Ginzberg, *Legends of the Jews*, 5:69–70, n. 12.

[55] *Kuzari*, 4.3, p. 162.   [56] *Ibid.*, 1.103.   [57] *Ibid.*, 1.25.

The important point to note here is that Halevi does not regard election itself, that is, the point in history when Israel receives the revelation from God, to be the origin of Israel's unique relationship with God. Her uniqueness is not purely relational, as it is for Scripture and the Rabbis. Instead, her uniqueness is substantial. That is, Israel already has a divine potential. What the event of revelation does is to actualize that potential by making all the people prophets (at least for the moment at Mount Sinai). Unlike Scripture and the Rabbis, Halevi does identify the element in Israel by virtue of which she was chosen by God.

And I shall tell you the nobility of this people ... For God chose them (*otam bahar*) for himself to be a people and a nation distinct (*mi-bayn*) from all the nations of the world. And this is because (*ve-khi*) the divine presence dwelled (*hal*) in the multitude of them so that all of them were fit (*r'uyyim*) to hear the divine word ... but before them [in history] the divine presence only occurred in those individuals to whom this special treasure (*segulah*) had passed from the first man.[58]

Thus it is not a mere possibility that is realized at Sinai. For that possibility does not contain its own realization; in fact, a possibility is only retroactively inferred after the event in which it is realized. But in the case of Israel, it is her divine potential that is being actualized; and it is certainly a divine potential of which she has been aware all along. Such a potentiality can have only one actualization, just as such an actualization can have only one potentiality.[59] The event at Sinai is the moment when Israel comes into her own substantial uniqueness. Furthermore, this means that Halevi's use of the term "choice" (*behirah*) must be taken metaphorically. For, as we have seen, a true choice entails two or more real options before the elector. But if that is the case, what other options did God have, since Israel's divine potentiality is already part of the created order? For, as we have seen, God's options are only logical, and they are only options before not after creation. Therefore, God's "choice" of Israel is not so much a choice as it is an inevitability of creation, the culmination of what began with his pri-

[58] *Ibid.*, 1.95, p. 31.   [59] See n. 21 above.

mordial and absolute will at the moment of the creation of the world. After that time, however, there are no more possibilities, even for God – that is, if one consistently follows the ontology that Halevi employs in his theology.[60]

What this designation of the substantial uniqueness of Israel leads to is that Halevi must now constitute the Jewish people as a species essentially separate from the rest of humankind. So when the king asks the sage why God did not give the Torah to all humankind, the sage answers that this would be like asking animals to have the power of speech.[61] In other words, because of the specific superiority of humans over animals, what is appropriate for the higher species is just as inappropriate for the lower species. He then continues,

> As I told you the divine presence was with an individual in every family, who was the one with most potential (*gar'in*) among the brothers and having the ancestral treasure (*u-segulat ha'av*) ... until the children of Jacob came, all of whom were a potentiality and a treasure, and they were separated from the rest of the children of man, having divine characteristics (*be-tekhunot elohiyot*) so that all of them were made as if (*k'ilu*) they were members of another species (*min aher*), one that is angelic (*mal'akhi*).[62]

Thus it is not a historical relationship (history being nothing but the sum total of all personal relationships that have been transmitted) that distinguishes Israel. It is her actualization as an entity separate and distinct from the rest of humankind, who themselves can only rise to the level of reason, that is, become philosophers. Israel can produce more than philosophers: she can produce prophets, because she is in essence supernatural.

Now, there does seem to be one prominent rabbinic precedent for this seemingly radical theological conclusion of Halevi. It is important for us to examine it now to see how close it is to Halevi's theological constitution of the *nature* of Israel.

"R. Simon ben Yohai says that the graves of gentiles do not cause defilement in an enclosure (*einan metam'ain b'ohel*) as Scrip-

---

[60] See appendix 4.   [61] *Kuzari*, 1.102–103.
[62] *Ibid.*, 1.103, p. 39. Cf. *ibid.*, 3.17.

ture states, 'For you My flock, flock that I tend, are men (*adam atem*)' (Ezekiel 34:31): you are called men, but the gentiles are not called men.'"[63] In the context of the original passage from Ezekiel, the meaning of this might very well be: Even though Israel enjoys a very special relationship with God, she must still recognize that she is ever human and never divine. *Adam* in biblical Hebrew much more often than not is used to remind humans who entertain illusions of their own invulnerability that they are still lowly creatures in comparison to God.[64] In the case of Israel, it is to remind her that even her election does not remove her from the creaturely status of all humankind. But in the context of the rabbinic passage just quoted, *adam* is taken to be a term of elevated differentiation. Israel, then, has a unique substantial status.

At this point, however, it is well to remember that the statement of R. Simon ben Yohai is made in a halakhic context, not a theological one. Accordingly, one should also recall the rabbinic principle of halakhic exegesis that posits: "A general principle (*kelal*) is limited to the specific example (*perat*) it characterizes."[65] In the case before us, this means that the substantial difference proposed by R. Simon ben Yohai is limited to certain questions of religious purity and impurity. The statement may be interpreted to mean that issues of religious purity are uniquely Jewish and, therefore, Jews and gentiles must be regarded as essentially different – in this context at least.[66] But even if R. Simon's view has wider

---

63 B. Yevamot 60b–61a. See *ibid.*, 103a–b.
64 See, e.g., I Sam. 15:29; II Sam. 24:14; Isa. 31:3; Ezek. 28:2, 9; Ps. 39:6–7; Job 5:7; also, *Midrash Mishlei*, 8, ed. Buber, 29b.
65 *Sifra*: Va-yiqra, ed. Weiss, 2a.
66 It must be emphasized that this is only the view of R. Simon (see B. Baba Batra 58a, Tos., s.v. "metsayyen"). Furthermore, even Maimonides, who accepts his halakhic conclusion (*Mishneh Torah*: Tum'at Met, 1.13), does not base it on R. Simon's reasoning concerning *adam*. Moreover, Rabbenu Tam questions R. Simon's whole line of reasoning and sides with the opposite opinion of the sages (see B. Yevamot 61a, Tos., s.v. "v'ein" and Nahmanides, *Hiddushei Ha-Ramban* thereon re M. Ohalot 18.9, and on B. Baba Batra 58a). See also R. Israel Lipschütz, *Tif'eret Yisra'el*: M. Avot 3.14 (Bo'az); M. Guttmann, *Das Judenthum und seine Umwelt* (Berlin, 1927); D. Novak, *The Image of the Non-Jew in Judaism* (New York and Toronto, 1983), 265ff. Cf. T. Eruvin 5.19 and Saul Lieberman, *Tosefta Kifshuta*: Mo'ed (New York, 1962), 404–405.

meaning, it must be remembered that he was teaching at the height of Roman persecution of the Jews and Judaism, and that his generally negative view of the gentiles is well evidenced.[67] Accordingly, his statement can be historically qualified to a certain extent.

It would seem, though, that Judah Halevi did take a view quite similar to the view of R. Simon ben Yohai taken theologically, that is, Israel is a species separate and distinct from the rest of humankind.[68] But there is one considerable addition. That addition is due to the mediation of philosophy in Halevi's theology.

It will be recalled that philosophy's usefulness for theologians is twofold: in the area of theoretical reason, and in the area of practical reason. In the area of theoretical reason, philosophy's service to theology is that it cogently affirms God as the absolute and helps us remove any literal anthropomorphisms from our religious discourse. When Halevi is dealing with the subject of what we today call "God-talk," he readily employs philosophical reason qua metaphysics.[69] In the area of practical reason, philosophy's service to theology is that it cogently affirms a natural-law morality, that is, it acknowledges that there are certain essential political structures necessary for a society worthy of integral human allegiance, and that these structures are known to ordinary (that is, nonprophetic, even nonmetaphysical) human reason.[70]

What theology does, because it is based on supernatural revelation, is twofold. First, it adds a whole new and higher dimension to both the *vita contemplativa* and the *vita activa*. Second, it provides specific details about both God and morality that unaided human reason, confined as it is to generalities, cannot obtain for itself.[71] Thus philosophy provides a floor for

[67] See B. Shabbat 33b.
[68] In the Kabbalah, the ontological distinctiveness of Israel is a major theme; however, the kabbalists go even further than Halevi. For them, Israel is not just a separate created species, but is actually part of the Godhead itself. See *Zohar*: Bere'sheet, 1:20b; Emor: 3:104b; R. Judah Loewe (Maharal), *Gevurot Ha-Shem* (Cracow, 1582), chap. 44; R. Hayyim ibn Attar, *Or Ha-Hayyim*: Gen. 1:27.
[69] *Kuzari*, 2.1ff.   [70] *Ibid.*, 2.48.
[71] *Ibid.*, 1.24; 3.7. See R. Joseph Albo, *Iqqarim*, 1.8.

theology, so to speak. It indicates the bottom limit below which theology cannot cogently go; but it does not provide a ceiling for theology, an upper limit. The heights to which theology on the wings of revelation can soar are not held down by any philosophical gravity.

For this reason, Halevi cannot argue that the Jews possess any inherent theoretical or moral superiority over the rest of humankind.[72] Virtue will be rewarded by God when done by any human being.[73] The only thing he can argue is that prophecy, the most immediate link possible between the divine and the human, is unique to Israel. On the basis of this substantial differentiation of Israel from the rest of humankind, he also argues that like any other unique nature, Israel requires special environmental conditions in order to fulfill its inherent potential, in her case, the potential for prophecy. That is how he assigns special substantial status to the land of Israel.[74] And, if prophecy is something that all Jews inherently seek, then it stands to reason why at the end of the dialogue in *Kuzari*, the sage takes his leave of the king of the Khazars and departs for the land of Israel, the only land by nature (that is, supernature) in which prophets can prophesy – a departure that Halevi himself was to replicate personally at the end of his own life.[75]

There is another factor in Halevi's theology of election that makes the separation of Israel from the other nations not seem like a form of misanthropy. That factor is Halevi's comparison of the relation of Israel to the nations with the relation of the heart to the rest of the body. He argues that just as the heart feels the pain of the rest of the body most intensely, so does Israel bear the sorrows of the world most intensely.[76] Thus her suffering in this world is not just her particular historical lot; it has cosmic significance. (And it also has the effect of purifying

---

[72] See Guttmann, *Philosophies of Judaism*, 127.

[73] *Kuzari*, 1.111. See R. Judah Moscato, *Kol Yehudah* thereon, who sees Talmudic basis for this view of Halevi in B. Sanhedrin 105a re Ps. 9:18 (the opinion of R. Joshua), and similarity to the view of Maimonides, *Mishneh Torah*: Teshuvah, 3.5 (also, Edut 11.10; Melakhim, 8.11).

[74] *Kuzari*, 1.95, 99. Cf. *ibid.*, 1.1.   [75] *Ibid.*, 5.27–28.   [76] *Ibid.*, 2.36ff.

her by making the least spiritually fit members of the people fall away.[77]) Furthermore, Halevi sees Israel's presence among the nations as having ultimate historical effect on them too. His biological analogy (his favorite type) is that of a seed planted in foreign elements, which in its continued growth transforms these foreign elements into itself.[78] In this process, Halevi like Maimonides after him assigns a special mediating role to the two "daughter" religions of Judaism: Christianity and Islam.[79]

The *Kuzari* was written not only as a defense of Judaism but also as an argument *for* it. The literary point of the dialogue between the Jewish sage and the king is to get the king to accept Judaism as the only sufficient solution to his human dilemma of how to live a coherent life with both God and his fellow humans, and for the king to grow in his newly acquired Jewish status. And, following this literary line, the theology of the book sees the culmination of history in the total conversion of humankind to Judaism. But if this is indeed the case, is it not quite odd that Halevi also insists that converts, no matter how sincere and perceptive, cannot themselves reach the level of prophecy, which is the unique human attraction of the Jewish people to begin with? The best that they can achieve, according to Halevi, is to become sages (*hakhamim*).[80]

The answer to this dilemma is, I think, connected to Halevi's views on choice discussed above. It will be recalled that God does not really "choose" in the way humans do. Humans do choose, however. Halevi has the philosopher in his dialogue speak of "choosing the truth."[81] As for human practice, this same philosopher talks about the desirability of human inventiveness, which is a recognition of the more innovative role of practical reason and its choices than obtains in

---

[77] *Ibid.*, 2.44.   [78] *Ibid.*, 4.23.

[79] *Ibid.* See Maimonides, *Mishneh Torah*: Melakhim, 11.4, uncensored ed.

[80] *Kuzari*, 1.27, 115. It has been suggested that this indicates that Halevi was not addressing his book to potential gentile converts to Judaism, but to Spanish Jewry in order that they might rededicate themselves to Judaism. See M. S. Berger, "Toward a New Understanding of Judah Halevi's *Kuzari*," *Journal of Religion* (1992), 72:224ff.

[81] *Kuzari*, 1.1.

theoretical reason (a point most fully developed later in the history of philosophy by Kant).[82]

Now it is precisely the fact that choice is such a human act that would make Halevi minimize its connection to the divine presence (*ha'inyan ha'elohi*) which distinguishes Israel. For even though, as we saw in the previous chapter, converts do not elect themselves to be Jews but are elected by a rabbinical tribunal acting *in loco Dei*, as it were, there is still more choice in their being Jews than is the case with those who are born Jews.[83] They can only *be converted* if they themselves first choose to convert. Thus if the covenant were essentially a matter of human volition, then it would seem that converts should have a higher status than native-born Jews. However, the covenant is a matter of divine volition and only one of human confirmation of that prior volition on God's part.[84] As such, converts are seen as if they are "born again"; native-born Jews, conversely, are not seen as if they chose to be Jews, that is, as if they are converts. That is why, it seems, the progeny of converts, but not converts themselves, can eventually become prophets. For they have *already* become part of the body of Israel, whereas their parents are still only grafted onto it.[85] This should dispel the notion that Halevi's theology of Israel has "racist" implications – at least in the modern sense of that loaded term. A racist theology could not tolerate the institution of conversion at all.[86]

RELATIONAL OR SUBSTANTIAL DISTINCTIVENESS

We have seen that Halevi puts considerable emphasis on the substantial distinctiveness of the Jewish people. I have also distinguished substantial distinctiveness from relational dis-

---

[82] *Ibid.* See also *ibid.*, 2.49.   [83] See pp. 177–188 above.

[84] See L. Bodoff, "Was Yehudah Halevi a Racist?," *Judaism* (1989), 38:177.

[85] For the difference between converts and the children of converts, see D. Novak, "The Legal Question of the Investigation of Converts," *Jewish Law Association Studies* (1987), 3:181ff. For a rabbinic debate whether converts are immediately integrated into Israel or whether it takes several generations, see B. Shabbat 146a (cf. B. Sanhedrin 94a). For Halevi's opaque views on this subject, see Bodoff, "Was Yehudah Halevi a Racist?," 180ff.

[86] Even in Kabbalah, where the ontological basis of Jewish distinctiveness is constituted more radically than in Halevi (see n. 68 above), conversion must be consti-

tinctiveness, the latter being what I consider to be the authentic biblical–rabbinic teaching. But what is the difference between the two? That is important to determine before I conclude this reflection on Halevi's theology of election by showing my main theological and philosophical problems with it.

In a situation of relational distinctiveness, the distinctiveness of the participants in the relationship is only meaningful in the context of the relationship itself. The best example is marriage, which is a model that plays a regular role in both biblical and rabbinic teaching. In a marriage deeply lived by its participants, the husband and wife believe themselves both chosen and choosing in unique ways, ways having a significance beyond the mere experience of *a* man and *a* woman. To and for each other, he is *the* man and she *the* woman. Moreover, in this profound situation, the husband and wife make very special demands on each other, demands that would be totally unreasonable if extended outside their own communion. But in their relations with the outside world, he is just a man and she is just a woman.[87]

So it is with the covenantal relationship between God and the Jewish people. In this communion, when the participants are living in mutual presence, God is *the Lord* (YHWH) and the Jewish people is *Israel*, both of which are unique proper names. But in relation to the rest of the world, God is the highest power and authority (*elohim*), whose distinction from the other powers and authorities in the world is one of degree, not one of kind.[88] As for Israel, in this relation she is just one people among many. In other words, the distinctiveness of both the Lord and Israel is not one that can be established by any external criterion. It is not something that could be demonstrated empirically to an uninvolved spectator. *Tertium non datur.*

---

tuted because it is such an integral part of halakhic tradition. However, like Halevi, the kabbalists emphasize the inequality of converts and native-born Jews. See *Zohar: Va-yiqra*, 3:14a–b; also, *Shelah*, 3:168a.

[87] See Franz Rosenzweig, "Divine and Human," trans. F. C. Golffing in N. N. Glatzer, *Franz Rosenzweig*, 2nd rev. ed. (New York, 1961), 243.

[88] See *Kuzari*, 4.3, 15.

However, Halevi wants to argue that the distinctiveness of Israel is empirically demonstrable. He locates that distinctiveness in the phenomenon of prophecy. Nevertheless, he has an empirical problem. Where are the Jewish prophets today? And, moreover, do the Jews appear to be any holier than other peoples?

Because prophecy has long ceased to manifest itself in Israel, Halevi has to base his current claims about Judaism on tradition *from* the prophets.[89] So he writes,

No one wherever can draw near to God, may he be exalted, except by means of the commandments of God, may he be exalted. And there is no entry (*mav'o*) to the knowledge of the commandments of God except through prophecy (*be-derekh ha-nevu'ah*), but not by means (*al yedei*) of reason or opinion ... Those men who through tradition (*be-qabbalah*) handed these commandments over to us were not lone individuals but were, rather, a great assembly, all of them great sages, who received it from the prophets. But in the absence of prophecy (*u-ve-he'ader ha-nevu'ah*), they received it from those who bear the Torah ... Since the days of Moses the tradition has never ceased in Israel.[90]

If, though, there is no longer immediate prophecy but only mediated tradition in Israel, then how is the Jewish people different from any other religious community grounded in revelation, that is, how is it different from the Christians and the Muslims? If all we are left with is traditions *from* prophetic revelation, then do not Christianity and Islam have traditions from prophetic revelation every bit as coherent as the tradition of the Jews? In other words, where is the demonstrable superiority of Judaism over Christianity and Islam? Even the earlier argument that Christianity and Islam base their claims on prior Jewish revelation is not very conclusive inasmuch as both Christianity and Islam claim that *their* respective *traditions* are closer to the essence of the *original* prophecy than is Jewish tradition. Since Jews make the same claims for their own tradition, and all we have are tradition*s*, there is hardly any way to demonstrate which tradition is true or even truer than the others.[91] Only an immediate revelation could possibly

[89] *Ibid.*, 3.24. [90] *Ibid.*, 3.53, pp. 139–140.
[91] See Novak, *Jewish–Christian Dialogue*, 17ff.

resolve this issue, and as Halevi admits about his epoch, quoting Scripture itself, "no vision (*hazon*) has sprung forth" (I Samuel 3:1).[92] Only a pagan religion like Hinduism, one without one authoritative revealed *book* and what seems (at least to Jews, Christians and Muslims) to be an incoherent tradition, comes off as being less plausible by comparison.[93] Therefore, the *Kuzari* has only really shown that religion*s* based on revelation and tradition, being forms of divine wisdom, are superior to philosophy, being a form of human wisdom, in relating humans to God (the theoretical concern) and humans to each other (the practical concern). For unlike pagan religions, these religions of revelation and tradition incorporate all the true strengths of philosophy and then transcend them. Nevertheless, Halevi has not demonstrated the superiority of Judaism, which is after all the original intent of his theological opus. He has only demonstrated the religious superiority of revealed religion per se over metaphysical philosophy.[94] (And in an age like ours, when most philosophers have long since lost interest in the "God question," Halevi's arguments have a largely antiquarian ring.)

Finally, concerning the question of the demonstrably greater holiness of the Jews, Halevi knows quite well that this cannot be demonstrated; in fact, it is doubtful that it can even be believed by anyone but a chauvinist, which he certainly was not. Moreover, since prophecy has long ceased to function, Halevi sees the burden of religion as resting on those who collectively can be termed "the saints" (*he-hasid*). They are the ones who are just below the level of the prophets, the ones whom the Talmud describes as being able to hear "the heavenly echo" (*bat qol*).[95] Not only are they the true leaders of Israel, but Halevi actually says about them that they are exemplified by

the man (*adam*) who affirms (*ha-modeh*) these things with a complete apprehension (*hakarah gemurah*), he is the true (*amiti*) Israelite. And it is right for him to aspire to becoming attached (*le-hitdabqut*) to the

[92] *Kuzari*, 3.1, p. 98.   [93] See *ibid.*, 1.61.
[94] See Strauss, *Persecution and the Art of Writing*, 140–141.
[95] *Kuzari*, 3.11. See, e.g., B. Eruvin 13^b re *bat qol*.

divine presence. He alone (*raq*) is attached to the children of Israel as distinct from (*mi-bein*) the rest of the nations.[96]

However, cannot Christianity and Islam make the exact same claims about their sages and saints? And, unlike the philosophers, who Halevi believes always function as isolated individuals, do not these "saints" – whether Jewish, Christian, or Muslim – form sacred communities respectively, which are physically part of the larger religious body, but for all intents and purposes separate from it spiritually?[97] Is this not, then, the insuperable problem of Halevi's attempt to give the Jewish people the status of a separate substance in the ontological sense?[98]

MAIMONIDES' INDIFFERENCE TO DISTINCTIVENESS

Despite the fact that he did more to represent Jewish law and theology than anybody else in history, and despite the fact that he has been the most widely revered postbiblical personality by the Jewish people, Maimonides did not assign any special ontological status to the Jewish people.[99] Because of this, he did not theoretically constitute the doctrine of the election of Israel, even though he did mention it when his representation of the tradition itself required it.[100] In other words, it was a part of the tradition he had received, but it was not part of the tradition that he chose to constitute theologically. In this section, we must discover why and how Maimonides came to place so little emphasis on the doctrine of election. For no full discussion of any Jewish doctrine can ignore what Maimonides

---

[96] *Ibid.*, 3.17, pp. 113–114.   [97] *Ibid.*, 3.1. Cf. *ibid.*, 4.3.

[98] For the Neoplatonic metaphysics that seems to underlie Halevi's substantialism, see Guttmann, *Philosophies of Judaism*, 130.

[99] See Menachem Kellner, *Maimonides on Judaism and the Jewish People* (Albany, N.Y., 1991), 81ff. Much of this section of the book has been influenced by Prof. Kellner's excellent study. For Maimonides' designation of certain acquired, not innate, virtues of the Jewish people, see, e.g., *Mishneh Torah*: Teshuvah, 2.10; Mattnot Aniyyim, 10.2.

[100] See, e.g., *Mishneh Torah*: Tefillah, 7.10; 12.5; Shabbat, 29.2. All of these examples are liturgical, i.e., where Maimonides has simply codified certain Talmudic formulations that must be kept intact (see B. Berakhot 40b and *Mishneh Torah*: Berakhot 1.5 and R. Joseph Karo, *Kesef Mishneh* thereon).

said – or even what he did not say. Finally, I shall attempt to argue just why Maimonides' position is even less defensible today than it was in his own time.

Despite the fact that Maimonides and Halevi are usually seen as opposite on just about every issue in Judaism, they both accepted the Platonic and Aristotelian notion of the eternity of God. For this reason, both of them can attribute will to God, but neither is prepared to attribute choice to God because, as we have seen, choice presupposes not only that God is the cause of the temporal realm, but that God actually enters into it, both to effect it and to be effected by it *from within*.[101] After this generic agreement, the specific disagreement between them is that Halevi sees the people of Israel as being a unique entity, having all the excellences of human nature plus excellences that could not have come from human nature. And because the Torah is what is given to them for their own sake, it too shares this unique status in the cosmic order created by God. There is a difference of kind between Israel/Torah and the rest of creation. For Maimonides, the difference between the Torah and the Jewish people on the one hand and the rest of creation – especially created humanity – on the other hand is one of degree, not one of kind.[102] By focusing on this ontological disagreement between Maimonides and Halevi as it pertains to the issue of election, we can see how the role each assigns to choice itself largely determines why Israel has the special status for the one that it does not have for the other.

For both Halevi and Maimonides, choice is something that characterizes the human condition more than anything else. Humans, being intelligent persons subject to the exigencies of time, are, therefore, required to make choices.[103] There is no way they can escape this burden – at least in this world. But for Halevi, as we have seen, the status of the Jewish people is not a

---

[101] See *Guide of the Perplexed*, 2.25; cf. *ibid.*, 3.26. Maimonides' use of the term "choice" (*behirah*), unlike his use of the term "will" (*ratson*), must be taken to be metaphorical. See *ibid.*, 2.48. Cf. *ibid.*, 3.17, where the distinction between *ratson* and *behirah* is more carefully maintained.

[102] Thus the Torah is the best, but not necessarily the only, "divine law." See *Guide of the Perplexed*, 2.35ff.

[103] See *Mishneh Torah*: Teshuvah, 5.1ff.

matter of choice precisely because it is something created for
them by God. Jews, either collectively or individually, have no
more choice to be Jews than any other species has a choice to
be what it has been made to be. Having human freedom,
however, the only choice Jews have is to pretend to be something that they are not, that is, to act (but not be) contrary to
their *created* status. That is why, as we have also seen, converts
do not fully become part of Israel in their own generation just
because their Jewish*ness* (as distinct from their adoption of
Juda*ism*) is still too much a matter of *their* own volition.

However, human choice does play a more important role in
Maimonides' theology because the primary initiation of the
relationship between God and man in this world is more
human than divine. This comes out in an illuminating
responsum of Maimonides.

The Talmud discusses the precise wording of the blessing
one is to recite in the morning before beginning the study of the
Torah, which itself is considered to be a daily requirement.
Three formulations are put forth, the second of which praises
God as the One who "teaches (*ha-melamed*) Torah to his people
Israel."[104] The conclusion of the final editor of the text is that
all three formulations are to be recited. But Maimonides argues
on purely theological grounds that this second blessing is not to
be recited "because God did not teach it [the Torah] to us, but
commanded us to study it and teach it. This derives from a
fundamental root of our religion (*banui al iqqar dattenu*),
namely, the performance of the commandments is in our
hands, that it is not something forced (*be-hekhreh*) upon us by
God either to do it or not to do it."[105]

Now, it seems that Maimonides is operating here with a very
Aristotelian notion of action.[106] That is, one must see four
principles at work in any intelligent human action. These four
principles have come to be known as: (1) the material cause;
(2) the efficient cause; (3) the formal cause; and (4) the final

---

[104] B. Berakhot 11b.

[105] *Teshuvot Ha-Rambam*, ed. Blau, 2:331–333 (no. 182). See Blau's note on p. 333. Cf.
Mishneh Torah: Tefillah, 7.10.

[106] See *Physics* 194b16ff.; *Metaphysics* 1044b1ff.; *Nicomachean Ethics* 112a20ff.

cause. In the case of a commandment of the Torah – especially one so central as the study of the Torah – the action to be performed can be broken down as follows: (1) the material cause is the content of the commandment as received from tradition; (2) the efficient cause is the person who chooses to do this specific act; (3) the formal cause is the anticipated relationship with God as originally given in prophetic revelation; (4) the final cause (*telos*) is the actualized relationship with God.[107] With this scheme in mind, we can now see that the choice to perform the commandment – to do the act – is the choice by the actor himself or herself of a *means* to an anticipated *end*. The commandment is both from God (*min ha-shamayim*) and for the sake of God (*le-shem shamayim*).[108] But the act itself can only be performed out of the free choice of the human person to whom and for whom it is addressed. In other words, actual choice can only be human and not divine. The efficient cause, in contrast to the three other causes, is always man and never God. That is why Maimonides insists that nothing in the Torah can be seen as contradicting the primacy of choice for humans. Anything that *seems* to do that must be explained figuratively, not literally.[109]

This view of human action is consistent with Maimonides' overall view of revelation. Now, initially, any discussion of revelation must emphasize that it is essentially an event. It happens at a definite time in a definite place. The question is: For whom is revelation an event? For many Jewish theologians, revelation is an event both in the life of God and in the life of Israel. It is only with this concept of revelation that one can constitute revelation as the foundation of a *covenantal* relationship *between* God and his people.[110] Accordingly, there is a history to their mutual relationship, and that history is something both parties share together. God appears to the

---

[107] See, e.g., *Mishneh Torah*: Shemittah Ve-Yovel, 13.13; Me'ilah, 8.8.
[108] See *Guide*, 2.35, 39; also, *Commentary on the Mishnah*: Sanhedrin, chap. 10, intro., principle 8, trans. Y. Kafih (Jerusalem, 1976), 143.
[109] See *Mishneh Torah*: Teshuvah, 6.1ff.
[110] See D. Novak, *The Theology of Nahmanides Systematically Presented* (Atlanta, 1992), 103–104, 110.

people to elect them, and out of this event the structure and content of the covenant – the Torah – emerges. But for Maimonides, this cannot be the case because God does not have a life in the sense of a temporal continuum. Thus there are no events in the "life" of God. The Torah, then, is essentially an expression of the eternal truth of God. It is something that those who are blessed with prophetic experience discover at a certain time in a certain place. The event of revelation, as distinct from its actual content, is a human experience, not a divine one.[111]

For this reason, Maimonides, most unlike Halevi, cannot confine prophecy to Israel. Prophecy is a possibility of human nature itself.[112] It is something that should ideally follow after the full exercise of ratiocination by humans, although even Maimonides must admit that there is a factor of grace involved in this final vision of the truth.[113] Nevertheless, what is necessary (although never wholly sufficient) for this exalted state to occur is the result of a series of rational choices by certain very gifted individuals. Prophecy, for Maimonides, is clearly the final object of human rational desire.[114] However, even though prophetic revelation is something that is, at least in principle, a human propensity, he is still a *Jewish* theologian who is committed to the superiority of Judaism to both philosophy per se and to the other two religions of revelation: Christianity and Islam.[115] But if that superiority is relative rather than absolute (as it is for Halevi), then, according to Maimonides, by what criterion is Jewish revelation to be preferred – that is, chosen – by rational persons?

The answer to this basic question comes out in this central text in his theological masterwork, the *Guide of the Perplexed*. The text concerns the essential difference between a law that

---

[111] The final *telos* of the commandments of the Torah is to attain the world-to-come, and Maimonides emphasizes that this is not "the world that is to come in time (*she'ayno matsui attah*)" but, rather, "that which is eternal (*matsui ve'omed*)," namely, being related to God in perpetual bliss (*Mishneh Torah*: Teshuvah, 8.8).

[112] See *Mishneh Torah*: Yesodei Ha-Torah, 7.1; *Guide of the Perplexed*, 2.36; also, Kellner, *Maimonides on Judaism and the Jewish People*, 26ff.

[113] *Mishneh Torah*: Yesodei Ha-Torah, 7.5; *Guide of the Perplexed*, 2.32.

[114] *Guide of the Perplexed*, 2.32.

[115] See, e.g., *ibid.*, 2.35.

can be termed "divine" and one that can only be termed "human."

If, on the other hand, you find (*ke-she-timtsa*) a Law all of whose ordinances are due to attention being paid, as was stated above, to the soundness of the circumstances pertaining to the body and also to soundness of belief – a Law that takes pains to inculcate correct opinions with regard to God ... and that desires (*ve-hishtadel*) to make man wise, to give him understanding, and to awaken his attention, so that he should know the whole of that which exists in its true form (*al tekhunat ha'emet*) – you must know that this guidance (*ha-hanhagah*) comes from Him (*me'itto*) ... and that this Law is divine (*elohit*).[116]

Now every traditional law, in one way or another, claims for itself a divine *origin*. In this respect, the Jewish Torah is no exception. Maimonides himself codifies that basic Jewish claim into the seventh and eighth of the thirteen dogmas he insists are indispensable in Judaism (the sixth of which is the insistence on the reality of prophecy per se).[117] But the chief factor making for a divine law is not its historical source (what we have seen functions as a material cause in Maimonides' theory of action) but its ultimate intent, its teleology (what we have seen is anticipated as a formal cause and actualized as a final cause).

A divine law, then, is the integral combination of norms that inculcate both practical and theoretical excellence. Only that combination can bring about the polity that is truly worthy of rational/social human nature. In stressing this possible combination, Maimonides has placed himself with Plato as opposed to Aristotle.[118] For, as we have seen, Plato is convinced that the theoretical life, essentially concerned with God, and the practical life, essentially concerned with human society, can be united in one person as in one community. Aristotle, on the other hand, is equally convinced that consistent attention to the theoretical life removes one from the arena of human society. The theoretical person (the philosopher per se) must still respect society as the place where ordinary people

---

[116] *Ibid.*, 2.40, pp. 38–384 (Hebrew text of Samuel ibn Tibbon).
[117] *Commentary on the Mishnah*: Sanhedrin, chap. 10, intro., pp. 142–144.
[118] See S. Pines, "Translator's Introduction," *Guide of the Perplexed*, lxxxviff.

fulfill their ordinary needs (and where even he or she still has some of these ordinary needs, however minimal). Furthermore, he or she must appreciate the fact that without first having practical excellence, which controls the passions, it is most unlikely that the theoretical person would have ever been attracted to the *vita contemplativa* and its intellectual concerns in the first place. Nevertheless, despite this respect and appreciation, the theoretical person cannot be truly engaged in society.[119] As such, he or she could hardly function as society's leader, which is the precise role Plato assigns to the philosopher, and which Alfarabi, Halevi (*mutatis mutandis*), and Maimonides assign to the prophet.

It is in this sense that Maimonides sees the superiority of Judaism. It is superior to philosophy because philosophy is unable to combine practical and theoretical excellence in any real society known heretofore. (Plato, it should be recalled, was a political failure.) But the Torah has been and is the constitution of the very real community of the Jews, a community that had a complete state and which Maimonides seems to believe could be imminently reconstructed under more favorable political circumstances.[120] And Judaism is superior to Christianity and Islam because of the theoretical shortcomings of the former and the practical shortcomings of the latter.[121] Christianity is theoretically inferior because of its doctrine of the Trinity, which compromises pure monotheism. And Islam is practically inferior because its law cannot measure up to the Mosaic Torah (that Torah which the Christians, conversely, do accept as the word of God). But because of affinities of these two "daughter" religions to Judaism, members of both are ripe candidates for conversion to Judaism. In fact, as I have argued elsewhere, Maimonides seemed to have been in favor of a form of proselytizing.[122]

---

[119] *Nicomachean Ethics* 1178b30ff.   [120] See *Mishneh Torah*: Melakhim, 11.3ff.

[121] See D. Novak, "The Treatment of Islam and Muslims in the Legal Writings of Maimonides," in *Studies in Islamic and Jewish Traditions*, ed. W. Brinner and S. D. Ricks (Atlanta, 1986), 244ff.

[122] See Novak, *Jewish–Christian Dialogue*, 59ff.

THE PRIMACY OF HUMAN CHOICE

Because of their association with the Torah, the Jews do have a privileged human position in Maimonides' view. But that is their only privilege.[123] It is a privilege that is almost entirely contingent on their making the right choices. For this reason, one can appreciate the prominent role Maimonides assigns to the convert, the person whose Juda*ism* (as opposed to his or her Jewish*ness*) is initiated by his or her choice to become a candidate for conversion.[124]

This primacy can be seen in Maimonides' codification of the Talmudic procedure for the reception of converts.[125] After reiterating the Talmud's stipulation that the candidate for conversion first be told of the precarious political situation of the Jews (to discourage those who might see conversion as having some material benefit), Maimonides perceives the beginning of the actual indoctrination of the would-be convert to consist of informing him or her of "the fundamental roots of the religion (*iqqrei ha-dat*), namely, the uniqueness of God (*yihud ha-shem*) and the prohibition of idolatry."[126] Now, there does not seem to be any manuscript evidence to suggest that Maimonides had an actual literary source for this prescription, one that does not appear in the text of the Babylonian Talmud as we have it today. Therefore, it is reasonable to assume that it is the result of his theological transformation of Halakhah in this important situation.[127] Furthermore, it seems to contradict his insistence elsewhere that the first two commandments of the Decalogue, concerning acceptance of the reality of God (and along with it his uniqueness) and the prohibition of idolatry, are evident to any rational person.[128] If so, then why does he make them appear to be something distinctly Jewish here?

Maimonides' theological transformation of Halakhah is also

---

123 See Kellner, *Maimonides on Judaism and the Jewish People*, 81ff.
124 See *ibid.*, 49ff.
125 B. Yevamot 47a–b.   126 *Mishneh Torah*: Isurei Bi'ah, 14.2.
127 See I. Twersky, *Introduction to the Code of Maimonides (Mishneh Torah)* (New Haven, Conn., 1980), 474–475.
128 *Guide of the Perplexed*, 2.33. Cf. *Mishneh Torah*: Yesodei Ha-Torah, 8.1ff.

evident in another departure from the text of the Talmud;
again another departure for which there does not seem to be
any manuscript evidence. He states that the would-be convert
is to be told, "know that the world-to-come is only held in store
(*tsafun*) for the righteous and they are Israel."[129] Furthermore,
this seems to contradict Maimonides' designation of the world-
to-come as a place where not only the righteous of Israel but
those of "the nations of the world" (*hasidei ummot ha'olam*) will
experience their final beatitude too.[130] Understanding the significance of these two departures from the traditional text of
the Talmud will help us better understand how Maimonides'
views on the role of human volition in the relationship with
God applied in the legal institution of conversion. The answers
to these questions help us to see how central voluntary conversion is to Maimonides' theological constitution of the Jewish
people.

As for the first question concerning belief in the uniqueness
of God and the prohibition of idolatry, even though these are
acts that can be expected of everyone in principle, they are acts
that form the foundation of the entire Mosaic Torah. It is the
Mosaic Torah that gives concrete expression to these two
principles. It is the Mosaic Torah that constructs the most
perfect monotheistic society possible in this world.[131] Thus
even though it is possible to be a gentile monotheist, it is more
than likely that a gentile living in a gentile society will be a
monotheist in spite of his or her society, not because of it.[132] In
other words, one is much more likely to be a consistent monotheist if one lives in a society where monotheism permeates
every aspect of communal and individual life.

As for the designation of the world-to-come being for Israel
only, one has to remember that this is being told to someone
who is converting to Judaism, someone who is already a monotheist. Therefore, there is no sense in telling such a person

---

[129] *Mishneh Torah*: Isurei Bi'ah, 14.4. See note of R. Zvi Hirsch Chajes (Maharats
Chajes) on B. Yevamot 47a–b.
[130] *Mishneh Torah*: Teshuvah, 3.5; Edut, 11.10; Melakhim, 8.11.
[131] See *Guide of the Perplexed*, 2.35.
[132] See Novak, *The Image of the Non-Jew in Judaism*, 115ff.

about the prospects for other-worldy salvation for *gentile* monotheists. If that were done, then the whole raison d'être of
conversion to Judaism would thereby be mitigated. At this
stage of his or her spiritual development, the would-be convert
is passing from a stage of abstract and practically partial
monotheism to one of concrete and practically complete monotheism. As such, it is only the choice to be included in this
complete monotheistic community and tradition that can be
addressed. But here as in the case before, the element of choice
is what is central. The convert is in essence being told about the
ends that the Jews themselves are supposed to be striving for.
One can conclude, therefore, that for Maimonides the volition
of the convert and its ultimate intentionality are the true
paradigms for the relationship of the Jewish people with
God.[133]

Maimonides' innovative approach to conversion can be
better grasped if we contrast it with the rabbinic teaching
expressed in the Talmudic text that he, in effect, theologically
transposed. For in that text, after the candidate for conversion
is told of the precarious condition of the Jewish people in this
world, his or her optimal answer is to be "I am unworthy" (*eini
ked'ai*).[134] Now, what sort of a response is that? It would seem
that the candidate is to accept that he or she is unworthy of
being chosen just as Israel is unworthy of being chosen. In fact,
the same phrase appears in a midrash that paraphrases Jacob's
admission that he is unworthy of God's grace: "I am too little
(*qatonti*) for all the kindnesses and faithfulness that You have
done with Your servant" (Genesis 32:10).[135] In other words, in
the original rabbinic version, the initiation of conversion is
divine, not human. The choice of the human being is to
respond to God's call, and this is despite the fact that there is no

---

[133] This comes out most strikingly in Maimonides' acceptance of one rabbinic opinion
(that of R. Judah) that a convert may recite the liturgical formula "our God and
God of our fathers" because all Jews are equally connected to Abraham himself,
and he was the first convert to monotheism/Judaism. See *Mishneh Torah*: Bikkurim,
4.3 re Y. Bikkurim 1.4/64a (cf. M. Bikkurim 1.4) and notes of R. David ibn Abi
Zimra, *Radbaz* and R. Judah Rozanis, *Mishneh Le-Melekh* thereon. See, also,
Teshuvot Ha-Rambam, 2:725–728 (no. 448); Twersky, *The Code of Maimonides*, 485ff.
[134] B. Yevamot 47a.   [135] *Bere'sheet Rabbah* 76.5.

reason for it if one follows the immediate criteria of self-interest in this world. The convert, like Israel herself, must accept the truth that the full reconciliation of the world with the reality of the covenant must come from the transcendent future (*olam ha-ba*). As the Talmudic text puts it: "At this time Israel is not able to receive either most of her reward or most of her punishment."[136]

Maimonides, of course, does codify the Talmudic phrase concerning being "unworthy," but his own emphasis is clearly on the initiating factor of human choice based on the universal criteria of monotheism.[137] That is why he prescribes that instruction in the commandments begin with matters of rational belief. For him, the choice in essence is human, not divine. For the Rabbis, on the other hand, immediately after the acceptance of election by the convert, he or she is informed of those commandments that are distinctly Jewish because, I think, they emphasize the truth that becoming part of Israel is an end in itself, that is, to be in covenant with God directly.[138]

THE QUESTION OF APOSTASY

Maimonides has been considered by much of posterity to have been the most consistent thinker in the history of Judaism. In fact, in many of the great centers of rabbinic learning in Eastern Europe, one's scholarly prowess was largely demonstrated by showing apparent contradictions among Maimonides' own statements, and apparent contradictions between Maimonides' own statements and those of the Rabbis themselves. One has to show that all these contradictions are only apparent and not real, and that incisive analysis can demonstrate that assumption.[139] Now, consistency is not difficult if one confines his or her attention to a small area of interest. But since Maimonides had something to say about every area of Judaism, his consistency was no mean achievement.

That amazing quality of consistency, which can only be the

---

[136] B. Yevamot 47a–b.   [137] *Mishneh Torah*: Isurei Bi'ah, 14.1.
[138] See pp. 187–188 above.
[139] See Twersky, *The Code of Maimonides*, 526ff.

virtue of an extraordinarily systematic thinker, is clearly evident in the connection between Maimonides' view of conversion and his view of apostasy. These are the two poles of Jewish identity: the way into Judaism and the way out of it. In both of these institutions, Maimonides posits the primacy of human volition.

After presenting the thirteen dogmas that he assumes are the *sine qua non* of Judaism, Maimonides concludes as follows:

When all these foundations (*ha-yesodot*) are perfectly understood and believed in by a person he enters into the community (*kelal*) of Israel ... Even were he to commit every possible transgression, because of lust and because of being overpowered by the evil inclination, he will be punished according to his rebelliousness, but he has a portion [of the world to come]; he is one of the sinners of Israel (*mi-posh'ei yisra'el*). But if a man doubts any of these foundations, he leaves the community (*yatsa min ha-kelal*) because he has denied the fundamental (*kafar b'iqqar*) ... One is required to hate him and destroy him.[140]

As the American-Israeli scholar Menachem Kellner points out in his study of Maimonides' views on Jewish identity: "That Maimonides took this theological answer to the question: 'Who is a Jew?' seriously is evidenced by the fact that he attaches to the acceptance of his principles the *halakhic* rights that Jews may demand of their fellows."[141]

Maimonides' refusal to include apostates, who deny willfully, in the same category as ordinary sinners, who sin more out of appetite than out of will, is illuminating.[142] We should contrast this view with the view of Rashi and other medieval halakhists, which was discussed in the previous chapter.[143] For they extend the Talmudic phrase "even though he sinned he is still a Jew" (*af-al-pi she-hata yisra'el hu*) to apostates. In other words, they refuse to acknowledge that *any* Jew can remove himself or herself from Israel willfully – at least in this world. Their view, as we have seen, although it is not the literal

---

140 *Commentary on the Mishnah*: Sanhedrin, chap. 10, intro., pp. 144–145 (trans. from Kellner, *Maimonides on Judaism and the Jewish People*, 5–60). Also, see Menachem Kellner, *Dogma in Medieval Jewish Thought* (Oxford, 1986), 21ff.

141 *Maimonides on Judaism and the Jewish People*, 60.

142 Cf. B. Avodah Zarah 26b; Hullin 5a; *Mishneh Torah*: Avodah Zarah, 10.1.

143 See pp. 191–192 above.

meaning of the Talmudic passage that it invokes, is still closer to the whole rabbinic teaching on Jewish identity than that of Maimonides typified by the above statement. For Maimonides, one can remove himself or herself from Israel even in this world and not just in the world-to-come.

However, it should be noted that even Maimonides cannot carry his own view of what we might term "volitional Judaism" to its full logical conclusion. For if that were the case, he would have to admit that one can opt for another religion *rather than* Judaism and actually be recognized as being a real member of that *other* religious community, however much such apostasy could not be done with impunity. To my knowledge, Maimonides never drew that conclusion. One can only see the apostate *as if* he or she were part of another religious community, but even that recognition is a *fictio juris*, and it is confined to some areas where the Halakhah assigns certain specific rights to Jews from their fellow Jews.[144] Such an option to change one's religious community is one he is only willing to allow to gentiles.[145] The weight of the overwhelming tendency of the Jewish tradition that allows no way out of Judaism for Jews is simply too ubiquitous to be interpreted otherwise, even by one as brilliant as Maimonides.

The assumptions behind Maimonides' avoidance of constituting the doctrine of election per se are even more problematic today than they were in his own time. They are problematic theologically, philosophically, and politically. Theologically, as we have already seen, they are problematic in terms of how much they depart from the tendency of the whole tradition, both Scripture and the teachings of the Rabbis. Philosophically, they are problematic because Maimonides sees the validity of Judaism in terms of its being the best combination of intellectual and practical excellence, a combination that is hierarchal: first *theoria*, then *praxis*. Yet, as I have argued

---

[144] See *Mishneh Torah*: Teshuvah, 3.14, where twenty-four types of sinners (including apostates, *ibid.*, 3.9) are still considered to be "of Israel" (*me-yisra'el*) and only "like a gentile" (*ke-goy* – *ibid.*, 3.12); also, see Shehitah, 4.14; Hovel U-Mazeeq, 7.6. Cf. p. 192, n. 105 above.

[145] See *ibid.*, Melakhim, 8.7; 10.9.

elsewhere, this assumption is based on a view of the hierarchal relation of metaphysics and ethics that itself presupposes an irretrievable Aristotelian natural science.[146] Intellectual excellence (*aretē*) is concerned with God, whose existence is demonstrated by a now irretrievable teleological physics. Without that foundation, however, the hierarchal superiority of *theoria* over *praxis* is lost, and their working combination is thereby lost as well. So, if one still wants a rationalist justification of Judaism in the modern world, it is better argued by Hermann Cohen than anyone else precisely because his view of God is not founded in such an irretrievable natural science. But, as we have already seen, Cohen's philosophy and theology themselves entail difficulties every bit as problematic for us today as those of Maimonides.[147]

The final and, I think, most serious problem for Maimonides' view of election is political. In Maimonides' own time, all societies were religiously grounded. The notion that one could live philosophically without allegiance to a historical religion was only a real option for lone individuals, and even these lone individuals would have had to hide their individual convictions carefully in order to remain part of the societies in which they too had to live.[148] However, by the time of Spinoza and the rise of *secular* states, such a dual life was no longer the only option.[149] One could practice the intellectual excellence of philosophy individually (and for Spinoza that still entailed a relation to God) and practical excellence socially, and neither way of life requires an allegiance to *any* historical religion any

---

[146] *Jewish–Christian Dialogue*, 67ff.; also, *Jewish Social Ethics*, 141ff. In the history of philosophy, there have been three major attempts to constitute this hierarchal relation of *theoria* and *praxis*, that is, where *praxis* is ultimately for the sake of *theoria*: those of Plato, Aristotle, and Spinoza. Aristotle's constitution is the most cogent and simultaneously the most vulnerable because unlike the other two it attempts to derive meta-physics from physics. Hence metaphysics has a demonstrably objective point of reference. In the case of Plato and Spinoza, the problem with their respective constitutions of this relation is that they can easily be dismissed as fanciful, subjective projections of an imagined reality onto the external universe. (Even Spinoza's claim to be reasoning *more geometrico* is based on an analogy to mathematics, not anything scientifically demonstrable.)

[147] See pp. 72–77 above.
[148] See Strauss, *Persecution and the Art of Writing*, intro.
[149] See pp. 46–47 above.

more. Hence historical religion is no longer the political necessity Maimonides thought it was.

In this uniquely modern reality of a secular political life,
Maimonides really has no satisfactory justification for
Judaism's unique role in the world. What is *now* still distinctive
about Judaism and the Jews in this world if we remain with
Maimonides' philosophical theology?

Despite the reverence for him that I share with virtually all
other traditional Jews, I cannot see how even his most devoted
contemporary disciples can derive an answer from his theology
to this overriding modern problem. Jews now have the real
option of being participants in anonymous secular societies in
the Diaspora, or being participants in their own secular society
in the State of Israel. And although it can be argued that either
of these two political options is consistent with adherence to the
historical Jewish religion, none of them (at least none of them
so far) can actually be *grounded in* historical Jewish religion. At
best, one can only argue that a foundation in *a* historical
religion offers one *a* better *approach to* the issue of political life
than a purely secularist one (and today such a secularist
approach is inevitably an atheistic one, which was definitely
not the case with Spinoza).[150] But one cannot argue that his or
her approach is *the* best approach now available, as Maimonides still could in his own time. So, at least at present, the
Maimonideans have no satisfactory answer to the Spinozists.[151]

---

[150] See Novak, *Jewish Social Ethics*, esp. chaps. 8–11.

[151] In our time, the late Leo Strauss, with his great philosophical ability, argued better
than anyone else for the plausibility of the Maimonidean political option. His
argument against Spinoza and his modern followers was that the liberal democracies, in which they placed such hope, do not have the inner strength to constitute a
virtuous society, nor do they have the inner strength to resist the public transformation of philosophy into statist ideology. Strauss seemed to suggest that a
society based on a revealed law could provide a better foundation for both
practical (exoteric) and theoretical (esoteric) excellence. Aside from the fact that
he could not suggest how such a society could ever be retrieved in the modern
world, and aside from the fact that he did not develop a *Gotteslehre* (as did
Maimonides and Spinoza) to constitute the *vita contemplativa*, his arguments are at
best plausible only for the political benefit of *a* revelation, but not for anything
singularly Jewish. (That probably explains Strauss' attraction for a number of
cultural and political conservatives today.) See his new introduction to the English
translation by E. M. Sinclair of his 1925 book, *Spinoza's Critique of Religion* (New
York, 1965), and his 1935 book, *Philosophy and Law*, trans. F. Baumann (Philadel-

But as we have seen at the beginning, the philosophical retrieval of Judaism itself, and especially the doctrine of the election of Israel, requires such an answer. We have thus come full circle. Our return to the sources must be more radical than a full stop in the Middle Ages.

phia, 1987), esp. 51ff. A Jewish response to Spinoza and his modern followers must, therefore, come out of a philosophical retrieval of more elementary Jewish sources, wherein we encounter the singular God of Israel, rather than out of Maimonides' own philosophical theology.

Conclusion

A happy alternative to the inadequacy of the secularist survivalism we have briefly examined in the introduction is the very recent attempt to renew discussion of the theology of Jewish identity by the contemporary Jewish thinker Michael Wyschogrod. Wyschogrod's work is an important revival and it is the work of a religiously committed Jew, one who is theologically serious and philosophically astute. It also comes closest to what I would consider to be the authentic teaching of Biblical-Rabbinic Judaism. Nevertheless, I do have some important differences with it. But because of the great similarity of our concerns, I want to discuss it at this point and then go directly into my own theological view on the subject.

In his recent book, *The Body of Faith: Judaism as Corporeal Election*, Wyschogrod forcefully argues for the centrality of the election of Israel. His basic point seems to be, in his own words,

Why does God proceed by means of election, the choosing of one people among the nations as his people? Why is he not the father of all nations, calling them to his obedience and offering his love to man, whom he created in his image? . . .

We must avoid an answer that does too much. Any answer that would demonstrate that what God did was the only thing he could have done or that it was the right thing to do would be too much of an answer. God must not be subject to necessity or to a good not of his making, and must not be judged by standards external to him.[1]

---

[1] *The Body of Faith* (New York, 1983), 58.

As Wyschogrod develops this key point, he invokes the
Buberian model of the I–Thou relationship. Like Buber, Wyschogrod maintains that such a relationship has no antecedents.
Nothing prepares us for it, let alone leads us into it. Unlike
Buber and more like Franz Rosenzweig, however, Wyschogrod
does see this relationship as having consequents, primarily the
Torah and its commandments.[2] In other words, like Rosenzweig and most unlike Buber, Wyschogrod sees an integral
connection between faith and law. God's election of Israel is a
presence, one that itself can lead to other factors, but one that
cannot be included in any larger whole.

The questions that now need to be addressed to Wyschogrod
are those that need to be addressed to any serious theorist of
election. They are: (1) How is this relationship between Israel
and God different from any other relationship between a
nation and its "god"? (2) How is this relationship connected to
God's creative relationship with the rest of the world,
especially all the other peoples? (3) How does the Torah
function in this relationship between God and Israel?

To begin with the last question, Wyschogrod clearly sees the
Torah as having been given for the sake of the election of
Israel, that is, it is the Torah which structures this relationship
and gives it true content.

> But the law is addressed only to Israel. It is not a universal law,
> obedience to which is expected of all peoples. Apart from the Noa-
> chide commandments, the Torah is addressed only to Israel . . . Israel
> is not the accidental bearer of the Torah. The Torah grows out of
> Israel's election . . . the Torah is not a demand that exists apart from
> the being of Israel.[3]

Along these lines, it is evident why Wyschogrod forcefully
argues against any suggestion that Jewish identity is contingent
on acceptance of the teachings of the Torah and the practice of
its precepts. Obviously, he believes that such acceptance and
practice enhance a Jew's sense of his or her election and give it

---

[2] See Buber, *I and Thou*, trans. W. Kaufmann (New York, 1970), 62–63; also,
pp. 86–87 above.
[3] *The Body of Faith*, 211.

meaning. Nevertheless, he seems to argue that the election of Israel is something *sola gratia* and is true even when Jews ignore the obligations of the covenant, even when they reject them.[4]

That is the reason why Wyschogrod insists on the total historicity of the Torah; it contains no natural law at all. Israel's election by God is the primary event and the giving/ receiving of the Torah is the secondary event, one that is for the sake of the continued meaning of this primary event. It is what makes this event found an unending process. In this view, there seems to be nothing primordial about the Torah. It is thoroughly within history, and history is always something local.[5] There is no *H*istory as some overarching cosmic category.

We have already seen that the difference between Israel's relationship with God and the relationship of any other nation with its "god" is that Israel's God is simultaneously the creator of the world.[6] Accordingly, there is a connection between the way one views God's relationship with Israel as its elector and the way one views God's relationship with the rest of the world as its creator. In fact, only this latter relationship enables Israel's relationship with God to be essentially and recognizably different from the relationship of any other nation with its "god."

In Wyschogrod's particular approach, indeed in the last quotation from his book, he refers to "the Noachide commandments." Inasmuch as he has given no indication that he advocates anything like natural law theory, one can only assume that he regards these Noahide commandments as just as historically contingent as is the Torah given to Israel. Both are the products of God's specific revelation in history. The doctrine of the Noahide commandments indicates the belief that God has not left the rest of the world without his governance, even after his election of Israel. God did not simply turn the rest of the world loose on its own, over to its own devices, as Deism and its cognates would have it. The question is: How is the revelation to the nations of the world related to the revelation to Israel?

[4] See *ibid.*, 174ff.   [5] See *ibid.*, 177–179.   [6] See pp. 115–138 above.

Wyschogrod himself does not raise this question. Nevertheless, it is very much implied by his theological typology and,
therefore, it can be raised and an answer attempted by someone
interested in the implications of his position on the election of
Israel, a position having precedent in Jewish tradition.

In a somewhat enigmatic passage, Wyschogrod does state,

And it is also true that a father loves all his children, so that they all
know of and feel the love they receive, recognizing that to substitute
an impartial judge for a loving father would eliminate the preference
of the specially favored but would also deprive them all of a father.
The mystery of Israel's election thus turns out to be the guarantee of
the fatherhood of God towards all peoples, elect and nonelect, Jew
and gentile.[7]

Looking at this passage in the context of his views on the total
historicity of revelation, one might say that God is related to
the gentiles *through* his relationship with Israel. What that
means is that the gentiles learn they too are the children of the
living God by accepting the fact that God's fullest relationship
is the one with Israel, which is presented and given normative
content in the Torah.[8] For that Torah also expresses God's

---

[7] *The Body of Faith*, 65.

[8] What Wyschogrod has overlooked, however, is the fact that in the Bible, God is only
called "father" directly in his relationship (although ultimately metaphorically: see
pp. 11–12 above) with Israel (see, e.g., Jer. 31:8) as Israel are called "children"
(see, e.g., Deut. 14:1) in their relationship with God. Even a favorite passage of
Liberal Jews, "Have we not one father, has not one God created us all?" (Malachi
2:10), concludes with an admonition to those who have "profaned the covenant of
our fathers" (*berit avoteinu*). Furthermore, the "father" mentioned here could very
well be Jacob, the progenitor of the people of Israel (see Ibn Ezra's comment
thereon; also, see comment of Ibn Ezra on Job 34:36; cf. comment of Rashi thereon).
And, finally, the reference to God as creator could very well be to God as the *creator of
the covenant with Israel* rather than as creator of the world (see Isa. 43:1). In other
words, God's relationship with the other nations is not one as intimate as that of a
father, but something else, namely, that of creator, judge, even benefactor (see, e.g,.
Ps. 148:5; 96:13; 145:9). That does not mean that God is not interested in the nations
of the world or is unconcerned with them. However, love is something that Israel
alone experiences in biblical teaching. Although some have seen oblique implications of God's universal fatherhood in some isolated biblical passages (see, e.g.,
Midrash Mishlei on Prov. 10:1 re Ps. 68:6, ed. Buber, 32b; Hizquni, *Commentary on the
Torah*: Exod. 4:22), the notion of God's love for the world seems to be more central to
the teaching of the New Testament (see John 3:16; also, Matt. 28:18–20). Cf.
pp. 121–123 above.

continuing concern with them, however secondary it might be. By acknowledging the truth of that relationship and appreciating at least some of its content in their own collective and individual lives, these gentiles can be subsequent participants in the covenant.[9]

That acknowledgment and appropriation, since it is totally within history, can only be consistently made by a prior acknowledgment that Israel is God's elect people and that she has received God's most direct and fullest revelation. Moreover, this revelation also includes norms by which these gentiles are to live in a less direct and more fragmentary relationship with God.

It would seem that the only gentiles who have ever made any such acknowledgment, however ambivalent they have so often been about it, are Christians. Only Christianity has accepted the historical truth of God's election of Israel and the revelation of the Torah to her, however much it has departed from Jewish interpretations and applications of it. Nevertheless, those Christians who are today attempting to come closer to the Jewish roots of their Christian faith, Christians with whom Michael Wyschogrod has been a major personality in intimate dialogue, seem to be prepared to acknowledge not only the necessity of Judaism for that faith but equally the continued primary presence of the Jewish people for it. Indeed, one can see the current theological project of the Protestant theologian Paul van Buren, which van Buren impressively presents as being about "the Jewish-Christian reality," as the Christian counterpart of Wyschogrod's theology of the election of Israel.[10] Thus this new Christian interest in the Judaism of the living Jewish people is the historical demonstration of a gentile response to God's concern for all of his creation, a concern that can only be understood and lived *through* a lasting contact with Israel as the elect of God.

[9] Cf. D. Novak, *Jewish–Christian Dialogue* (New York, 1989), 117–118.
[10] See *A Theology of the Jewish-Christian Reality* (2 vols., San Francisco, 1980, 1983), 1:132, 156.

THE CORRELATION OF ELECTION AND THE TORAH

Although his emphasis on the irreducibility of the election of Israel corresponds to much classical Jewish teaching, I cannot accept Wyschogrod's theory for two reasons: one theoretical, the other practical.

In classical Jewish teaching, there is a dialectic between a theology of grace and a theology of merit. On the one hand, God has chosen the people of Israel and that choice is clearly not due to any prior merit on Israel's part. It is *sola gratia*, as we have already seen in detail in chapter 4. But on the other hand, the covenant requires that the people of Israel merit it by keeping God's commandments in the Torah. Thus in spite of "even though Israel has sinned, she is still Israel," it has been recognized by normative Jewish tradition that there are cases when Jews can stray so far from the Torah that for all intents and purposes, they – and even more so their children and grandchildren – do indeed forfeit their election and its privileges.[11] In other words, Wyschogrod's biblicism and his effective subordination of the Torah to the Jewish people are not adequate to the genuine dialectic between grace and merit, between election and obligation, within classical Jewish teaching.[12] The Jewish people is at least as much for the sake of the Torah as the Torah is for the sake of the Jewish people.[13] Here there must be something about the Torah, for which they live as much as it lives for them, that is part of the prehistorical, created order.

If the Torah is only for the sake of Israel's election, then it

---

[11] See B. Kiddushin 68b re Deut. 7:4; B. Yevamot 17a and Meiri, *Bet Ha-Behirah* thereon, ed. Dickman, 91; pp. 189–197 above.

[12] For Wyschogrod's explicit biblicism, see *The Body of Faith*, xiv–xv. Yet he explicitly eschews Karaism, the Jewish version of *sola scriptura*, and sees Rabbinic Judaism as the authentic continuation of Scripture. Wyschogrod rightly insists that Jewish theology must be biblically rooted, even to the point of having to devise ontological categories consistent with it rather than relying on the categories of ancient or modern metaphysics that are inconsistent with it. With that premise, I am in full agreement.

[13] See *Kohelet Rabbati* 1.9 and *Midrash Ha-Gadol*: Bere'sheet, ed. Margulies, 245 re Isa. 65:22; also, M. Kadushin, "Some Aspects of the Rabbinic Concept of Israel: A Study in the Mekilta," *Hebrew Union College Annual* (1945), 19:7off.

could also be taken to be for the interest of her nationalistic self-interest. For if the people of Israel is the sole raison d'être of the Torah, there is no room left for any higher standard in it by which nationalistic self-interest can be judged. But clearly, the prophets of Israel taught otherwise. In their teaching, the Lord of nature and history judges Israel as he judges the whole world. Thus the standard of divine judgment (*mishpat*) must be seen as transcending what is being judged by it. "Do you say that the way of the Lord is not right (*lo yitakhen*)? Each man according to his ways shall I judge (*eshpot*) you, O House of Israel!" (Ezekiel 3:20) Israel is required to obey the Torah even if it is not in her nationalistic self-interest. So, the acceptance of the academy of Yavneh rather than the capital city of Jerusalem and its Temple by Rabban Yohanan ben Zakkai in the first century of the Common Era surely indicates that national sovereignty was very much qualified in order that the Torah might be supreme.[14]

The practical implication of assuming that the Torah is solely for the sake of affirming the election of Israel is to see no transcendent standard governing Israel's relationships with the nations of the world. The only relationship possible, then, is one where gentiles accept Jewish sovereignty and dominance, be it political or only "religious."[15] That does not mean, of course, that this theological stance necessarily leads to political programs where Jews are to dominate non-Jews coercively. Fortunately, in Jewish tradition, practice is not to be simply deduced from theory, especially from theology.[16] In cases where coercion is the issue, a variety of norms need to be considered before any final practical decision is made. Nevertheless, this type of theology can all too easily lend itself to such a practical program of coercive dominance. (A discussion of how this is actually the case in the correlation of nationalist politics and a type of religious Zionism and its theology today is

---

[14] See B. Gittin 56b.
[15] See Maimonides, *Mishneh Torah*: Melakhim, 8.10 and 9.14. Cf. Nahmanides, *Commentary on the Torah*: Gen. 34:13.
[16] See Y. Pe'ah 2.4/10a; *Otsar Ha-Ge'onim*: Hagigah, ed. B. M. Lewin (Haifa and Jerusalem, 1932), vol. 5, nos. 67–69.

beyond the purview of this book, however much it is in mind.) Indeed, a consistent proponent of it would have no theological arguments that I can anticipate with which to argue against such programs, however much he or she might be morally offended by them.

The only way out of this theological–political conundrum, it seems to me, is to constitute philosophically the doctrine of the election of Israel so that, at least in dialectical interaction, the doctrine of the revelation of the Torah is not reducible to it. It would seem that one has to search the tradition for a view of the Torah that applies equally, even if only on certain points, to both Israel and the nations of the world. Only such a discovery can save us from confusing – God forbid – the idea of the chosen people with the odious idea of a *Herrenvolk*, an idea whose adherents are directly responsible for our greatest agony in history. (A discussion of how election has been misused by many post-Holocaust Jewish thinkers is beyond the purview of this book, however much it is in mind.) Surely, recent Jewish experience, an experience that most of us are determined to share with the world, must also be a factor in formulating our theology.

PHENOMENOLOGY OF THE COMMANDMENTS: GOD, ISRAEL, AND THE WORLD

In the course of this study, I have tried to present the doctrine of election consistently in correlation with the doctrine of revelation. They are not identical because the Torah's concern with justice (*mishpat*) is general and not reducible to the singularity of election. This is the concern with the universal character of nature as created by God (*elohim*).[17] I have been critical of those views that seem to reduce even the universal aspect of revelation to election: the world to Israel, and those views that reduce singular election to universal revelation: Israel to the world. Both have appeared inadequate to me because both cannot constitute the full truth that the Jewish

[17] See R. Judah Halevi, *Kuzari*, 4.15.

observance of the commandments intends. In modern Jewish thought, I criticize Hermann Cohen for slighting election for the sake of universal revelation and Michael Wyschogrod for slighting revelation in its universality for the sake of the singularity of election.

It is now time to conclude this reflection of mine with a phenomenological constitution of the commandments and their intentionality. For it is here that we see the correlation of the singular and the general in the midst of the most authentic area of Jewish action and experience. It is here that we can see election in its essential correlations. The main referent of this concluding reflection is the most central covenantal observance, that of Passover.

In the book of Deuteronomy, when Moses is preparing the people of Israel for their imminent entrance into the Promised Land, he anticipates the following question that children will ask their parents about the commandments of the Torah: "What (*mah*) do these testimonies (*edot*), statutes (*huqqim*), and norms (*mishpatim*) mean which the Lord our God has commanded you?" (6:20).[18] In the Passover Haggadah this question becomes the all-inclusive question of the "wise son." In other words, it deals with the three basic types of commandments. It is the most important question any Jew can ask about Judaism.

The *mishpatim* are civil and criminal laws that justly govern interhuman relationships. According to the Rabbis, reason would have dictated them even if they had not been written in the Torah.[19] They are, nonetheless, seen as part of revelation because they participate in a larger covenantal context, one that reason could not dictate since it is rooted in unique historical events, not uniform universal processes (nature). In the case of Passover, one can see this concern for justice in the commandment given prior to the actual covenantal observance of the Passover event, namely, "and a woman shall ask

[18] The LXX has "commanded us (*hēmin/otanu*)," as do Y. Pesahim 10.4/37d and *Mekhilta*: Bo, ed. Horovitz–Rabin, 73. Cf. M. M. Kasher, *Haggadah Shlemah* (Jerusalem, 1967), 121.

[19] *Sifra*: Aharei-Mot, ed. Weiss, 86a; B. Yoma 67b re Lev. 18:4.

(*ve-sha'alah*) her neighbor and whoever dwells with her in her house for vessels of silver and gold ... and you shall despoil Egypt" (Exodus 3:22). Even though the end of the verse seems to imply that the Israelites could simply take whatever they wanted from the Egyptians at the time of the Exodus, some commentators have pointed out that the commandment itself prescribes a request not a threat, an exercise of right not might. Such elementary justice must not be violated even in appearance (since a case could be made that the Israelites had the right to take what they wanted because of the centuries of slavery).[20]

The *edot* are those laws which testify to covenantal events by symbolic celebration. They comprise that part of revelation that gives tradition its historical intentionality and continuity. They are most directly concerned with the election of Israel because they celebrate it.[21] Passover, of course, is the archetype of this type of celebration. All celebrations are considered "remembrances of the Exodus from Egypt" (*zeker yetsi'at mitsrayim*).

Finally, the *huqqim* are those laws having neither natural nor historical reasons, laws accepted because of God's authority alone. They are laws that have no analogues in the positive law of any other people.[22] Regarding Passover, one commentator notes that there are laws connected with it that have no ostensive reason, such as those that require that no bone of the

[20] See comments of Rashbam (ed. Bromberg, 81 and see n. 16) and Rabbenu Bahyah thereon.

[21] See Nahmanides, *Commentary on the Torah*: Exod. 13:11; Deut. 6:16, 20.

[22] See pp. 174–175 above; also, B. Sanhedrin 21b re Deut. 17:16–17; B. Shabbat 108a re Exod. 13:9 and Deut. 14:21; Y. Shabbat 3.3/6a; *Bere'sheet Rabbah* 44.1; *Bemidbar Rabbah* 19.4; *Midrash Leqah Tov*: Huqqat, ed. Buber, 119b. In this common rabbinic view of the *huqqim*, their very unintelligibility is not just apparent but real. The very phenomenology of their observance requires the suspension of both natural and historical reason. However, for most of the medieval theologians, both rationalist and nonrationalist, the unintelligibility of the *huqqim* is only apparent. Inherently, they are *ratio per se*, even though they are not *ratio quoad nos*, i.e., immediately intelligible to us. See, e.g., Maimonides, *Guide of the Perplexed*, 3.26 and Nahmanides, *Commentary on the Torah*: Lev. 19:19; 26:15; R. Menahem Recanati, *Commentary on the Torah*: Huqqat, beg. re *Bemidbar Rabbah* 19.3 à la Eccl. 7:23. My view of the *huqqim* is closer to the common rabbinic view than it is to the one prevalent among most of the medieval theologians. I think that the dialectical role of *hoq* as a surd is important for the phenomenological constitution of the commandments.

Paschal lamb be broken and that the Paschal lamb be eaten by one intact group (Exodus 12:46).[23]

In this scheme, the election of Israel – which is most directly experienced and celebrated in the study and practice of the *edot* – must be correlated with the practice of the *mishpatim* and the practice of the *huqqim*.

The *mishpatim* are the antecedents of the *edot* inasmuch as Israel is part of the universal order of nature (specifically, human nature) before she participates in the singular covenantal order.[24] The covenant presupposes humanity. Since a presupposition is a condition, not a ground, as I have been emphasizing, the *edot*, therefore, transcend the *mishpatim* in intensity and detail. They are not reducible to them as parts to a larger whole, nor are the *mishpatim* simply the means to the *edot* as ends. The *edot* are the modes of Israel's active, responsive experience of God's electing and nurturing love for her in the covenant. Hence the *edot* are intercovenantal, involving the collective relationship of Israel with the Lord and simultaneously with each other.[25] The *mishpatim*, though, are included in the covenant but not subsumed by it. They also govern Israel's extracovenantal relationships with the other nations of the world, her human neighbors in the order of creation.

The *huqqim* are the limits of Israel's election that she actively experiences in the *edot*. They are limits in the sense that they prevent the covenant from being taken as a symbiosis of God and Israel, a symmetry of God and Israel as functioning equals.[26] Precisely because they have neither universal nor historical reasons, because their sole authority is God's mysterious will, they are able to function as active reminders that Israel is totally defined by the covenant, whereas God partici-

---

[23] R. Yom Tov ben Abraham Ishbili (Ritva), *Commentary on the Passover Haggadah*, ed. Y. Leibowitz (Jerusalem, 1983), 23.

[24] See Nahmanides, *Commentary on the Torah*: Exod. 15:25 and Lev. 18:4; also, D. Novak, *The Theology of Nahmanides Systematically Presented* (Atlanta, 1992), 107ff.

[25] See, e.g., Deut. 5:13–15.

[26] Thus the Buberian I–Thou model can be seen as a correlation of man and God, that is, no I (human) without Thou (divine), and no Thou without I. As such, this type of theology shares the same basic logical problem that plagues Hermann Cohen's theology (see pp. 59–60 above). See, e.g., David Hartman, *A Living Covenant* (New York, 1985), 302.

pates in the covenant but is not defined by it. In kabbalistic terms that illustrate this point most perceptively, God is both *in* the *sefirot* (manifestations) and beyond them as *Ayn Sof* (infinity).[27] The *huqqim*, then, being nothing but the active experience of God's will, are as mysterious as creation itself. This is a point that God stresses to Job when the human temptation to judge God by a common standard arises. "Where were you when I established the earth ... when I prescribed its limit (*huqqi*)?" (Job 38:4, 10) The ubiquity of the story of the binding of Isaac (*aqedah*) in Jewish consciousness reiterates this point. God's commandment to Abraham and Isaac is the archetypal *hoq*.[28] Only God is to be obeyed without question.

Whereas the *mishpatim* by their intention of universal order function as the intelligible precondition or general antecedent of the covenantal *edot*, the *huqqim* function as their unintelligible or mysteriously divine limit. For that reason, no system of Jewish theology (especially the one now being presented) can ever be complete. The *huqqim* intend the unassimilable surd of revelation. (This could be a theological illustration of Gödel's Theorem.) The *huqqim* intend God's primal authority, which transcends both humanity in general and even the specific history of the covenant with Israel. They declare that in the normative order of the cosmos, existence is prior to essence and that everything is contingent upon that which no finite creature can ever comprehend.[29]

The ultimate consequent of the election of Israel is the final redemption itself (*ge'ulah*). However, it is not the automatic result of what transpires now in the present.[30] It is not the mere project of either election or revelation. It should not be seen as

---

[27] See Gershom Scholem, *On the Kabbalah and its Symbolism*, trans. R. Manheim (New York, 1969), 35ff.

[28] See Maimonides, *Guide of the Perplexed*, 3.24. This might also be the reason why this was once considered to be the Torah reading in the synagogue for Rosh Hashanah when it was celebrated for only one day even in the land of Israel. For the festival of creation, it expresses the doctrine that creation is rooted in the inscrutable will of God, for which no reason can be found. See B. Mandelbaum, intro., *Pesiqta De-Rav Kahana* (2 vols., New York, 1962), 1:xiv (re Ms. Carmoli). Cf. J. Mann, *The Bible as Read and Preached in the Old Synagogue* (Cincinnati, 1940), 1:178.

[29] See pp. 124–138 above.   [30] See pp. 152–162 above.

the fulfillment of the hegemony of the covenant (*torat yisra'el*) inasmuch as the Torah in toto is concerned with more than Israel, but also with the elementary norms that the creator has enabled all humans to discover with intelligence and good will in their own social nature. And it is also concerned with God's absolute decrees (*gezerot*), which seem to have no historical meaning at all and, hence, no covenantal intent.[31] Furthermore, it should not be seen as the fulfillment of the hegemony of the Torah qua universal moral law inasmuch as the Torah is mostly concerned with the irreducible singularity of Israel's historical existence. Accordingly, the final redemption should not be taken as a projection from either of these two modes of the Torah. All that can be known about the final redemption, then, is that the estrangement between God and Israel and God and the world will ultimately be overcome. And God's redemption of Israel will be central to this cosmic redemption.

Only when the election of Israel or the revelation of the Torah is seen as a means to another evident end – be that end the hegemony of the covenantal Torah or the hegemony of the universal Torah – only then is the redeemed future seen as a simple projection from the present into the future rather than as a divine trajectory from the future into the present. In the modern age, such projections have frequently declared themselves here and now to be some humanly achieved "beginning of redemption" (*atehalta de-ge'ulah*) in one form or another.[32] However, as a new divine trajectory into history and nature the final redemption can only be hoped for; it cannot be predicted, let alone achieved by humans. We can only have faith *that* it will come; we cannot have any knowledge of *what* it will be.[33]

This philosophical approach to the theological doctrine of the election of Israel has profound implications for the two most pressing political questions facing the Jewish people today: (1) Who is a Jew? (2) What is the relationship of Jews with non-Jews to be?

---

[31] See B. Berakhot 33b.
[32] See M. M. Kasher, *Israel Passover Haggadah* (New York, 1964), 274ff. Cf. Yeshayahu Leibowitz, *Yahadut, Am Yehudi U-Medinat Yisra'el* (Jerusalem, 1976), 181ff.
[33] See B. Berakhot 34b re Isa. 64:3.

As for the question of who is a Jew, the doctrine of the election of Israel constituted here says more – but not less – than the halakhic answer concerning matrilineal descent or legally valid conversion. It says that a Jew is one who with his or her people has been chosen by God in love. That love justifies the commanded response to love God in return (*ahavat Ha-Shem*) and to love every other member of the covenanted people (*ahavat yisra'el*).[34] As such, the doctrine of election teaches that, within the parameters of Halakhah, of course, every effort must be made to practice that love towards every other Jew. Appreciation of the chosenness of the Jewish people in correlation with the authority of the Torah teaches that no halakhic option be exercised that would further exacerbate separation among Jews when another more unifying halakhic option is available.[35] To add strictures, whose effect is to exclude more and more Jews from one's conception of the covenanted community (*kenesset yisra'el*), is to reduce the election of Israel to the Torah – that is, one's own theological view of the Torah's true intent (*da'at torah*). That, as we have seen, is theologically arguable. But the doctrine of election also teaches that valid halakhic distinctions between Jews and non-Jews be continually respected so that a Jew can have objective criteria for determining who the recipient of his or her covenantal love truly is. To alter the laws of the Torah and tradition for the sake of "Jewish unity" is to sever the election of Israel from its correlation to the Torah. And it is only the Torah that instructs us *that* Israel is chosen and *how* her chosenness is to be lived.[36]

As for the question of what the relationship of Jews with non-Jews is to be, the doctrine of election, when rightly constituted, removes the temptation of chauvinism. It does not say that Israel is somehow more human than anyone else. It does not place Israel above the nations of the world in any area of

---

[34] Therefore, the preponderance of Jewish opinion has been that the commandment "You shall love your neighbor as yourself" refers to one's fellow Jew. See Maimonides, *Mishneh Torah*: De'ot, 6.3–4; *Evel*, 14.1. Justice, however, is commanded towards all human beings. See B. Baba Kama 113a-b re Lev. 25:50. Cf. n. 8 above.

[35] See *Sifre*: Devarim, no. 96 and B. Yevamot 13b re Deut. 14:1.

[36] See R. Saadiah Gaon, *Emunot Ve-De'ot*, 3.7.

purely human interaction. It says that Israel's election is an intimate matter between her and God.[37] By not reducing the entire Torah to this relationship, but rather by emphasizing its universal aspect as well, the doctrine of election enables Jews to function as equals with non-Jews in those areas where common human issues of peace, justice and righteousness are at stake between them. It does not say that election creates any special privileges in the world, even those of *noblesse oblige*. And by not seeing the redeemed future as any kind of projection from a present human state of affairs, Israel cannot claim to be any more redeemed than anyone else. This lack of redemption, either Jewish or universal, is a point Jews have always emphasized when the adherents of other religions and ideologies have made triumphalist claims against us, claiming that the world is already redeemed.[38] But what God will finally do with the world is as mysterious as what God has been doing with Israel in the past and the present. Against the hidden horizon of the final redeemed future, everything past and present is ultimately provisional. God has not yet fulfilled his own purposes in history.

May God's kingdom come speedily, even in our own day!

[37] See *Tanhuma*: Ki Tissa, printed ed., no. 34.
[38] See Nahmanides, "Disputation," in *Kitvei Ha-Ramban*, ed. Chavel, 1:315–316.

Appendix 1
Some major Jewish thinkers cited

Aha Ha'Am (1856–1927). Russian Jewish essayist and nationalist theoretician. Major influence on the revival of the Hebrew language as a vehicle for modern thought by Jews. Founder of "Cultural Zionism," which advocated the spiritual (but nonreligious) revival of Jewish nationhood through group values. Spent last years in Palestine.

Albo, Joseph (fifteenth century). Spanish Jewish theologian and active polemicist against Christianity, especially as principal Jewish spokesman at Disputation with Catholic theologians at Tortosa in 1413. Disciple of anti-Aristotelian Jewish theologian Hasdai Crescas. First Jewish thinker to use term "natural law" (*dat tiv'it*), which reflects influence of Thomas Aquinas. Chief work *Sefer Ha'Iqqarim* (*Book of Roots*), the most systematic Jewish theology ever written.

Buber, Martin (1878–1965). Viennese born and educated; leading German Jewish thinker. First holder of a chair in Jewish thought at a German university (Frankfurt-on-Main). Settled in Israel in 1938 and taught at the Hebrew University in Jerusalem. Considered a founder of modern religious existentialism through influence of major work *I and Thou*. Early proponent of Spiritual Zionism along religious, but nontraditionalist, lines. Wrote (with Franz Rosenzweig) a radical new translation of the Bible into German.

Cohen, Hermann (1842–1918). Leading German philosopher and liberal Jewish theologian. The major influence on the revival of Kant in late ninteenth- and early twentieth-century philosophy in Europe. Worked out a systematic Jewish theology through the critical appropriation of Kantian principles. Major promoter of post-Enlightenment German–Jewish synthesis. Teacher of Franz Rosenzweig.

Halevi, Judah (1075–1141). Spanish Jewish theologian and poet. In major work *Kuzari* argued for the superiority of revelation and tradition (of which Judaism is the epitome) over rationalist philosophy. Major influence on subsequent mystical developments in late medieval Judaism. Fervent lover of the land of Israel. According to legend, killed just as he was to enter Jerusalem. Religious poetry an important component of Jewish liturgy.

Heschel, Abraham Joshua (1907–1972). Scion of Hasidic dynasty, then later educated as a philosopher in Germany. Came to the United States in 1940 and taught at the Jewish Theological Seminary in New York. Adapted the methods of phenomenology for his theological reflections on Jewish religious life. The major influence on the growth of Jewish theology in America after the Second World War, especially through most important English work *God in Search of Man*.

Maimonides (1135–1204). Born in Muslim Spain; spent most of his career as physician and communal leader in Egypt. Most important medieval Jewish jurist and theologian. Codified all of biblical and rabbinic law in encyclopedic work *Mishneh Torah*. Developed new methods in theology through the critical appropriation of Aristotle and Islamic rationalists, especially in *The Guide of the Perplexed*. Most influential Jewish thinker on subsequent generations.

Nahmanides (1194–1270). Leading Spanish Jewish exegete and theologian. Most important single influence on emerging Kabbalah. Developed an anti-Aristotelian, but not anti-rationalist, theology under the impact of the thought of Saadia Gaon and Judah Halevi. Major work *Commentary on the Torah*. Greatly influenced subsequent development of Jewish law through synthesis of methods of various Talmudic schools. Representative of Jews of northern Spain in Disputation with Dominicans at Barcelona in 1263. Forced to leave Spain for Israel in 1267.

Rashi (1040–1105). Most important Jewish exegete on the Bible and the Talmud. Leader of Franco-German Jewry during First Crusade and developed methods for dealing with new religious and social problems. Cited most often by subsequent Jewish thinkers when using biblical or Talmudic texts.

Rosenzweig, Franz (1886–1929). Leader of the movement in German Jewry away from assimilation towards reappropriation of Jewish tradition. Major figure in post-rationalist philosophy after the First World War. Major work *The Star of Redemption* written when officer in the German army at the eastern front (1914–1918). Studied with Hermann Cohen and collaborated with Martin Buber. Most important influence on postmodern Jewish thought and Jewish–Christian dialogue after 1945.

Saadiah Gaon (882–942). Born in Egypt, but career spent as leader of Babylonian Jewry. One of the earliest Jewish thinkers to confront the issues raised by Greek philosophy. Theological method heavily influenced by Islamic dialectical theology known as Kalam. Major work *Sefer Emunot Ve-De'ot* (The Book of Beliefs and Opinions). Set the stage for all subsequent philosophical theology by Jews in the Middle Ages.

Soloveitchik, Joseph B. (1903–1993). Scion of leading family of Lithuanian talmudists, later educated as a philosopher in Germany. Came to the United States in 1932. Greatest influence on American Jewish Orthodoxy, especially as teacher of Rabbis at Yeshiva University in New York. Applied Neo-Kantian methodology and later existentialism to the explication of the deeper significance of Jewish law.

Appendix 2

Because Rosenzweig is quite unclear on this issue, interpreters have often seen his position on the traditional Jewish commandments as advocating subjectivism, that is, he seems to saying that only those laws each *individual* can experience as commandments revealed by God are to be observed. His difference from Buber, then, is that he does not see the traditional Jewish laws as being antithetical to a response to God's personal commandments *ipso facto*. (For more on their difference, see G. Bonola, "Franz Rosenzweig und Martin Buber: Die Auseinanderstezung über das Gesetz," in W. Schmied-Kowarzik [ed.], *Der Philosoph Franz Rosenzweig* [Munich, 1988], 1:225ff.) I myself have drawn that same conclusion in earlier works. (See *Law and Theology in Judaism* [2 vols., New York, 1974–1976], 2:14–15; *Jewish–Christian Dialogue* [New York, 1989], 89ff.) I now believe, however, that much of what Rosenzweig had to say along these lines was *only* the expression of his *own* individual situation, and that he was not advocating it as a general standard for the Jewish community as a whole. Thus in his well-known letter to the faculty of the *Lehrhaus* in November 1924, he calls this approach of not observing a *Gesetz* until he has experienced it as *Gebot* as *das Besondere unsrer Situation* (*Briefe*, ed. E. Rosenzweig [Berlin, 1935], no. 413, p. 521). Here *unsrer* surely refers to his own situation as one who was coming into Jewish faith and observance from an estranged background. But, for those Jews who "have remained at home at Judaism" (*heimgeblieben Juden – ibid.*), it is another matter, i.e., they are to observe all the traditional laws and *then* strive to experience them as commandments (cf.

B. Shabbat 88a re Exod. 24:7). Furthermore, in a letter to the Orthodox Jewish leader Jakob Rosenheim, written almost immediately after the letter cited above, Rosenzweig says that "the danger of individualism truly exists only for individuals, but not for the collective (*Gemamtheit*)" (*ibid.*, no. 414, p. 522).

Nevertheless, Rosenzweig's continuing ambivalence is expressed in his letter to the *Lehrhaus* faculty when he says, "to what extent ... this law of election covers the traditional Jewish law, only that is doubtful (*zweifelhaft*) for us" (*ibid.*, no. 413, p. 518). And even later than that, Rosenzweig reiterates the point that "the connection (*Verbindung*) of God and man is the only content of revelation" (*Jehuda Halevi*, 29).

I would suggest that one could see some possible halakhic basis for Rosenzweig's distinction between the collective approach and the individual approach in the Talmudic concept of the "kidnapped child" (*tinoq she-nishbah*). This seems to apply to his situation and to that of those like him (who are legion today) in the sense that this term designates someone who comes to traditional Jewish observance from a background in which there had never been such observance before. (The concept does have to be stretched somewhat, though, inasmuch as people like Rosenzweig have observed some Jewish rituals, but they have not done so in the context of obligation [*hiyyuv* – see R. Vidal of Tolosa, *Magid Mishneh* on Maimonides, *Mishneh Torah*: Shofar, 2.4 re B. Rosh Hashanah 28a–29a]. In the Talmudic source of this context [B. Shabbat 68a], however, the "kidnapped child," like the "ignorant convert" [i.e., a convert who was never instructed in Jewish practices before conversion: see Tos., s.v. "ger" thereon re B. Yevamot 47a] with whom he or she is compared, seems never to have observed any Jewish religious practice in any context whatsoever.) In this sense, then, Rosenzweig and those like him are not really *ba'alei teshuvah*, even though that is what they are usually called today, unlike Rosenzweig's teacher Hermann Cohen, who Rosenzweig reports as having said "Ich bin ja ein Baal t'schuwoh" (introduction to Cohen's posthumously published *Jüdische Schriften*, ed. B. Strauss [3 vols., Berlin, 1924], 1:xxi, and *Kleinere Schriften*, ed. E. Rosenzweig [Berlin,

1937], 307). However, unlike Rosenzweig, Cohen's *Heimkehr*, was real, for he came from an observant and learned Jewish background. Thus Cohen was re-turning to where he had been before, whereas Rosenzweig was more radically "returning" to where he had never been before. When it comes to such people, it would seem that the Talmudic concept of *tinoq she-nishbah* offers some support for Rosenzweig's suggestion that those "coming into" Judaism should not do so more rapidly than they can intellectually and emotionally handle. (See his August 1924 letter to Eugen Rosenstock in *Briefe und Tagebü- cher*, ed. R. Rosenzweig and E. Rosenzweig-Scheinmann [2 vols., The Hague, 1079], 2:984–985.) What Rosenzweig has done, it seems to me, is to give a good theological rationale for that gradual integration into Jewish observance that worked so well in his own case.

Appendix 3

In early rabbinic teaching, there does not seem to be any clear distinction between "the days of the Messiah" (*yemot ha-mashiah*), "the resurrection of the dead" (*tehiyyat ha-metim*), and "the world-to-come" (*olam ha-ba* – see, e.g., M. Avot 2.16). Moreover, even in later rabbinic teaching, where such distinctions are made (see B. Berakhot 34b), all these realms are constituted as temporally transcendent. This is the case even with *olam ha-ba* (see Y. Yevamot 15.2/14d re Ps. 140:8). It is not seen as an eternal, unchanging, preexistent realm as it is for Maimonides (see *Mishneh Torah*: Teshuvah, 8:8; cf. note of Rabad thereon re B. Sanhedrin 97a on Isa. 2:17, and Novak, *The Theology of Nahmanides*, 129).

The inclusion of the idea of eternity in Jewish theology, whatever its historical origins might be, presupposes the notion of divine unchangeability. That notion, however, is neither biblical nor rabbinic (see Franz Rosenzweig, "Der Ewige," in *Kleinere Schriften*, ed. E. Rosenzweig [Berlin, 1937], 197). Thus the verse, "I the Lord do not change (*lo shaniti*)" (Mal. 3:6) does not mean that God does not change in the context of his covenantal relationship. For if that were the case, God could not respond to his covenantal partners, which is an essential aspect of covenantal mutuality. Response is a transitive act (see Gen. 6:6, 8:21; Exod. 32:14; Zech. 1:3). What the verse means, I think, is that God *does not change into something else*. God never loses his personal identity (see Y. Sanhedrin 1.1/18a re Isa. 44:6). God's unchangeability for us is his fidelity to the promises of the covenant (see Y. Ta'anit 2.1/65a re Num. 23:19), one of which is that God will change from exercising strict justice to exercise mercy (*ibid.*, re Isa. 26:21) when his people truly turn back to him (*ibid.*, re Joel 2:13).

God is *everlasting*, spanning world time (*l'olam*) but not limited by it (*va'ed*) (see Exod. 15:18 and the translation of Martin Buber and Franz Rosenzweig, *Die Fünf Bücher der Weisung* [Olten, 1954], 193). Creatures, even human creatures, do *change into something else*. They do lose their personal identity; they become nameless "dust" (see Gen. 3:19; Ps. 49:10ff.; Eccl. 12:7). And humans also lose their personal identity because, unlike God, they are unfaithful to the covenant. Because they inevitably sin, they die (see B. Shabbat 55a re Ezek. 18:20; also, B. Sanhedrin 10a and Rashi, s.v. "malqot"). Furthermore, being generative beings, creatures leave part of themselves behind in their descendants, who biologically transcend them in time future as their ancestors transcend them in time past (see Gen. 38:8; Deut. 25:5ff.). But God is not a generative being; there is nothing before him and nothing after him in time (see Isa. 43:10; Arakhin 31b re Lev. 25:30 and Rashi, s.v. "she'ayn lo dorot"). Therefore, if there is life after death for human creatures, it is bodily resurrection, i.e., God returning to them what they have really lost (see B. Pesahim 68a re Deut. 32:39). Immortality, on the other hand, which many later Jewish theologians accepted, is based on the idea of eternity. And it involves the same ontological difficulties for Jewish theology as does the idea upon which it is based. A creator God is everlasting, not eternal, and only a creator God can effect resurrection of the dead (see Maimonides, *Ma'amar Tehiyyat Ha-Metim*, in *Igrot Ha-Rambam*, ed. I. Shailat [2 vols., Jerusalem, 1987], 1:366–367).

Appendix 4

Recently, the Israeli scholar Yohanan Silman has argued that the later sections of *Kuzari*, those that seem to be more philosophical, were written before the earlier sections, those that seem to be more theological. Following this thesis, then, would require one to interpret the earlier sections more literally and the later sections more figuratively in order to explicate Halevi's final position. See *Bein Filosoph Le-Navi: Hitpat'hut Haguto Shel Rabbi Yehudah Halevi Be-Sefer Ha-Kuzari* (Ramat-Gan, 1985), 134ff.; 239ff. If I were to follow Silman, that would require my approaching the text of *Kuzari* as less than an integral work of thought and, therefore, I would be unable to draw some of the conclusions that I have drawn in this section of the book.

Like all attempts at the isolation of different sources (*Quellenscheidung*) in a work accepted by posterity as a unitary classic, it assumes that one can return to an "original" reading of a text. Nevertheless, the method is questionable. First, the conclusions drawn by means of this method (one that became established in the nineteenth century by scholars who were influenced by the "Higher Criticism" of the Bible) are always tentative. Second, it seems to assume that the final editor of a literary work drawn from composite sources (let alone when the editor is also the very same author of these sources) could have done a better job of reworking these sources so as to avoid specific contradictions and more general inconsistencies. Third, it does not deal with the fact that when texts are read in the context of a continuing tradition, especially a religious one, the *Tendenz* of the tradition is always more synthetic than analytic. The latter is ultimately for the sake of the former (which still leaves a wide range of operation for historical-critical researches within a religious tradition – *pace* various fundamentalisms). In other words, what might very well have been fragmentary originally is *subsequently taken* by posterity as unitary. In the case of Judah Halevi, or any other theologian whose thought has become part of the tradition of Judaism, that thought has to be taken to be systematic (*sheetati*) with apparent inner contradictions interpreted and reinterpreted for the sake of unitary order. This is the sense in which I read Halevi (or Maimonides, etc.). And because I read him within the context of a larger tradition with which I myself do identify, my critique of him is more synthetic than analytic, i.e., I criticise (with great respect) points that do not seem to fit into the larger *Tendenz* of the tradition rather than points that seem to suggest his own internal inconsistencies.

Bibliography

CLASSICAL JUDAIC TEXTS

Abrabanel, Isaac, *Commentary on the Torah*. Warsaw, 1862
  Rosh Amanah, ed. M. Kellner. Ramat-Gan, 1993
Abraham ibn Ezra, *Commentary on the Torah*, 3 vols., ed. A. Weiser. Jerusalem, 1977
Albo, Joseph, *Sefer Ha'Iqqarim*, 5 vols., ed. and trans. I. Husik. Philadelphia, 1929–1930
Apocrypha and Pseudepigrapha of the Old Testament, 2 vols., ed. and trans. R. H. Charles. Oxford, 1913
Avot De-Rabbi Nathan, ed. S. Schechter (reprint). New York, 1967
Bahya ibn Pakudah, *Hovot Ha-Levavot*, 2 vols., trans. Judah ibn Tibbon (reprint). Jerusalem, 1962
Bahya, Rabbenu, *Commentary on the Torah*, 3 vols., ed. C. B. Chavel. Jerusalem, 1971
Batei Midrashot, 2 vols., ed. A. J. Wertheimer. Jerusalem, 1950
David ibn Abi Zimra, *Teshuvot Ha-Radbaz*, 2 vols. Warsaw, 1882
Duran, Simon ben Zemah, *Teshuvot Tashbats*, 2 vols. Lemberg, 1891
Gersonides, *Milhamot Ha-Shem*. Riva di Trento, 1560
Halevi, Judah, *Kuzari*, trans. Y. Even-Shmuel. Tel Aviv, 1972
  Kuzari, trans. H. Hirschfeld (reprint). New York, 1964
  Kuzari, trans. Judah ibn Tibbon (reprint). New York, 1946
  Selected Religious Poems, ed. H. Brody. Philadelphia, 1924
High Holyday Prayerbook, 2 vols., ed. and trans. P. Birnbaum. New York, 1960
Hizquni, *Commentary on the Torah*, ed. C. B. Chavel. Jerusalem, 1982
Isaac of Vienna, *Or Zaru'a*, 2 vols. Zhitomir, 1862
Israel Isserlein, *Teshuvot Terumat Ha-Deshen* (reprint). B'nai B'rak, 1971
Jacob ben Asher, *Tur*, 7 vols. (reprint). Jerusalem, 1969
Jacob ibn Habib, *Ein Ya'aqov*, 3 vols. (reprint). New York, 1953
Karo, Joseph, *Shulhan Arukh*, 7 vols. Lemberg, 1873

Maimonides, *Commentary on the Mishnah*, 3 vols., trans. Y. Kafih. Jerusalem, 1976

Guide of the Perplexed, trans. S. Pines. Chicago, 1963

Igrot Ha-Rambam, 2 vols., ed. I. Shailat. Jerusalem, 1987

Mishneh Torah, 5 vols. (reprint). New York, 1957

Moreh Nevukhim, trans. Samuel ibn Tibbon (reprint). New York, 1946

Sefer Ha-Mitsvot (reprint). Jerusalem, 1962

Sefer Ha-Mitsvot, ed. C. Heller. Jerusalem, 1946

Teshuvot Ha-Rambam, 3 vols., ed. Y. Blau. Jerusalem, 1960

Meiri, *Bet Ha-Behirah*: Yevamot, ed. S. Dickman. Jerusalem, 1968

Mekhilta, ed. H. S. Horovitz and I. A. Rabin (reprint). Jerusalem, 1960

Midrash Aggadah, ed. S. Buber. Vienna, 1894

Midrash Bere'sheet Rabbah, 3 vols., ed. J. Theodor and C. Albeck (reprint). Jerusalem, 1965

Midrash Ha-Gadol: Bemidbar, ed. Z. M. Rabinowitz. Jerusalem, 1973

Midrash Ha-Gadol: Bere'sheet, ed. M. Margulies. Jerusalem, 1947

Midrash Leqah Tov, 2 vols., ed. S. Buber. Vilna, 1884

Midrash Mishlei, ed. S. Buber. Cracow, 1893

Midrash Rabbah, 2 vols. (reprint). New York, 1957

Midrash Vayiqra Rabbah, 3 vols., ed. M. Margulies. Jerusalem, 1953

Miqra'ot Gedolot: On the Prophets and Hagiographa, 3 vols. (reprint). New York, 1951

On the Torah, 5 vols. (reprint). New York, 1950

Mishnah, 6 vols., ed. C. Albeck. Jerusalem, 1957

Mishnat Rabbi Eliezer, 2 vols., ed. H. Enelow. New York, 1934

Mishnayot, 12 vols. (reprint). New York, 1969

Nahmanides, *Commentary on the Torah*, 2 vols., ed. C. B. Chavel. Jerusalem, 1963

Hiddushei Ha-Ramban, 4 vols. (reprint), ed. M. Hirschler *et al.* Jerusalem, 1973–1987

Hiddushei Ha-Ramban, 2 vols., ed. I. Z. Meltzer. B'nai B'rak, 1959

Kitvei Ha-Ramban, 2 vols., ed. C. B. Chavel. Jerusalem, 1963

Nissim Gerondi, *Derashot*, ed. L. A. Feldman. Jerusalem, 1973

Otsar Ha-Ge'onim, 13 vols., ed. B. M. Lewin. Haifa and Jerusalem, 1928–1943

Pesiqta De-Rav Kahana, 2 vols., ed. B. Mandelbaum. New York, 1962

Pirqei De-Rabbi Eliezer (reprint). Antwerp, n.d.

Rashbam, *Commentary on the Torah*, ed. A. Bromberg. Jerusalem, 1969

Rashi, *Commentary on the Torah*, ed. C. B. Chavel. Jerusalem, 1982

Rashi, *Teshuvot Rashi*, ed. I. Elfenbein. New York, 1943

Recanati, Menahem, *Commentary on the Torah*. Venice, 1523
Saadiah Gaon, *Book of Beliefs and Opinions*, trans. S. Rosenblatt. New Haven, Conn., 1948
Sefer Hasidim, ed. Bologna (reprint). Jerusalem, 1966
Septuagint, 2 vols., ed. A. Rahlfs. Stuttgart, n.d.
Sifra, ed. I. H. Weiss. Vienna, 1862
Sifre: Bemidbar, ed. H.S. Horovitz and I. A. Rabin. Leipzig, 1917
Sifre: Devarim, ed. Louis Finkelstein. New York, 1969
Solomon ibn Adret, *Hiddushei Ha-Rashba*, 3 vols. (reprint). Jerusalem, 1963
    Teshuvot Ha-Rashba, 5 vols. (reprint). B'nai B'rak, 1958
Solomon ibn Gabirol, *Selected Religious Poems*, ed. I. Davidson. Philadelphia, 1924
Talmud Bavli, 20 vols. Vilna, 1898
Talmud Yerushalmi, 7 vols., ed. Pietrkov (reprint). Jerusalem, 1959
    ed. Venice/Krotoschin (reprint). New York, 1948
Tanakh. Jerusalem, 1969
Tanhuma, printed ed. Jerusalem, n.d.
Tanhuma, 2 vols. (reprint), ed. S. Buber. Jerusalem, 1964
Yalqut Shim'oni, 2 vols. (reprint). New York, 1944
Yom Tov ben Abraham Ishbili (Ritva), *Commentary on the Passover Haggadah*, ed. Y. Leibowitz. Jerusalem, 1983
    Teshuvot Ha-Ritva, ed. Y. Kafih. Jerusalem, 1959
Zohar, 3 vols., ed. R. Margoliyot. Jerusalem, 1984

MODERN JUDAIC TEXTS

Ahad Ha'Am, *Kol Kitvei Ahad Ha'Am*, 2nd ed. Jerusalem, 1949
Baer, Yitzhak, *A History of the Jews in Christian Spain*, 2 vols., trans. L. Schoffman. Philadelphia, 1961
Bamberger, Bernard J., *Proselytism in the Talmudic Period*. New York, 1968
Baron, Salo W., *The Jewish Community*, 3 vols. Philadelphia, 1942
    "Yehudah Halevi: An Answer to an Historic Challenge." *Jewish Social Studies* 3 (1941)
Berger, M. S., "Toward a New Understanding of Judah Halevi's *Kuzari*." *Journal of Religion* 72 (1992)
Berkovits, Eliezer, *Man and God: Studies in Biblical Theology*. Detroit, 1969
Blumenkranz, B., *Juifs et chrétiens dans le monde occidental: 430–1096*. Paris, 1960
Bodoff, L., "Was Yehudah Halevi a Racist?" *Judaism* 38 (1989)
Borowitz, Eugene B., *Renewing the Covenant*. Philadelphia, 1991

Brinner, W. and S. D. Ricks (eds.), *Studies in Islamic and Jewish Traditions*. Atlanta, 1986

Buber, Martin, *I and Thou*, trans. W. Kaufmann. New York, 1970
  Ich und Du, 2nd ed. Heidelberg, 1962
  The Knowledge of Man: A Philosophy of the Interhuman, ed. M. Friedman. New York and Evanston, 1965
  Königtum Gottes, 3rd rev. ed. Heidelberg, 1956
  On the Bible: Eighteen Essays, trans. M. A. Meyer; ed. Nahum N. Glatzer. New York, 1968
  Two Types of Faith, trans. N. P. Goldhawk. New York, 1962

Buber Martin, and Franz Rosenzweig, *Die Fünf Bücher der Weisung*. Olten, 1954

Büchler, Adolf *Studies in Sin and Atonement in the Rabbinic Literature of the First Century* (reprint). New York, 1967

Chajes, Zvi Hirsch, *Kol Kitvei Maharats Chajes*, 2 vols. B'nai B'rak, 1958

Chazan, Robert, *Barcelona and Beyond: The Disputation of 1263 and its Aftermath*. Berkeley, Calif., 1992

Cohen, Arthur A., *The Tremendum: A Theological Interpretation of the Holocaust*. New York, 1981

Cohen, Hermann, *Der Begriff der Religion im System der Philosophie*. Giessen, 1915
  Ethik des reinen Willens, 4th ed. Berlin, 1923
  Jüdische Schriften, 3 vols., ed. B. Strauss; intro. Franz Rosenzweig. Berlin, 1924
  Kants Theorie der Erfahrung, 4th ed. Berlin, 1925
  Logik der reinen Erkenntnis, 3rd ed. Berlin, 1922
  Das Prinzip der Infinitesimal-Methode und seine Geschichte (reprint). Frankfurt-on-Main, 1968
  Religion der Vernunft aus den Quellen des Judentums, 2nd ed. Darmstadt, 1966
  Religion of Reason Out of the Sources of Judaism, trans. S. Kaplan. New York, 1972

Cohen, Richard A., *Elevations: The Height of the Good in Rosenzweig and Levinas*. Chicago, 1994

Efros, Israel, *Studies in Medieval Jewish Philosophy*. New York and London, 1974

Eisen, Arnold M., *The Chosen People in America: A Study in Jewish Religious Ideology*. Bloomington, Ind. and London, 1983

Emden, Jacob, *Sh'elat Yavets*. Lemberg, 1844

Encyclopedia Judaica, 16 vols. Jerusalem, 1972

Encyclopedia Talmudit, 22 vols. Jerusalem, 1946–1993

Epstein, Baruch Halevi, *Torah Temimah*, 5 vols. (reprint). New York, 1962

Fackenheim, Emil L., *God's Presence in History: Jewish Affirmations and Philosophical Reflections*. New York, 1970
　Quest for Past and Future. Bloomington, Ind., 1968
　To Mend the World: Foundations of Future Jewish Thought. New York, 1982
Finkelstein, Louis, "The Institution of Baptism for Proselytes." *Journal of Biblical Literature* 52 (1933)
　The Pharisees, 2 vols. Philadelphia, 1938
Fox, M. (ed.), *Modern Jewish Ethics*. Columbus, Ohio, 1975
Freedman, H., *Jeremiah: Translation and Commentary* Soncino Books of the Bible. London, 1949
Gelhaar, S. S., *Prophetie und Gesetz bei Jehudah Halevi, Maimonides und Spinoza*. Frankfurt-on-Main, 1987
Gibbs, Robert *Correlations in Rosenzweig and Levinas*. Princeton, 1992
Ginzberg, Louis, *The Legends of the Jews*, 7 vols. Philadelphia, 1909–1938
Glatzer, Nahum N., *Franz Rosenzweig: His Life and Thought*, 2nd rev. ed. New York, 1961
Goodman, L. E. (ed), *Neoplatonism and Jewish Thought*. Albany, N.Y., 1992
Gordis, Robert, *The Book of God and Man: A Study of Job*. Chicago, 1965
Goren, Shlomo, *Torat Ha-Mo'adim*. Tel Aviv, 1964
Greenwald, Yekutiel Y., *Kol Bo Al Avelut*. New York, 1965
Guttmann, Julius, *Philosophies of Judaism*, trans. D. W. Silverman New York, 1964
Guttmann, Michael, *Das Judenthum und seine Umwelt*. Berlin, 1927
Haberman, Joshua O., *Philosopher of Revelation: The Life and Thought of S. L. Steinheim*. Philadelphia, 1990
Halivni, David Weiss, *Meqorot U-Mesorot*: Nashim. Tel Aviv, 1968
Hartman, David, *A Living Covenant: The Innovative Spirit in Traditional Judaism*. New York, 1985
Heinemann, Isaak, *Darkhei Ha'Aggadah*, 2nd ed. Jerusalem, 1954
Heschel, Abraham Joshua, *God in Search of Man: A Philosophy of Judaism*. New York, 1955
　Man is Not Alone: A Philosophy of Religion. Philadelphia, 1951
　The Prophets. Philadelphia, 1962
Jewish Encyclopedia, 12 vols. New York, 1916
Judah Aryeh Leib of Gur, *Sefat Emet*, 5 vols., Brooklyn, 1985
Josephus, *Antiquities*, 6 vols., trans. H. St. John Thackeray *et al.* Cambridge, Mass., 1930–1965
Kadushin, Max, *The Rabbinic Mind*. New York, 1952
　"Some Aspects of the Rabbinic Concept of Israel: A Study in the Mekilta." *Hebrew Union College Annual* 19 (1945)

Kaplan, Mordecai M., *Judaism as a Civilization*. New York, 1934
  The Purpose and Meaning of Jewish Existence. Philadelphia, 1964
Kasher, Menachem M., *Haggadah Shlemah*, 3rd ed. Jerusalem, 1967
  Israel Passover Haggadah. New York, 1964
  Torah Shlemah, 11 vols. (reprint). Jerusalem, 1992
Kasher, M. M. *et al.* (eds.), *Leo Jung Jubilee Volume*. New York, 1962
Katz, Jacob, "Af-al-pi She-Hata Yisra'el Hu." *Tarbiz* 27 (1958)
Kaufmann, Yehezkel, *The Religion of Israel*, trans. M. Greenberg.
  Chicago, 1960
  Toldot Ha'Emunah Ha-Yisra'elit, 4 vols. Jerusalem and Tel Aviv, 1966
Kellner, Menachem, *Dogma in Medieval Jewish Thought: From Maimo-
  nides to Abravanel*. Oxford, 1986
  Maimonides on Judaism and the Jewish People. Albany, N.Y., 1991
Klatzkin, Jacob, *Hermann Cohen*. Berlin and London, 1923
Kohut, Alexander, *Aruch Completum*, 9 vols. New York, n.d.
Leibowitz, Yeshayahu, *Yahadut, Am Yehudi U-Medinat Yisra'el*. Jeru-
  salem, 1976
Levenson, Jon D., *Creation and the Persistence of Evil: The Jewish Drama
  of Divine Omnipotence*. San Francisco, 1988
  Sinai and Zion: An Entry into the Hebrew Bible. Minneapolis, 1985
Lieberman, Saul, *Tosefta Kifshuta*, 12 vols. New York, 1955–1988
Loewe Judah, (Maharal), *Gevurot Ha-Shem*. Cracow, 1582
  Netsah Yisra'el. Prague, 1599
Luzzatto, Samuel David, *Commentary on the Torah*, ed. P. Schlesinger.
  Tel Aviv, 1965
Malbim, Meir Leibush, *Commentary on the Torah*, 2 vols. (reprint).
  New York, 1956
Mann, Jacob, *The Bible as Read and Preached in the Old Synagogue*.
  Cincinnati, 1940
Mendes-Flohr, P. (ed.), *The Philosophy of Franz Rosenzweig*. Hanover
  and London, 1988
Mosès, Stéphane, *System and Revelation: The Philosophy of Franz Rosenz-
  weig*, trans. C. Tihanyi. Detroit, 1992
Neusner, Jacob, *A Life of Yohanan ben Zakkai*. Leiden, 1962
Novak, David "Before Revelation: The Rabbis, Paul, and Karl
  Barth." *Journal of Religion* 71 (1991)
  "Buber and Tillich," *Journal of Ecumenical Studies* 29 (1992)
  "Buber's Critique of Heidegger." *Modern Judaism* 5 (1985)
  Halakhah in a Theological Dimension. Chico, Calif., 1985
  *The Image of the Non-Jew in Judaism: An Historical and Constructive
  Study of the Noahide Laws*. New York and Toronto, 1983
  Jewish–Christian Dialogue: A Jewish Justification. New York, 1989
  Jewish Social Ethics. New York, 1992

Law and Theology in Judaism, 2 vols. New York, 1974, 1976
"The Legal Question of the Investigation of Converts." *Jewish Law Association Studies* 3 (1987)
"Response to Eugene Borowitz." *SH'MA* 22/426 (January 24, 1992)
The Theology of Nahmanides Systematically Presented. Atlanta, 1992
"When Jews Become Christians." *First Things* 17 (November, 1991)
Nuriel, A., "The Divine Will in the *Kuzari*." *Jerusalem Studies in Jewish Thought* 9 (1990)
Petuchowski, Jakob J., *Ever Since Sinai*. New York, 1961
Prayerbook Reform in Europe: The Liturgy of European Liberal and Reform Judaism. New York, 1968
Pines, Shlomo, "Shi'ite Terms and Conceptions in Judah Halevi's *Kuzari*." *Jerusalem Studies in Arabic and Islam* 2 (1980)
Reischer, Jacob, *Teshuvot Shevut Ya'aqov* (reprint). Jerusalem, 1971
Rosenbloom, N. H., *Tradition in an Age of Reform: The Religious Philosophy of Samson Raphael Hirsch*. Philadelphia, 1976
Rosenzweig, Franz, *Briefe*, ed. E. Rosenzweig. Berlin, 1935
Briefe und Tagebücher, 2 vols., ed. R. Rosenzweig and E. Rosenzweig-Scheinmann. The Hague, 1979
Jehuda Halevi: fünfundneunzig Hymnen und Gedichte (reprint). The Hague, 1983
Kleinere Schriften, ed. E. Rosenzweig. Berlin, 1937
On Jewish Learning, trans. W. Wolf, ed. Nahun N. Glatzer. New York, 1955
Die Schrift: Aufsätze, Ubertragungen und Briefe, ed. K. Thieme. Königstein, 1984
The Star of Redemption, trans. W. W. Hallo. New York, 1970
Der Stern der Erlösung. Frankfurt-on-Main, 1921
Understanding the Sick and the Healthy: A View of the World, Man, and God, trans. T. Luckman. New York, 1954
Schechter, Solomon, *Some Aspects of Rabbinic Theology* (reprint). New York, 1936
Schnied-Kowarzik, W. (ed.), *Der Philosoph Franz Rosenzweig*. Munich, 1988
Schoeps, Hans-Joachim, *Ausfrühchristlicher Zeit: Religionsgeschichtliche Untersuchungen*. Tübingen, 1950
Scholem, Gershom, *Major Trends in Jewish Mysticism*, 3rd rev. ed. New York, 1961
The Messianic Idea in Judaism, trans. M. A. Meyer. New York, 1971
On the Kabbalah and its Symbolism, trans. R. Manheim. New York, 1969

Pirqei-Yesod Be-Havanat Ha-Kabbalah Ve-Simleiha, trans. Y. Ben-Shlomo. Jerusalem, 1980

Sabbatai Sevi: The Mystical Messiah, trans. R. J. Z. Werblowsky. Princeton, 1973

"Schöpfung aus Nichts und Selbstverschränkung Gottes," *Eranos Jahrbuch* 25 (1956)

Schreiber, Moses, *Teshuvot Hatam Sofer*, 3 vols. (reprint). New York, 1958

Sed-Rajna, G. (ed.), *Rashi 1040–1990: Hommage à Ephraim E. Urbach*. Paris, 1993

Siegel, S. and E. B. Gertel (eds.), *God in the Teachings of Conservative Judaism*. New York, 1983

Silberg, Moshe, *Ba'in K'Ehad*. Jerusalem, 1981

Silman, Yohanan, *Bein Filosof Le-Navi: Hitpat'hut Haguto Shel Rabbi Yehudah Halevi Be-Sefer Ha-Kuzari*. Ramat-Gan, 1985

"Ha-Ta'amim Ha-Shitatiyyim Le-Rayon Behirat Yisra'el Be-Sefer Ha-Kuzari." *Sinai* 80 (1977)

Simon, Marcel, *Verus Israel: A Study of the Relations Between Christians and Jews in the Roman Empire (135–425)*, trans. H. McKeating. New York, 1986

Soloveitchik, Joseph B., *The Lonely Man of Faith*. New York, 1992

Sperling, Abraham, Isaac, *Sefer Ha-Minhagim U-Meqorei Ha-Dinim*. Jerusalem, 1972

Strauss, Leo, *Persecution and the Art of Writing*. Glencoe, Ill., 1952

Philosophy and Law, trans. F. Baumann. Philadelphia, 1987

"Quelques remarques sur la science politique de Maimonide et de Farabi." *Revue des Etudes juives* 100 (1936)

Tewes, J., *Zum Existenzbegriff Franz Rosenzweigs*. Meisenheim am Glan, 1970

Tishby, Isaiah, *Mishnat Ha-Zohar*, 2 vols. Jerusalem, 1961

Twersky, Isadore, *Bibliography to the Code of Maimonides (Mishneh Torah)*. New Haven, Conn., 1980

Urbach, Ephraim E., *Hazal: Pirqei Emunot Ve-De'ot*. Jerusalem, 1971

Uziel, Ben Zion, *Teshuvot Mishpatei Uziel*: Even Ha'Ezer. Jerusalem, 1964

Wolfson, Harry A., *Philo*, 2 vols. Cambridge, Mass., 1947

Wyschogrod, Michael, *The Body of Faith: Judaism as Corporeal Election*. New York, 1983

Yosef, Ovadia, *Teshuvot Yabi'a Omer*, 6 vols. Jerusalem, 1980

Zac, Sylvain, *La Philosophie religieuse de Hermann Cohen*. Paris, 1984

GENERAL TEXTS

Abbott, W. M. (ed.), *The Documents of Vatican II*, trans. J. Gallagher *et al*. London and Dublin, 1966

Alexander, Samuel, *Spinoza and Time*. London, 1921

Allison, H. E., *Benedict de Spinoza*. Boston, 1975

The Apostolic Fathers, 2 vols., trans. K. Lake. Cambridge, Mass., 1912

Arendt, Hannah, *Lectures on Kant's Political Philosophy*, ed. R. Beiner. Chicago, 1982

    The Life of the Mind, 2 vols. New York, 1978

Aristotle, *Metaphysics*, 2 vols., trans. H. Tredennick. Cambridge, Mass., 1933

    Nicomachean Ethics, trans. H. Rackham. Cambridge, Mass., 1926

    Physics, 2 vols., trans. F. M. Cornford. Cambridge, Mass., 1929

    Politics, trans. H. Rackham. Cambridge, Mass., 1932

Ashby, G., *Sacrifice: Its Nature and Purpose*. London, 1969

Augustine, *The Basic Writings*, 2 vols., ed. W. J. Oates. New York, 1948

Avineri, Shlomo, *The Social and Political Thought of Karl Marx*. Cambridge, 1968

Barth, Karl, *Church Dogmatics*, 2/2, trans. G. W. Bromiley *et al*. Edinburgh, 1957

Bergson, Henri, *Time and Free Will*, trans. F. L. Pogson. New York, 1910

Boman, T., *Hebrew Thought Compared with Greek*, trans. J. L. Moreau. London and New York, 1970

Buckley, Michael J., *At the Origin of Modern Atheism*. New Haven, Conn., 1987

Buren, Paul van, *A Theology of the Jewish-Christian Reality*, 2 vols., San Francisco, 1980, 1983

Calvin, John, *Institutes of the Christian Religion*, 2 vols., trans. F. L. Battles. Philadelphia, 1960

Caspar, Bernhard, *Das Dialogischen Denken: Eine Untersuchung der religionsphilosophischen Bedeutung Franz Rosenzweigs, Ferdinand Ebners und Martin Bubers*. Freiburg, 1967

Clark, R. W., *Einstein: The Life and Times*. New York, 1971

da Costa, Uriel, *Schriften*, ed. G. Gebhardt. Amsterdam, 1922

Eichrodt, W., *Theology of the Old Testament*, 2 vols., trans. J. A. Baker. Philadelphia, 1961

Ellul, Jacques, *The Technological System*, trans. J. Neugroschel. New York, 1980

    The Theological Foundation of Law, trans. M. Wieser. Garden City, N.Y., 1960

Feuer, Lewis S., *Spinoza and the Rise of Liberalism*. Boston, Mass., 1958

Hampshire, Stuart, *Spinoza*, rev. ed. Middlesex, 1987

Hegel, G. W. F., *Phänomenologie des Geistes*, ed. J. Hoffmeister. Hamburg, 1952

Phenomenology of Spirit. trans. A. V. Miller. Oxford, 1977

Philosophy of Right, trans. T. M. Knox. Oxford, 1952

Heidegger, Martin, *Being and Time*, trans. J. Macquarrie and E. Robinson. New York and Evanston, 1962

An Bibliography to Metaphysics, trans. R. Manheim. Garden City, N.Y., 1961

Hessing, S. (ed.), *Speculum Spinozanum: 1677–1977*. London, 1978

Spinoza: Dreihundert Jahre Ewigkeit, 2nd enlarged ed. The Hague, 1962

Hume, David, *A Treatise of Human Nature*, ed. L. A. Selby-Bigge. Oxford, 1888

Husserl, Edmund, *Ideas: An Bibliography to Pure Phenomenology*, trans. W. R. B. Gibson. New York, 1962

Kant, Immanuel, *Critique of Judgment*, trans. J. H. Bernard. New York, 1951

Critique of Practical Reason, trans. L. W. Beck. Indianapolis, 1956

Critique of Pure Reason, trans. N. Kemp Smith. New York, 1929

Groundwork of the Metaphysic of Morals, trans. H. J. Paton. New York, 1964

Religion Within the Limits of Reason Alone, trans. T. M. Greene and H. H. Hudson. New York, 1960

Kaufmann, Walter, *Hegel: A Reinterpretation*. Garden City, N.Y., 1966

Levinas, Emmanuel, *Totality and Infinity*, trans. A. Lingis. Pittsburgh, 1969

Levy, Ze'ev, *Baruch or Benedict: On Some Jewish Aspects of Spinoza's Philosophy*. New York, 1989

Lindbeck, George A., *The Nature of Doctrine: Religion and Theology in a Postliberal Age*. Philadelphia, 1984

Lonergan, Bernard, *Insight*, 3rd ed. San Francisco, 1970

Lucas, J., *The Oldest Biography of Spinoza*, ed. A. Wolf. New York, 1927

McShea, Robert, *The Political Philosophy of Spinoza*. New York, 1967

Marx, Karl, *Zur Judenfrage*. Berlin, 1919

Meek, T., "The Translation of Gêr in the Hexateuch." *Journal of Biblical Literature* 49 (1930)

Mendenhall, George, *Law and Covenant in Israel and the Ancient Near East*. Pittsburgh, 1955

Nicene and Post-Nicene Fathers, 2nd series, vol. 5. Grand Rapids, Mich., 1983

New Testament, trans. E. J. Goodspeed. Chicago, 1923
Novak, David, *Suicide and Morality*. New York, 1975
Nygren, Anders, *Eros and Agape*, trans. P. Watson. Chicago, 1982
Origen, *Contra Celsum*, ed. M. Borret. Paris, 1967
Pallière, Aimé, *The Unknown Sanctuary*, trans. L. W. Wise; intro. David Novak. New York, 1985
Pannenberg, Wolfhart, *Systematic Theology*, vol. I, trans. G. W. Bromiley. Grand Rapids, Mich., 1991
Pines, Shlomo, "Spinoza's *Tractatus Theologico-Politicus*." *Scripta Hierosolymitana* 20 (1968)
Plant, R. *Hegel*. Bloomington and London, 1973
Plato, *Euthyphro*, trans. H. N. Fowler. Cambridge, Mass., 1914
Laws, 2 vols., trans. R. G. Bury. Cambridge, Mass., 1926
Philebus, trans. H. N. Fowler. Cambridge, Mass., 1921
Republic, 2 vols., trans. P. Shorey. Cambridge, Mass., 1930
Theaetetus, trans. H. N. Fowler. Cambridge, Mass., 1925
Timaeus, trans. R. G. Bury. Cambridge, Mass., 1929
Popper, Karl, *The Open Society and its Enemies*, 2 vols. Princeton, 1962
Rad, G. von, *Old Testament Theology*, 2 vols. trans. D. M. G. Stalker. New York, 1962
Rawls, John, *A Theory of Justice*. Cambridge, Mass., 1971
Ricoeur, Paul, *Hermeneutics and the Human Sciences*, ed. and trans. J. B. Thompson. Cambridge, 1981
The Symbolism of Evil, trans. E. Buchanan. New York and Evanston, 1967
Rowley, H. H., *The Biblical Doctrine of Election*. London, 1950
Ruether, Rosemary, *Faith and Fratricide: The Theological Roots of Anti-Semitism*. New York, 1974
Russell, Bertrand, *The Problems of Philosophy*. Oxford, 1959
Sachs, M., *Einstein versus Bohr: The Continuing Controversies in Physics*. La Salle, Ill., 1988
Sartre, Jean-Paul, *Anti-Semite–and Jew*, trans. George J. Becker. New York, 1965
Réflexions sur la question juive. Paris, 1946
Schwartz, Joel, "Liberalism and the Jewish Connection: A Study of Spinoza and the Young Marx." *Political Theory* 13 (1985)
Seneca, *De Clementia*, trans. A. Stewart. London, 1900
Sonderegger, Katherine, *That Jesus Christ was Born a Jew: Karl Barth's "Doctrine of Israel"*. University Park, Pa, 1992
Spinoza, Baruch, *Collected Works*, 2 vols., trans. E. Curley. Princeton, 1985
Correspondence, ed. and trans. A. Wolf. London, 1928
Opera, 4 vols., ed. J. van Vloten and J. P. N. Land. The Hague, 1914

Tractatus Politicus, trans. R. H. M. Elwes. New York, 1951
Tractatus Theologico-Politicus, trans. S. Shirley. Leiden and New York, 1989
Strauss, Leo, "The Mutual Influence of Theology and Philosophy." *Independent Journal of Philosophy* 3 (1979)
Spinoza's Critique of Religion, trans. E. M. Sinclair. New York, 1965
Tacitus, *Histories*, trans. K. Wellesley. Baltimore, 1975
Taylor, Charles, *Sources of the Self*. Cambridge, Mass., 1989
Theologische Aufsätze: Karl Barth zum 50. Geburtstag. Munich, 1936
Thomas Aquinas, *Basic Writings*, 2 vols. English Dominican trans.; ed. A. Pegis. New York, 1945
Tillich, Paul, *Systematic Theology*, vol. 1. Chicago, 1951
Vaux, Roland de, *The Early History of Israel: To the Exodus and Covenant at Sinai*, trans. D. Smith. Philadelphia, 1978
Voegelin, Eric, *Order and History*, vol. 1. Baton Rouge, La., 1957
Whitehead, Alfred North, *Process and Reality: An Essay in Cosmology*. New York, 1929
Wildberger, H., *YHWH's Eigentumsvolk: Ein Studie zur Traditionsgeschichte und Theologie des Erwahlungsdenkens*. Zurich, 1960
Wittgenstein, Ludwig, *Philosophical Investigations*, 2nd ed., trans. G. E. M. Anscombe. New York, 1958
Tractatus Logico-Philosophicus. London, 1961
Wolfson, Harry A., *The Philosophy of Spinoza*, 2 vols. Cambridge, Mass., 1934
Studies in the History of Philosophy and Religion, 2 vols., ed. I. Twersky and G. H. Williams. Cambridge, Mass., 1977
Yovel, Yirmiyahu, *Spinoza and Other Heretics*, 2 vols. Princeton, 1989
Zac, Sylvain, *Philosophie, théologie, politique dans l'œuvre de Spinoza*. Paris, 1979
Spinoza et l'interprétation de l'écriture. Paris, 1965

Index

DATE DUE

			Printed in USA